Profit and Power

Why are multinational corporations so powerful and elites so wealthy while still operating within nation-state rules? *Profit and Power* examines how firms engage in legal transgression, operating at the edges of legality to maximize profits. Offering a practical analysis of jurisdictional arbitrage, Ronen Palan exposes the hidden mechanisms behind corporate power in globalization and reveals how the rule-based transgressor elite emerged through strategic use of multinational corporation structures. Tracing the origins to the late nineteenth century, Palan focuses on centrally coordinated multi-corporate enterprises – networks of legally independent yet interconnected firms. He explores the gap between the legal entity and the corporate group, a loophole long exploited to arbitrage national regulations, including taxation. This is the first systematic study of jurisdictional arbitrage and its impact on states and society. By analysing corporate decision-making within fragmented regulatory environments, it unveils the systemic role of legal ambiguity in shaping modern capitalism and corporate dominance.

RONEN PALAN is Professor of International Political Economy at City St George's, University of London. He was the founding editor of the *Review of International Political Economy* and his previous books include *Sabotage: The Business of Finance* (with Anastasia Nesvetailova, 2020), *Tax Havens: How Globalization Really Works* (with Richard Murphy and Christian Chavagneux, 2010), and *The Offshore World* (2003).

Profit and Power

Arbitrage in the Era of the Multinational Corporation

RONEN PALAN
City St George's, University of London

CAMBRIDGE
UNIVERSITY PRESS

Shaftesbury Road, Cambridge CB2 8EA, United Kingdom

One Liberty Plaza, 20th Floor, New York, NY 10006, USA

477 Williamstown Road, Port Melbourne, VIC 3207, Australia

314-321, 3rd Floor, Plot 3, Splendor Forum, Jasola District Centre, New Delhi - 110025, India

103 Penang Road, #05–06/07, Visioncrest Commercial, Singapore 238467

Cambridge University Press is part of Cambridge University Press & Assessment, a department of the University of Cambridge.

We share the University's mission to contribute to society through the pursuit of education, learning and research at the highest international levels of excellence.

www.cambridge.org
Information on this title: www.cambridge.org/9781009605281

DOI: 10.1017/9781009605298

© Ronen Palan 2026

This publication is in copyright. Subject to statutory exception and to the provisions of relevant collective licensing agreements, no reproduction of any part may take place without the written permission of Cambridge University Press & Assessment.

When citing this work, please include a reference to the DOI 10.1017/9781009605298

First published 2026

A catalogue record for this publication is available from the British Library

A Cataloging-in-Publication data record for this book is available from the Library of Congress

ISBN 978-1-009-60527-4 Hardback
ISBN 978-1-009-60528-1 Paperback

Cambridge University Press & Assessment has no responsibility for the persistence or accuracy of URLs for external or third-party internet websites referred to in this publication and does not guarantee that any content on such websites is, or will remain, accurate or appropriate.

For EU product safety concerns, contact us at Calle de José Abascal, 56, 1°, 28003 Madrid, Spain, or email eugpsr@cambridge.org

The more you multiply enterprises, the more you multiply the centres of formation of something like an enterprise, and the more you force governmental action to let these enterprises operate, then of course the more you multiply the surfaces of friction between each of these enterprises, the more you multiply opportunities for disputes, and the more you multiply the need for legal arbitration. An enterprise society and a judicial society ... are two faces of a single phenomenon.

Michel Foucault, *The Birth of Biopolitics*

Contents

List of Figures	page viii
List of Tables	ix
Preface	xi
Acknowledgements	xxxii
Author Note	xxxvi
List of Abbreviations	xxxviii

	Introduction	1
1	Decoding Jurisdictional Arbitrage: Strategies, Implications, and Global Dynamics	44
2	The Advent of the Centrally Coordinated Multi-corporate Enterprise	62
3	Tools of Trade	90
4	Corporate Tax Arbitrage	113
5	How the European Union Became a Facilitator of Global Corporate Tax Avoidance	135
6	A World of Fuses and Splitters	143
7	How Not to Tell by Telling: Reporting and Disclosure Arbitrage	157
8	Geopolitics and Jurisdictional Arbitrage: Does the United States Arbitrage the World?	170
9	The Hidden Empire: How MNCs Redefine Power through Arbitrage	177
	Conclusions	191
References		198
Index		226

Figures

P.1	The rising value of intangibles among the S&P 500 companies.	*page* xvi
I.1	Volkswagen equity map, *c*. mid 2018.	14
I.2	Wells Fargo equity map, *c*. 2021.	15
I.3	Group structure of Apple Inc., highlighting Irish holding structure, *c*. January 2019.	16
2.1	A pyramidal holding company structure.	76
3.1	Direct and indirect ownership patterns.	94
3.2	Schematic representation of a split ownership structure.	95
4.1	Real-estate tax arbitrage scheme.	124
6.1	Corporate fuse.	153
6.2	Trump Organization equity map, *c*. 2021.	155
7.1	Weighted quality of signal received from OFC subsidiaries.	165
7.2	Prevalence of dormant companies among independent and integrated energy trading companies.	167
7.3	Dormant-like behaviour of corporate subsidiaries.	167
7.4	Income statement quality of OFC-based subsidiaries of independent and integrated oil trading companies.	168

Tables

I.1 The logic of jurisdictional arbitrage	*page* 21
I.2 Arbitraging and intangibles	27
3.1 CCMCEs and the object of jurisdictional arbitrage	91
3.2 CCMCEs as fractal structures in the light of the theory of simple and complex transactions	96
7.1 Independent and integrated trading companies (CORPLINK/OECD study)	165

Preface

As I was completing this book, the second Trump administration began to take shape. There are many unsettling aspects about this direction in American politics, but one in particular is closely tied to the theme of this book. The emerging administration is heavily influenced by business moguls who happen to be major shareholders controlling global corporations. The *Financial Times* aptly describes this new administration as 'plutocratic', a term reminiscent of the last days of the Roman Empire – a time of unprecedented concentration of wealth and power among the elite in a mode of governance that increasingly favoured the interests of a wealthy few.

Even more troubling, perhaps, is the fact that Trump is not alone. Around a tenth of the world's current billionaires have held or sought political office (Krcmaric et al., 2024). Billionaires represent an important but understudied subset of the 'global leadership class' (Gerring et al., 2019). According to the UBS Global Wealth Report 2024, global billionaire wealth surged by approximately 17 per cent over the year, reaching US$14 trillion, and the number of billionaires increased to 2,682 from 2,544, with significant gains in the United States (UBS, 2024). For comparison – although this is akin to comparing apples and pears – the world's billionaires collectively represent a 'second China', a country with a nominal gross domestic product of approximately US$14 trillion.

This book is a study of an aspect of global capitalism that, at first glance, seems only tangentially connected to the rise of figures such as Donald Trump and other billionaires of our era. It is a study of esoteric and opaque planning schemes set up by lawyers and accountants to arbitrage national rules and regulations. These schemes, referred to by corporate lawyers as *jurisdictional arbitrage*, are devised by business organizations to exploit regulatory discrepancies across different jurisdictions. While these schemes are increasingly drawing attention, particularly in the field of corporate taxation, they are often framed as cases of avoidance, evasion, or the manipulation of rules through 'artificial' constructs.

The more I learned about these schemes, the more it became clear that dismissing them as mere fringe activities is misleading. They play a constitutive role within a complex web of factors shaping contemporary capitalism. This intricate web has ultimately given rise to a distinct form of wealth concentration that defines our times. However, the relationship between wealth concentration, the corporate form, and the legal and political environment – an environment in which so many billionaires are actively and strategically involved nowadays – is frequently misunderstood.

To argue that we misunderstand capitalism – and that the study of certain technical forms of corporate organization, seemingly of interest only to a handful of specialists, holds the key to that misunderstanding – is a bold claim. Yet it is precisely the argument I will be advancing in this book.

As I see it, Marx's influence on modern thought was, in at least one crucial way, decisive. He not only coined the term 'capitalism' but also framed it as a system fundamentally driven by the circulation of capital. For Marx, the capitalist – an owner of the means of production – invests capital into the production of goods. Workers, in turn, use their wages to purchase these goods, generating profits for the capitalist, who then reinvests in production while skimming off wealth to sustain a life of luxury. The system perpetuates itself in this cycle, with everything else as an appendage to this core framework. Marx called this process 'capital accumulation'. The idea that modern billionaires continue this same relentless accumulation of wealth remains deeply ingrained in our understanding of capitalism. But, as I will argue, this assumption is fundamentally flawed. Capital is no longer accumulated in the way our ancestors imagined – it moves, circulates, and transforms in ways that defy the traditional narrative.

From its very inception, this dominant vision of capitalism has contained anomalies – elements that simply do not fit neatly within its narrative. My argument is that what appear to be inconsistencies in the conventional understanding of capitalism – often ignored or dismissed – are not anomalies at all. Rather, they reveal overlooked or misrecognized systemic relationships, signalling the existence of an alternative form of capitalism.

This 'other capitalism' emerged, thrived, and is now at risk – largely because we have been looking elsewhere. And at the heart of this neglected reality lies arbitrage, the proverbial canary in the coal mine. Understanding the full significance of arbitrage may require us to revisit these very anomalies, for they may hold the key to rethinking capitalism itself.

****

By modern capitalism, I refer to the system that emerged in the late nineteenth-century United States and subsequently spread across the globe. This capitalist economy is broadly recognized for bringing together a unique combination of factors that set it apart from other forms of capitalism. Some of these factors are well known and have been extensively discussed. The American model was characterized by large corporate organizations – what Alfred Chandler referred to as M-corporations – which combined economies of scale, technological innovation, advanced organizational structures, and large banking institutions to achieve significant leaps in productivity (Chandler, 1993). It was not only about large-scale production; it was equally about consumption. Furthermore, under the guidance of American hegemony, this model of capitalism introduced the post-Second World War international trading and investment regimes, collectively known as the rules-based liberal order.

However, the familiar narrative is marked by certain anomalies – facts that, while rarely disputed for their accuracy, were and are still consistently downplayed or dismissed because their significance is difficult to interpret. As a result, they remain isolated as niche topics among specialists, with no clear or obvious connection to the broader trajectory of modern history.

The first of these anomalies concerns the nature of business organization, particularly the structures at the heart of the corporate world. Alfred Chandler's concept of the M-form corporation eventually evolved into what we now recognize as the multinational corporation (MNC) – a global leviathan, roaming the world in search of profits, transcending national boundaries, and reshaping economies in its wake. Although numbering only a few thousands, MNCs account for about 33 per cent of global output, 49 per cent of global export, and 23 per cent of global employment (Garcia-Bernardo, 2021). Together with global banks, they form a core organizational and administrative vehicle driving the processes that are often described as 'globalization'.

There is no shortage of writing on the MNC. In fact, the sheer volume of literature on the subject raises an important challenge for anyone attempting to add yet another contribution. As Stephen Cohen aptly put it: 'Why is another book on this subject necessary?' (Cohen, 2007, 1). Any new analysis must not only justify its existence but also offer fresh insights that go beyond the well-trodden narratives of global expansion, corporate power, and market dominance. And yet the very concept of the MNC is, and has always been, a misnomer. Legally speaking, there is no singular corporation that is acting across borders. Despite its name, the MNC has never been truly multinational in the sense of being equally embedded in multiple nations. Rather, it has always remained anchored in specific legal, financial, and institutional frameworks – typically those of its home country – while projecting its influence globally. The terminology of the singular MNC is a convenient shorthand that is used to describe what in reality are increasingly complex networks of independent legal entities – corporations, partnerships, or other corporate forms – connected through equity ties.

'So what?' many might dismissively ask, viewing this anomaly as nothing more than a legal technicality. For all practical purposes – commercially speaking – MNCs do indeed function as singular entities. I agree. Yet corporate lawyers, some of whom became personal friends during the life of this project, including Reuven Avi-Yonah, Omri Marian, and Jean-Philippe Robé, are not convinced. For them, the concept of the MNC is inherently contradictory. After all, a corporation is a legal entity licensed by a state; it cannot be multinational by its very nature. The actual legal structure of these firms is what transforms abstract ideas, a plan hatched up among investors, into practical organizations capable of engaging in market activities. How can we ignore those practicalities?

Equally perplexed are accountants such as Robert Sterling or Yuval Millo of Warwick Business School (who also advised the CORPLINK project, see Acknowledgements). They question the value and validity of 'consolidated accounts' for these MNCs. The accounting practices that present these sprawling networks as unitary entities seem problematic, shielding a complex web of legal and financial arrangements beneath a single corporate identity.

But this is only the first anomaly in a series of contradictions that define our relationship with 'capitalism'. Another one of those 'things' that somehow seem misaligned with reality is the pervasive belief that those supposedly singular MNCs are primarily geared towards the manufacturing of physical goods or, at most, the provision of services to markets. The renowned economist Edith Penrose defines 'firms' as organizations that acquire 'resources from their environment for the production and sale of goods and services at a profit' (Penrose, 2009, 31). Albert Hirschman suggests that every firm produces, in essence, 'saleable outputs for customers' (Hirschman, 1990, 3). For Michael Jensen and William Meckling, the 'corporation' is a kind of input–output machine 'meeting marginal conditions related to inputs and outputs to maximize profits – or, more precisely, to optimize present value' (Jensen and Meckling, 1976, 306–307).

This axiomatic assumption has become an article of faith, most probably because traditional economic theories of the firm were, in fact, rooted in the Smithian model of the factory. The truth is that substantial empirical evidence shows MNCs are neither solely nor, perhaps, even primarily focused on the production of 'things'. This point was acknowledged by Penrose herself. As firms grow, she noticed, 'the firm will increasingly acquire the characteristics of a financial holding company, lose those of an industrial firm, and finally become virtually indistinguishable from an investment trust' (Penrose, 2009, 19). Penrose's solution for what she saw as the metamorphosis of the firm was to assign economic theory to that portion of the firm that still acted as an industrial enterprise. Neil Kay says that the implication of Penrose's work and the work of others in this vein was profound: economists simply had to accept that 'there was no irony or contradiction in the idea that in the theory of the firm, the firm was not a firm' (Kay, 2000, 14). The firm, in other words, is a 'theoretical construct' (Allen, 2005, 899) bearing little resemblance to 'its real-world namesake' (Demsetz, 1983, 377).

So not only is the concept of the MNC a misnomer, but the very idea that these 'firms' exist primarily to produce goods or services at transaction cost efficiency is equally dubious. The traditional view, rooted in transaction cost economics, suggests that firms emerge and grow as efficient solutions to market failures. Yet, in reality, many of the world's most powerful MNCs are not primarily in the business of production at all – in fact, they often leave the messy world of production of things to subcontractors. Their strategies, in turn, often centre on creating what is commonly referred to in business parlance

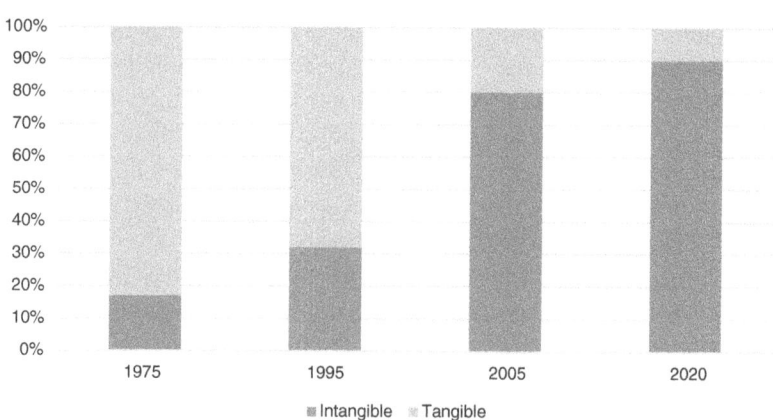

Figure P.1 The rising value of intangibles among the S&P 500 companies. Source: Graph created by the author, based on data from Ocean Tomo (2021)

as 'value'. Crucially, today, the value they generate is predominantly derived from another one of those anomalies, intangible assets.

Figure P.1 draws on estimates provided by Ocean Tomo to highlight the extent to which the modern economy seems to be focused on intangibles. As you will see from the chart, current estimates suggest that intangible assets account for approximately 90 per cent of the value of the S&P 500 companies (Ocean Tomo, 2021). According to Brand Finance's analysis, the total value of intangible assets owned by the world's largest companies reached USD79.4 trillion in 2024, a 28 per cent increase from USD61.9 trillion in 2023 (BrandFinance, 2024). Numerous statistics circulate that converge on a similar conclusion: the modern economy is fundamentally driven by intangibles.

How, then, do these supposedly input–output machines we call MNCs produce intangibles? The problem lies in the traditional narrative of capitalism and the market economy, which has left little room to seriously engage with the concept of intangibles. Instead of examining intangibles on their own terms, the prevailing tendency has been to conflate them with finance – a framing that obscures their distinct nature and significance. This conflation reduces intangibles, and that is the third important anomaly, to mere speculative assets or financial instruments, failing to account for how they reshape economic power, corporate strategy, and even the logic of value itself in the modern economy.

This has led to the mistaken conclusion that the corporate economy – or perhaps capitalism itself – at some point took a wrong turn. It is now all about 'shareholder capitalism' and 'short termism', resulting in profits in the corporate sector being derived primarily from what are often categorized as 'financial activities', rather than from the production of goods for markets. This perceived 'wrong turn' is often referred to as 'financialization', often ascribed to the ills of 'neoliberalism', and regarded with considerable apprehension. It reflects a growing sense that the global economy has become increasingly detached from the tangible world of goods and production.

What, then, exactly are intangible assets? Does an economy based on intangible value operate under the same market principles developed by neoclassical economics? Moreover, what is the connection between intangible assets, the decentralized structure of modern MNCs, and the rise of today's billionaires? Only by addressing these questions can we begin to appreciate the significance of what might initially seem like merely technical issues related to arbitrage.

****

Let us start with the question that I touch upon at the beginning of this Preface: the rise of those enormously wealthy individuals, the billionaires. What does the 'wealth' of a billionaire signify in today's world? And by implication, what does it actually mean to be wealthy? The question is multifaceted, with several elements fused and often conflated. We can dismiss from the outset two common misconceptions about the source of today's billionaires' power and wealth. The first is the belief that they are extraordinary entrepreneurs. While some certainly fit this description, and most are eager to portray themselves this way, entrepreneurship alone is not enough. Countless superb entrepreneurial individuals never reach billionaire or even millionaire status.

The second is the common misconception that billionaires maintain their wealth by avoiding or evading taxation and by engaging in illicit financial activities more generally. While the elites of many countries can be defined as kleptocratic (Cooley and Heathershaw, 2017; Findley et al., 2014; Pitcher and Soares de Oliveira, 2022), and nearly all of today's wealthy employ the services of the wealth management industry, famous and infamous for its tax avoidance acumen, the wealth industry excels at *preserving* wealth, not creating it (Harrington, 2016).

Wealth is often seen, even today, as something that can be 'accumulated', assets or control over resources (Rowlinson and McKay, 2011). In popular discourse, wealth is often depicted as the accumulation of a lot of 'things', a world where the rich surround themselves with an abundance of luxurious items at their disposal. The term accumulation originates from the Latin word *accumulare*, 'to heap up' or 'to pile together'. The root, *cumulus*, conveys the idea of a physical or metaphorical mass being gathered or increased over time. In its earliest uses, accumulation referred to the process of amassing or collecting things, often physical items, into a larger group or quantity.

'Things', however, have no inherent value. The car I proudly own, the machinery I invest in – they are tomorrow's junk, burdensome and costly to dispose of. The water in a billionaire's pool, the bricks and wood in a mansion, are merely elements assembled in a certain way, assigned worth because society deems them symbols of wealth. Outside this collective, if tacit, agreement, things possess no inherent value. Wealth, in other words, is a social construct, what sociologists refer to as 'intersubjective'. Value is created and sustained not by physical objects but by the collective beliefs, trust, and shared perceptions within society. Modern wealth is far more abstract and elusive, tied less to tangible possessions – a form of power embedded in ownership structures of the corporate economy (Robé, 2020).

A century ago, John R. Commons wrote: 'Words are deceptive if they do not convey the meaning intended; numbers are liars if they do not indicate the actual quantities' (Commons, 1924, 9). To understand the nature of wealth today and its relationship to the concept of intangibles, and ultimately to the corporate form, we must trace its origins back, he argues, to the American railway system and the rise of the American version of the *Raubritter*, or robber barons (Josephson, 1962).

In England, the earliest railway lines that began exactly 200 years ago, in 1825, were modest in scale, mostly local endeavours. These lines typically spanned 20–30 miles, connecting towns and industrial centres to facilitate the movement of goods and passengers over relatively short distances. In the United States, in contrast, the same steam railway technology had a dramatically different impact. The vast geography of the United States and its relatively sparse population in many regions created a demand for long-distance transport that the railway uniquely fulfilled. Raw materials such as coal, timber, and steel could be transported efficiently over great distances, while finished goods could reach previously inaccessible consumers. The railroads became the backbone of the emerging US economy, knitting together the disparate republics into a unified state and enabling large-scale industries to prosper by capitalizing on economies of scale and accessing far-reaching markets.

The American railway companies exemplified, as we know, a new kind of enterprise: complex, capital-intensive organizations capable of managing extensive networks and requiring unprecedented levels of investment, coordination, and innovation. But there was something more to these industries. Crucially, they intentionally and knowingly created new markets, and, as Commons later theorized, the anticipation of the volume of trade produced in these markets became an intrinsic part of their value (Commons, 1934).

Thorstein Veblen, an inspiration to Commons, wrote about how investors recognized the potential of these railway companies not only to charge for transporting increasing volumes of people and goods but also to create their own markets (Veblen, 1908). By buying shares in these companies, investors hoped to benefit not only from current profits distributed as dividends but also from the future profits of those anticipated markets the companies were poised to create. As companies expanded and the anticipated demand for transport materialized, their share value reflected both current earnings and the projected growth and revenue potential of the emerging markets. The same was true in England as well, but on a much smaller scale.

Crucially, companies were increasingly valued in the United States on the basis of the anticipation of their future earning capacity. In the early 1890s, New Jersey amended its incorporation rules to allow companies to own stocks in other companies. This change set off a wave of acquisitions, with companies purchasing controlling shares in others, which soon became known as subsidiaries. Often, the purchasing company – frequently organized as a holding company – would pay a premium for the company it acquired. This premium was justified by the belief that the combined entities could generate greater future income streams than either could on its own. The amount paid above the tangible value of the acquired company was recorded in the accounting books as 'goodwill'.

Similarly, holding companies began to proliferate, creating subsidiaries with initial capital investments but recording higher values on the subsidiaries' accounts based on the same logic. This practice reflected the growing emphasis on the anticipated value of the combined operations. American courts increasingly began to accept that these valuations of future earning capacity of the 'corporation' were not merely behavioural traits but were actual 'assets' possessed by these investors – specifically, intangible assets owned by the corporation itself, with claims over those assets represented by the shares held by investors. The courts accepted that when states intervened directly or indirectly in the pricing charged by corporate groups, which states often did, then they have taken something valuable from the investor, future income streams.

Commons argued that those practices became in effect a new form of property, intangible property. They were profoundly different and distinct from another category of intangible assets, which he referred to as incorporeal or financial assets. Financial assets are tradeable debt promises or 'I owe you' instruments. But intangible assets consisted of what I believe are two distinguishable categories. The one that Commons discussed at length was 'industrial goodwill'. It was broadly the value investors put on the company's future earning capacity (Commons, 1934). The other, trademarks, patents, or proprietary technologies and data became recognized as a different type of intangible 'assets'. But they became to be treated by the courts as assets only from around the 1920s.

A unique characteristic of the two intangible assets (as opposed to financial or incorporeal assets), Commons observed, was that they changed the broader meaning of property. It was not entirely a novelty for a company such as H. J. Heinz to place a standardized image on its food products. But it was novelty that the image began to have a financial value entered on the corporate groups as an asset (Foroudi et al., 2017). Later, as we will see, this 'asset' could be assigned to a corporation within the family or corporate group that we call MNC, and that corporation would trade with others within the group, 'charging' for the use of these assets.

In an article titled 'Transcendental Nonsense and the Functional Approach', Félix Cohen lamented the 'thingification' of this type of assets: There was once a theory that the law of trademarks and trade-names was an attempt to protect the consumer against the 'passing off' of inferior goods under misleading labels. Increasingly the courts have departed from any such theory and have come to view this branch of law as a protection of property rights in divers economically valuable sale devices. (Cohen, 1935, 86)

The value of company trademarks could fluctuate over time, thus superficially resembling a financial instrument. Unlike a financial asset, the worth of a trademark or a logo was inherently tied, however, to the notion of exclusivity and hence to law. The same Félix Cohen lamented that a 'vicious circle' emerged, in which the courts intervened in the production of value and wealth creation:

Courts and scholars ... have taken refuge in a vicious circle ... if commercial exploitation of the word 'Palmolive' is not restricted to a single firm, the word will be of no more economic value to any particular firm than a convenient size, shape, mode of packing, or manner of advertising, common in the trade. Not being of economic value to any particular firm, the word would be regarded by courts as 'not property'. (Cohen, 1935, 87)

In other words, contrary to the traditional concept of markets and states, the value of those 'intangibles' in markets hinged from the outset on the legal system and courts' interpretations. Indeed, by the 1920s, US courts were emboldened to determine the 'value' of public utilities as well, based on similar principles (Richberg, 1927).

Accountants had to rethink the nature of various items that made up the value of the corporation. They began to theorize that value of corporate intangible assets were inherently tied to perceived ability to command a premium price or secure greater market share (Allan, 1889). Value lay, in other words, in subjective perceptions of the future. The price of intangibles became a forward-looking calculation, tied to the company's ability to withhold use and maintain exclusivity in the market.

Such 'value' cannot be 'accumulated', and hence the idea that wealth is accumulated today is highly dubious. Unlike tangible and incorporeal assets, intangibles are deeply intertwined with the corporate form. Tangible assets, such as buildings, machinery, or inventory, can be imagined to exist independently and can be transferred, sold, or utilized, at least in theory, outside the framework of a corporation. Similarly, incorporeal assets, such as financial instruments or contractual rights, can operate and hold value within a broader legal and economic context, often independent of any specific corporate entity. Intangible assets, however, are fundamentally tied to the identity and operations of the corporate entity itself. Today, a trademark or logo is only valuable if it is judged to enhance a company's ability to generate superior income streams. If the presence of the logo does not allow a company to charge a higher price for its product or increase the volume of its sales, then the ability to withhold the logo – that is, to deny others from using it (the same theory applies to an idea or a patent) – has no economic value. Exclusivity, rather than scarcity, defines the economic worth of an intangible asset.

This is particularly true with regard to 'assets' such as goodwill. These assets derive their value not just from legal ownership but also from the ongoing activities, strategies, and narratives of the corporation as a 'going concern'. The theory is that the worth of corporate goodwill is tied to the corporation's ability to leverage its 'culture' or other intangibles in the marketplace, and requires active management, sustained innovation, and reputational upkeep. In this sense, intangibles are not passive properties but dynamic extensions of the corporation's identity and strategy. They are inseparable from the corporate form, both in practical application and in the valuation frameworks that define their economic significance.

There are other differences between financial and intangible assets. Financial assets are time-sensitive, and their value is often influenced by the duration of the holding period. The longer a financial asset is held, the greater its exposure to market volatility, possibly leading to price fluctuations. As a result, lenders typically demand higher interest or returns on financial assets with longer maturities to compensate for the increased risk. Time plays a different role in the valuation of intangible assets. The value of a patent does not increase simply because it is held for a longer period. On the contrary, according to accounting standards, intangible value is subject to amortization over time. This process gradually reduces the value of these intangible assets on financial statements, reflecting their consumption, use, or decline in usefulness over a specified period.

It is crucial, therefore, for the argument I present in this book to differentiate between financial and intangible assets, and then between financial assets and the concept of the financial system. Financial assets, such as bonds or cash reserves, serve as tools for investment, liquidity, or risk management. While they are vital for maintaining financial stability of corporate groups and are enabling growth – such as funding projects or acquisitions – they are not core drivers of the corporate operational or strategic decisions. Intangible assets, in contrast, occupy a central position in corporate growth strategies and play an increasingly significant role in corporate valuation. Unlike financial assets, intangibles are directly tied to a company's operations and competitive positioning, shaping its ability to innovate, differentiate, and succeed in the marketplace. The financial system, however, specializes in trading in both assets, hence the common confusion of all intangible assets with finance.

****

The economy of intangibles Commons described was entirely a market-based relationship, and in that sense could be thought of as 'capitalism', although it represented a fundamentally different capitalism from the one described by Ricardo, Marx, or neoclassical thinkers. This has led to a misleading sense of continuity. Over time, the historical and political economic analysis of the origins of intangible assets in the late nineteenth century has largely been forgotten.

Today, the definition of the two (in fact, three) types of assets, financial and intangible, is a subject of debate in accounting, but financial assets are broadly seen as contracts or claims on the future cash flows of an entity. They represent ownership or a contractual right to receive payments. Such claims can be in the form of *stocks*, bonds, bank deposits, mutual funds, or derivatives (Fiechter, 2011, emphasis mine). In contrast, intangible assets are typically seen as non-physical assets that provide economic value through their influence on operations, brand recognition, or intellectual property. They include patents, trademarks, copyrights, brand equity, customer relationships, and, most elusive of all, goodwill (Hussinki et al., 2024).

From the perspective of Commons, today's approach tends to conflate, however, financial assets with intangible assets. The conflation of intangible and incorporeal assets makes sense to some extent, as they share a key characteristic: they are both intangible, and they are deeply intertwined. In fact, it is challenging to conceive of intangible assets as having value outside the context of an advanced financial system. One needs an advanced financial system to provide standardized methods for the valuation of intangibles such as discounted cash flow analysis or market comparisons. The trade in debt instruments underpins, in addition, much of the liquidity and speculation driving financial markets, while the valuation of future income streams serves as the anchor for the perceived worth of assets such as intellectual property or corporate equities. Together, these systems create a feedback loop in which expectations of future value and the mechanisms of financial exchange reinforce one another, amplifying both perceived value and market activity.

It is also true that the large and ever-expanding industry of financial intermediation – encompassing investment management firms, investment banks, wealth advisors, and other actors – tends to blur the distinction between different types of assets (Millo et al., 2025). This industry, commonly associated with financial markets, typically treats investments in intangibles and incorporeal assets as equivalent. Both types of property tend to be viewed, therefore, as financial investments' contribution to the financialization of the economy.

Why do I return to Commons's distinction rather than adopting contemporary views on intangibles? I return to Commons because his perspective allows us to have a more nuanced understanding of the dynamics of economics growth and wealth concentration. It also sheds light on the relationship between wealth concentration and the corporate entity for the simple reason that, unlike tangible or financial instruments, intangibles have a much closer relationship to the corporate form. From Commons's viewpoint, *futurity* – the strategies employed by corporate management and their professional helpers, to enhance the value of a company's shares – is fundamentally tied to intangible assets.

Today, as we saw, the category of shares or stocks is typically classified as a financial asset. This perspective makes sense from the viewpoint of individual investors, who indeed treat stocks as purely financial instruments, reflecting their role as passive participants in the corporate structure. These investors aim solely for financial gain, without bearing liability for the performance, decisions, or malfeasance of the companies they invest in. For investors, stocks in companies are a financial asset.

For corporations, however, shares play a far more complex role. Corporations can, and often do, purchase shares in other corporations purely as financial investments, acting in this regard much like individual investors. But corporations also use shares strategically to establish subsidiaries and affiliates around the world. But under such circumstances, shares held in these subsidiaries are not treated as merely financial assets; they are integral components of the corporate group's structure and operations as a going concern. Shares have, therefore, this strange dual role in today's economy: they can serve as financial instruments, and they can serve as the building blocks of corporate organizations, and they can do both simultaneously – the latter, as we will see, has more to do with the question of power, specifically the relationship between the corporate group and its institutional and political environment.

This dimension of the use of equity holding is very well known. But while the literature abounds with references to terms such as 'subsidiaries' or 'affiliates', the common tendency is to ignore the legal meaning of these terms and treat subsidiaries under the metaphor of the 'limb', as an organic part of the corporate organization. The metaphor supports the impression that these clusters of companies operate as a single entity – an MNC.

In reality, however, the legal definition of a subsidiary refers to a company controlled by another company, typically called the parent or holding company. Control is most commonly established through ownership of more than 50 per cent of the subsidiary's voting stock, although it can also be achieved through other mechanisms, such as the ability to appoint the majority of the subsidiary's board of directors. Similarly, in legal and business terms, an 'affiliate' refers to a company related to another through common ownership or control. Unlike a subsidiary, an affiliate does not need to be majority-owned by the parent company.

Writing a century ago, Commons could not fathom, for instance, the situation we have today, whereby, for example, David Beckham's 'wealth' can be his image. For example, a company called Gillette may believe it can secure superior future income streams by linking its razors to David Beckham's image. Of course, David Beckham must secure rights over his own image in law, and then sell those rights to someone else, in this case Gillette, and pocket the money. The more he sells those rights, the less he withholds the right to his image from others, and the less valuable the rights are going to be. In a powerful example of how this works, Paul McCartney's imagination, as it appeared in musical scores, was bought by Michael Jackson, thus preventing Paul McCartney from using these scores without paying Michael Jackson. Michael Jackson obtained the right of withholding Paul McCartney's use of Paul McCartney's own ideas and music, for which he charged rent. By exercising withholding, Jackson maintained the value of his property.

I also could in theory have control over my own image. Unfortunately, no company seems to recognize its withholding from the market as capable of generating superior future income streams for them. As a result, my image does not contribute to my wealth. The intangible value of my image is currently zero.

****

If Commons offers a more nuanced account of the rise of intangibles that I will be using in this book, Veblen provides a theoretical framework linking intangibles to power. Veblen's theory plays an important role in my interpretation of modern wealth 'accumulation'. Veblen's theory focuses on the concepts of institutional delay or institutional dislocation, emphasizing how these create spaces for opportunistic behaviour. The transformation of the US economy into one dominated by intangibles occurred, Veblen argues, under the framework of an inherited set of rules, laws, norms, and habits of thought that evolved in Europe during the seventeenth century. Originally, smallholders and producers claimed a 'natural' right to the fruits of their labour – a principle tied closely to physical production. By the late nineteenth century, the universal right to ownership in the United States, rooted in seventeenth-century European concepts of 'natural law', had evolved.

Rather than owning the fruits of their own labour, the robber barons of America's nineteenth-century 'Gilded Age' appropriated these seventeenth-century ideas of ownership and reinterpreted them to fit the new industrial paradigm. They leveraged those outdated concepts of ownership to accumulate power by controlling organizations that claimed ownership over intangible assets. The concept of owning or 'holding' became in effect a concept of 'withholding' (Commons, 1924). In doing so, this new ownership class redefined property – not as a natural extension of productive labour, but as a tool for the accumulation and exercise of power.

In Veblen's view, these momentous events were not a concerted political action perpetrated by a class in the way Marx understood. Rather, they were the result of action by certain individuals who just happened to be in the right place at the right time. Technological advancements move quickly, following their own rhythms and often creating significant gaps between emerging innovations and inherited institutions such as laws, which move much more slowly. These gaps present opportunities, and those who seize them become the wealthy and powerful of their era. Such individuals are not merely fortunate beneficiaries of chance; they actively corner society's knowledge, expertise, institutions, and even habits of thought to serve their interests and corner the market (Veblen, 1908).

****

Of course, this is only a snapshot of Veblen's and Commons's perspectives on American capitalism in the late nineteenth century. What I take from Commons and Veblen is the following. First, we live in a world that, at least during the period covered in this this book, roughly 1980 to 2020, has been increasingly dominated by intangibles.

Second, as in earlier periods, new opportunities have emerged from the dynamics highlighted by Veblen – temporal dislocations between inherited institutions and their rules. Veblen explains that such opportunities arise when individuals exploit technological advances to arbitrage the existing institutional environment, enabling them to concentrate wealth. The wealth they concentrate is clearly largely in the form of intangibles, the augmented value of shareholding of large corporate groups.

Third, it follows that today's elites – our billionaires – probably like their predecessors have learned to exploit the gaps created by technological advancements within this institutional framework in the context of an intangible economy. These gaps enable them to redefine ownership and power in ways that capitalize on the evolving dynamics of intangibles and institutional inertia.

In the spirit of Veblen's and Commons's evolutionary ideas, then, I start where Veblen and Commons left off. I often think about my friend and mentor Susan Strange, who, as I have argued elsewhere, carried that tradition of thought forward while also challenging its limitations (Palan, 1999). Her intuition was that the older 'progressive' tradition had a fundamental flaw: it could not see much beyond the American border. When these economists talk about 'the market', what they had in mind was the American market.

Strange argued that political economy requires an 'I' – it must be international political economy. Today, we live in a world where markets operate within a fragmented state system. This is crucial. The world that eventually caught up with the large conglomerates and banking groups demanded a new social contract between private capital and society, represented by the state. The contract specifies that businesses benefit from public infrastructure, foundational services, and other societal support. In return, they pay taxes and adhere to regulations, recognizing the importance of social responsibility and financial stability. This notion of a social contract is at the heart of modern capitalism.

The social contract between the state and the corporation has a spatial dimension. This relationship has been institutionalized as a relationship between business and sovereign governments. This relationship is a form of constraint, but it also has a fatal flaw. In this sense, while each corporation is regulated by its respective country, the MNC as a whole, is not. That is what the anomaly in the discussion of the legal structure of the MNCs tends to miss out. Now consider a world increasingly dominated by intangibles. An MNC may choose to locate many of its intangible assets, such as trademarks or rights over patents, or data, or even 'goodwill', in low-tax jurisdictions and charge other subsidiaries hefty prices for using those assets. While each corporation within the group is subject to taxation in its own country and cannot avoid this, the group as a whole can reduce its overall tax burden.

This same principle can also be applied to liabilities, financial restrictions, and other regulatory constraints, as we explore further in due course.

Now, consider the following scenario. what if I, a business manager, can skew the balance? Suppose I manage to find a way to receive the same level of infrastructural support and services, but use certain mechanisms – whether legal loopholes, lobbying, or regulatory arbitrage – to reduce my tax obligations, avoid liabilities, sidestep financial restrictions, or bypass other regulatory constraints. Would not a business that takes advantage of those opportunities be judged by the market to be more valuable because its prospects for profitable future income are augmented? The ability to tilt the scales, to extract the same or greater resources from the environment while shouldering fewer costs, is precisely what makes such entities attractive to investors. They are seen as more efficient, more profitable, and ultimately better positioned to deliver long-term returns.

The market rewards such a corporate group, a group that harnesses its decentred legal structure to arbitrage rules, with significantly higher capitalization, reflecting its enhanced profitability and reduced risk profile.

That is what the Susan Strange's 'I' represents in the context of technology. It symbolizes a modern form of temporal dislocation, where technological advancements have outpaced the inherited institutions of the nineteenth-century nation-state.

This dislocation also explains why all MNCs are organized as clusters of independent companies. Their fragmented structure mirrors the fragmented markets in which they operate. They adopt this organization because it offers significant advantages for arbitraging rules. By exploiting these regulatory discrepancies, they not only reduce costs and liabilities but also enhance their market value by increasing the worth of their intangible assets

Who truly benefited from the future income streams capitalized into higher value of the shares of companies? The often-heard answer at the time of Veblen and Commons, as now, is that the beneficiaries are 'all of us': the millions of individuals with pension funds or shares in investment funds. This narrative conveniently glosses over the fact that many foreign investors lost their money, falling victim to the dubious characters and speculative schemes behind the sale of shares.

Veblen took a less charitable view, seeing these dynamics not as benign or merely unfortunate outcomes of risk-taking, but as symptomatic of deeper structural inequalities. To Veblen, the wealth generated by these enterprises was not evenly distributed among shareholders or reinvested for the public good. Instead, it was disproportionately concentrated in the hands of a few, exacerbating the economic disparities and power imbalances that defined his critique of capitalism. John Pierpont Morgan built his wealth in the late nineteenth century by reorganizing and consolidating the United States's largest railroads, raising capital in Europe, and actively managing these corporations. He was a powerful broker, who, with the aid of 'Commodore' Vanderbilt, forced the merger of steel companies around Pittsburgh on, among others, Andrew Carnegie, creating US Steel Trust in 1901 (Allen, 1979). Henry Goldman, son of the firm's founder Marcus Goldman, led Goldman Sachs in new directions in the early 1900s, including the practice of selling shares to families and expanding into the initial public offering market. Goldman is considered a great innovator in generating and capitalizing on industrial goodwill (Palan, 2015).

For Veblen, these individuals capitalized opportunistically on circumstances, exploiting institutional dislocation. Today's modern plutocracy operates similarly, thriving on their ability to arbitrage rules. They are a rule-based transgressor elite, composed of major shareholders in corporate groups whose wealth is predominantly denominated in intangibles. They avoid paying taxes not through theft, but by employing sophisticated strategies such as 'buy, borrow, and die'. This involves borrowing against the value of their shares to finance their lifestyles while deferring capital gains taxes, leaving those liabilities to their heirs. And when proposals such as a wealth tax emerge to counteract these techniques of wealth accumulation – as was central to Kamala Harris's plan – those who objected were notably seated in the front row and centre in the Rotunda, aligning with a president who will hear none of it.

This also tells us about the cynicism of our own age, exemplified by these elites, particularly those who seek to play a role in modern politics. Figures such as Donald Trump, who have amassed their wealth by taking advantage of the corporate form to transgress rules and exploit systemic loopholes, now position themselves as the saviours of those left behind by the very system they have profited from. In their boundless cynicism, these individuals craft a narrative of defiance against the establishment, those who benefit from jurisdictional arbitrage, conveniently ignoring that they are both its products and its beneficiaries. Their populist rhetoric exploits the frustrations of those who feel disenfranchised, while perpetuating the structures that entrench their right to continue acting as a rule-based transgressor elite. Jurisdictional arbitrage is not just a mechanism of exploitation; it is also a vital link in a chain of relationships defining the present-day politics and economy.

****

In his *Dialogue on the Two Chief World Systems*, Galileo Galilei speaks in the name of a sceptic who pointed out all sorts of anomalies (Galilei and Finocchiar, 1997). The heavens appear to obey all the expected rules, the sceptic pointed out, with celestial bodies moving predictably across the night sky. But there are anomalies: certain bright stars (what we now know as planets) suddenly deviate from the pattern. They turn sharply, move in reverse, or shift at unexpected angles. To avoid imprisonment (where he eventually ended up anyway), Galileo did not explicitly state the radical truth he was proposing: the conventional theory predicated on a radical separation of heaven and earth was based on an interpretation of a three-dimensional world through a two-dimensional lens. In a three-dimensional world where the Earth and other planets orbit the sun, their movements, when observed from Earth's perspective, appear anomalous and strange.

Similarly, in economics and international political economy, we continue to interpret the world economy – a three-dimensional system comprising tangibles, incorporeal assets, and intangibles – through the constrained lens of a two-dimensional perspective: one is called the 'real' economy, the other 'finance'.

This limited vantage point has left us grappling with an anomaly: the modern MNC, organized as a cluster of independent companies, seemingly preoccupied with dividing itself into an ever-growing number of subsidiaries structured along increasingly complex lines of control. At the same time, the company sheds as many tangible aspects of its activities as possible, outsourcing them to external contractors. These companies derive their value increasingly from intangibles. Why does this happen?

Only by understanding this model of capitalism as a systemic relationship among various components but facing also those strange anomalies of the modern MNCs can we uncover how a once-fringe activity such as arbitrage has come to play such a central role in today's corporate planning and strategies. My aim in this book is to bring jurisdictional arbitrage schemes to light, not to overstate their significance, but to situate them within the broader context of my understanding of the American model of capitalism at large, often referred to as globalization.

Acknowledgements

While most books are, in reality, the product of collective efforts, this one is even more so than most. The research for this book was conducted under the auspices of a five-year, large-scale research project, funded by the European Research Council Advanced Grant, titled Corporate Arbitrage and CPL Maps: Hidden Structures of Control in the Global Economy (CORPLINK). I am profoundly grateful for the support that made this work possible.

The research was deepened and expanded through a two-year research initiative undertaken by the same team as part of an Organisation for Economic Co-operation and Development (OECD) project on illicit finance in the energy trading sector. These collaborations have significantly enriched the scope and depth of the analysis, allowing for a comprehensive exploration of jurisdictional arbitrage and its broader implications for the global economy.

Throughout this period, I was fortunate to benefit from the help and support of many exceptionally talented individuals. I am deeply indebted to the advice and assistance of numerous colleagues, as well as experienced lawyers, accountants, and business professionals – far too many to name individually. Their insights and expertise played a crucial role in shaping the ideas and arguments presented in this book.

I extend my special thanks to my colleagues at City St George's, University of London, whose unwavering support and intellectual engagement greatly enriched this project. Their contributions – through countless discussions, critical feedback, and collaborative exchanges – have been invaluable. In particular, I would like to thank Amin Samman, Sandy Hager, Albena Azmanova, Inga Rademacher, Brunello Rosa, Photis Lysandrou, Lucio Sarno, Jean Chalabi, and Stefano Sgambati for their thoughtful insights, encouragement, and commitment to academic dialogue.

I am also deeply grateful to several friends who generously shared their time, insights, and expertise, helping to refine the ideas and

Acknowledgements

analyses presented in this book. Their intellectual generosity and critical engagement have been invaluable. In particular, I would like to extend my thanks to Reuven Avi-Yonah, Omri Marian, Lorraine Eden, Alex Cobham, Moran Harrai, Daniel Haberly, Eelke Heemskerk, Peter Jansky, Markus Meinzer, Javier Garcia-Bernado, Johnny West, Christopher Trautvetter, Paul Vaaler, Jenaline Pine, Corentin Cohen, Sol Picciotto, Janek Toporowski, and Mark Herman Schwartz. Their contributions – whether through discussions, feedback, or shared research – have profoundly shaped this work, and I am truly appreciative of their support.

A special mention goes to my friend David Sassoon, whose vast experience in managing some of the world's largest specialist commodity trading companies provided an invaluable perspective. His deep knowledge of the corporate world and willingness to share insights greatly enriched this research.

I am also deeply grateful to my son Michael Palan, now at McKinsey, whose corrective insights and sharp analytical perspective helped refine many of the ideas in this book. My son Sasha Palan produced many of the figures for this book. Additionally, Jonathan Glukhovski, formerly of Goldman Sachs, contributed to my understanding of the world of special purpose vehicles, shedding light on some of the more intricate financial structures examined in this work. Their contributions have been indispensable, and I am immensely thankful for their support.

Many of the ideas in this book were first introduced at the annual meetings of a unique group of scholars; we call our gathering the Offshore Group. These remarkable scholars include Brooke Harrington, Kimberly Kay Hoang, Alex Cooley, Ricardo Soares de Oliveira, Jason Sharman, Kristin Surak, and John Heathershow. Their contributions were invaluable, not only in shaping conceptual ideas but also in refining the presentation of the research.

This study also benefited enormously from our friends and colleagues involved in the OECD project. Catherine Anderson, Rebecca Engebretsen, and Douglas Porter challenged us to think critically about the implications of jurisdictional arbitrage in the global energy trading sector. Additionally, Phil Culbert of KPMG provided invaluable insights and expertise, enhancing our understanding of the sophisticated techniques employed by these organizations

Special thanks are due to three close friends. Leonard Seabrooke, who led a key stream of the CORPLINK project at the Copenhagen

Business School, and played a crucial role in helping secure the funding necessary for this research. Yuval Millo, a professor of accounting at Warwick Business School, provided invaluable advice on accounting matters central to the project and made a direct contribution to Chapter 7 of this book. Finally, Xinyi Wei, now of the United Nations Conference on Trade and Development (UNCTAD), who joined the team towards the end of the project, offered profound insights into the operations of Chinese companies and banks through Hong Kong's financial centre.

The core CORPLINK team consisted of Hannah Petersen, Richard Phillips, Anastasia Nesvetailova, and Jean-Philippe Robé. Hannah Petersen, now with Boston Consulting, was a key contributor to both the CORPLINK and OECD projects. She authored numerous background notes, managed much of the equity mapping, and contributed significantly to many of the project's publications.

My partner, Anastasia Nesvetailova, played a pivotal role in both projects from their inception. Now at UNCTAD, she is creatively advancing the ideas and methodologies outlined in this book into policy frameworks for developing countries. Her work is pioneering a new field of study that integrates corporate organization and arbitrage with core questions of development. These groundbreaking insights are reflected in chapter 7 of the *UN Trade and Development Report (TDR) 2022* and chapter 3 of *TDR 2023*.

This book would not have been possible without the help and support of Jean-Phillip Robé, a distinguished scholar and highly accomplished corporate lawyer with years of experience at the highest levels of industry. Jean-Phillip generously dedicated his time to meticulously reviewing our equity mappings of various corporate groups. He not only highlighted the diverse structures in use but also patiently explained the legal and business principles underpinning the organization of arbitrage. His extraordinary expertise in law and the corporate world, coupled with a profound knowledge of history and a remarkable ability to generalize and conceptualize, forms a critical foundation for the insights presented in this book.

Last but certainly not least, Richard Phillips, whose groundbreaking development of the equity mapping technique formed the foundation of both projects. Richard not only created the necessary coding and innovated the algorithm but also brought an extraordinary depth of knowledge about the business world, gained during his time at the

Manchester Business School. His profound understanding of data analysis transformed the study of corporate arbitrage into a true art form. All the empirical and conceptual work presented in this book was conducted in close collaboration with Richard Phillips, whose contributions were indispensable to its creation.

I would like to extend my gratitude to the team at Cambridge University Press, particularly to John Haslam and Carrie Parkinson, who went above and beyond to support this project. I am also deeply thankful to Elisabeth Thompson, who not only assisted with proof-reading and editing but also identified missing elements, ensuring the book's completeness. I would also like to thank Vidhya Ramamourthy, Claire Sissen, and Edward Street as members of the team for their work on the book.

While this book has benefited enormously from the insights, expertise, and contributions of these individuals, any errors or oversights remain entirely my own responsibility. Their support has been invaluable, but the final interpretations, conclusions, and any shortcomings in this work are solely mine.

Author Note

This study focuses on how firms engage in legal transgression by operating at the edges of legality – exploiting grey areas in the law to maximize profits. It provides a practical view of how jurisdictional arbitrage functions in real-world corporate behaviour, showing the dark side of globalization where corporate power often goes unchecked. This nuts-and-bolts book tells the story of the 'secret weapon' that led to the rise of the wealthiest and most power elites of today, the rule-based transgressor elite. It is not a story about a concerted attempt by a group of people to exploit others. Nor is this a narrative of a social class taking advantage of the state or some grand imperialistic design. Instead, it is a story of a social group that rose to unprecedented position of power and wealth by using the most powerful secret of a capitalist economy: the DNA of a multinational corporation (MNC).

The beginnings of the story go back to the late nineteenth century, the era of the ascent of large business going concerns organized as clusters of legally independent companies linked together through formal or informal linkages. These companies are typically described as multinational corporations (or enterprises). I prefer to see them as centrally coordinated multi-corporate enterprises (CCMCEs). This book centres on an important dimension of the CCMCE organizational structure that has remained relatively unexplored. It is the gap that opened between the legal status of the group, the 'going concern', and the legal entity, or the corporation. This gap has been exploited ever since to arbitrage national rules. It has become the principal technique by which modern corporate groups adjust to, but also avoid and evade, national rules and regulations, including taxation.

The book presents the first systemic survey and analysis of the techniques of jurisdictional arbitrage, their relationship to the CCMCE model of corporate organization, and impact on state and society. The book guides the reader through the dilemmas faced by corporate organizations in the chaotic regulatory environment of real markets that traverse many countries, each with their own rules and regulations, viewing the regulatory and political environment as seen from the perspective of managers and 'business planners' of modern organizations. The book describes the dynamics of the set of opportunities they uncovered, the penalties they have tried to avoid, and rewards they have reaped, to begin to understand the profound systemic impact that the ambiguity the concept of the corporation and that of the business concern have had on the development of modern capitalism.

Abbreviations

APA	Advance pricing agreement
ASI	Apple Sales International
BEPS	Base erosion and profit shifting
BOC	Bank of China
BVI	British Virgin Islands
CCB	China Construction Bank
CCMCE	Centrally coordinated multi-corporate enterprise
CEN	Capital export neutrality
CFC	Controlled foreign company
CIN	Capital import neutrality
DTA	Double taxation agreement
ECI	Effectively connected income
EM	Equity mapping
EU	European Union
FDI	Foreign direct investment
GP	General partner
GUO	Global ultimate owner
IB	International business
ICIJ	International Consortium of Investigative Journalists
IP	Intellectual property
IRS	Internal Revenue Service
ITA	International tax arbitrage
KG	Kommanditgesellschaft (German limited partnership structure)
LLC	Limited liability company
LP	Limited partner
MNC	Multinational corporation
MSF	Multi-subsidiary firm
NI	Netherlands Antilles
OBS	Off-balance sheet

List of Abbreviations

OECD	Organisation for Economic Co-operation and Development
OFC	Offshore financial centre
R&D	Research and development
SEC	Securities and Exchange Commission
SNA	Standard social network analysis
SPE	Special purpose entity
TCE	Transaction cost economics
TJN	Tax Justice Network
UBO	Ultimate beneficial ownership
UBTI	Unrelated business taxable income
UN	United Nations
UNCTAD	United Nations Conference on Trade and Development

Introduction

On May 21, 2013, the Permanent Subcommittee on Investigations of the US Senate Homeland Security and Government Affairs Committee held a hearing into an alleged tax avoidance scheme perpetrated by the Apple group. One of the more outrageous tactics used by Apple, the committee concluded, was to set up two Irish affiliates in such a way that they ended up being tax residents neither of Ireland nor of the United States. The affiliates reported a net income of US$30 billion and US$74 billion respectively between 2009 and 2012, more than a quarter of Apple's annual income during those years. Yet they 'declined to declare any tax residence, filed no corporate income tax return, and paid no corporate income taxes to any national government for three years' (Levin et al., 2013, 2).

An even more elaborate scheme was set up by another paragon of contemporary capitalism, Google. In this scheme, known as *Double Irish, Dutch Sandwich* (Beebeejaun, 2020; Darby and Lemaster, 2007), Google transferred ownership of intellectual rights over vital patents and trademarks to a subsidiary incorporated in Ireland (Burke-Kennedy, 2020; House of Commons, Committee of Public Accounts, 2013; Zucman, 2015). That subsidiary, although registered in Ireland, was domiciled in Bermuda, a zero-tax jurisdiction. The scheme ensured Google paid almost no tax at all. A variant of the scheme known as *Double Irish and Single Malt* (Coyle, 2017; Kelly, 2015; Loomis, 2011) emerged recently, replacing the Netherlands with Malta.

The discovery of the tactics employed by Apple, Google, Amazon, and many other leading corporate groups opened a Pandora's box, revealing a shady world of modern corporate tax and regulatory planning consisting of an unknown number of schemes described by corporate lawyers as *jurisdictional arbitrage* (Avi-Yonah, 2017; Kerber, 1999; Marian, 2013; Panayi, 2006a, 2006b, 2015). Jurisdictional arbitrage refers to tax planning and regulatory avoidance strategies that exploit gaps, loopholes, or inconsistencies in one country's laws to circumvent the rules of another. These schemes are highly complex, shrouded in secrecy, and deeply embedded within intricate corporate structures.[1]

'Few, if any phenomena', note Jan Friedrich and Mathias Thiemann, 'threaten the goal of law-makers, market regulators or accounting standard-setters to issue adequate rules and ensure their rigorous application as does regulatory arbitrage' (Friedrich and Thiemann, 2021, 81). Yet such concerns have not given rise to anything approaching a systemic study of jurisdictional arbitrage. On the contrary, the literature on jurisdictional arbitrage in law and accounting, notes Annalise Riles, is 'surprisingly thin' (Riles, 2013, 68). In other disciplines – such as economics, business, and political science – the literature is scarcer, bordering on non-existent.[2] Jurisdictional arbitrage schemes tend to be portrayed as isolated actions that take place on the margins, in offshore financial centres (OFCs). The European Union's Anti-Tax Avoidance Directive, for instance, targets what it calls 'artificial constructions' designed to exploit differences between national tax laws to minimize the tax burden.[3] More broadly, jurisdictional arbitrage schemes are typically depicted using derogatory language, such as 'gamesmanship', 'manipulation', 'artificial constructions', 'exotic planning devices', or 'phantom investments', suggesting they raise few if any significant systemic issues (Damgaard et al., 2019a; Freedman, 2008; Kaye, 2014; Mitchell, 2008; Post et al., 2002).

---

[1] Complexity may mask a degree of communality: 'While there can be several layers of complexity, arrangements exploiting differences in the tax treatment of instruments ... are often based on similar underlying elements and aim at achieving similar effects' (OECD, 2012, 7). This suggests these schemes could lend themselves to comparative analysis as they draw on similar sets of tools and principles. Hence, contrary to common impressions, there can, in principle, be a theory of jurisdictional arbitrage.

[2] The literature in international business, political science, and international political economy is replete with examples of how MNCs structure their operations to minimize taxes, bypass regulations, and exploit divergences in national regulatory frameworks. Yet this literature tends to be anecdotal and rarely if ever makes connection between these practices and jurisdictional arbitrage.

[3] In EU law, for instance, artificial constructions refer to business practices or legal arrangements that lack real economic substance or commercial purpose and are designed to gain tax or regulatory advantages (see Avi-Yonah, 2000; Panayi, 2015; Reurink and Garcia-Bernardo, 2021)

Is this approach justified? I do not think so. Far from being a fringe activity, jurisdictional arbitrage has become systemic, deeply embedded in the fabric of corporate strategy. In advancing this argument in the following pages, we must move beyond the traditional perspectives of economists, who focus on markets and actors, and political scientists, who emphasize the role of the state. Instead, we need to adopt the vantage point of corporations themselves – seeing the world through the eyes of their managers and shareholders. Paradoxically, it is only by seeing through the eyes of the corporation that we come to recognize the full extent to which modern multinational corporations (MNCs) are political entities – shaping and being shaped by the very systems they are presumed to merely operate within.

To support this argument, I will be making throughout this book seven interrelated points.

First, whereas most of what has been written about arbitrage tends to be from the perspective of corporate taxation, the strategic exploitation of differences in laws and regulations to minimize costs or avoid regulation extends well beyond taxation.[4] Taxation was, after all, only one facet of the broader emergence of the rise of what is described in scholarly circles as the regulatory state (Majone, 1997). During the twentieth century, states increasingly replaced the nineteenth-century private litigation regimes with regulatory agencies and enacted a plethora of rules and regulations affecting businesses across various domains Today, business is subject to regulations extending from civil to administrative and sometimes criminal liability in all of the world's major legal systems. Business is subject, in addition, to privately designed (or quasi-private) accounting rules, a 'collection of

---

[4] This is not to say taxation is unimportant. The latest estimates of global corporate tax avoidance suggest around US$1 trillion a year, or approximately 1 per cent of global gross domestic product, most of which is attributed to the few thousand MNCs that dominate the world economy (Alstadsæter et al., 2018, 2022; Cobham and Janský, 2018a, 2019; Zucman, 2015). Current estimates of corporate tax avoidance focus on the revenue side of the equation, however, and multinational firms take advantage of futures and derivatives instruments to manipulate the timing and place of transactions, and those can be used for tax purposes as well. Two decades ago, such techniques were estimated to cost in excess of US$100 billion in tax avoidance annually in the United States alone (CFA, 1998; Donohoe, 2015; Schizer, 1999). In addition, most quantitative analyses of corporate tax avoidance would find it difficult to factor in the manipulation of accounting categories at the subsidiary level, and may underestimate the degree of avoidance that is taking place.

dialects' that evolved 'when professionals applied quantitative methods to qualitative endeavours' (King, 2006, 203).[5]

The point, as argued cogently by Annalise Riles (2013), is that any rules, however well designed, can be arbitraged, and most are likely to be arbitraged by someone, somewhere. Arbitraging schemes, she notes, are indeed most lucrative when spilling into new, often unsuspected regulatory spheres, not least because that is where money can be made (Riles, 2013). The scope for arbitrage in the international sphere is far greater than commonly assumed.

Second, the focus on taxation has contributed to what seems to me fairly widespread (though often implicit) perception that MNCs behave like large profit harvesting machines. The corporate group is designed, or so it is believed, so that the parent company accumulates group-wide profits, which are then distributed as dividends to shareholders. The parent use subsidiaries in OFCs to avoid taxation.

While this model may seem reasonable, a moment's reflection reveals major strategic and financial problems with such an approach. If all profits were systematically funnelled to the parent company, the corporate group would be disproportionately dependent on the tax and regulatory environment of the parent's home country. This would expose the group to several risks. Many home countries tax worldwide income of their corporations, meaning that once profits are repatriated to the parent, they become fully taxable. For instance, a US-based parent would be subject to US tax rules on all repatriated profits, potentially eliminating the benefits of offshore tax planning.[6]

I argue that when viewed from the perspective of capital market augmentation, the function of subsidiaries of MNCs changes

---

[5] These include, in the words of Thomas King, financial accounting, tax accounting, operational accounting and specialized accounting rules for those 'lucky banks, insurers, utilities, and transportation firms' that are required to file reports demonstrating solvency or compliance with government rules (King, 2006, 4).

[6] The United States' Global Intangible Low-Taxed Income introduced in 2017 applies to foreign subsidiaries' income even if it's not repatriated. But then, some countries, for example China and Brazil, impose restrictions on how and when foreign companies can repatriate profits. Furthermore, the harvesting machine model would expose the group to foreign currency volatility, particularly if the parent's home country has an unstable exchange rate or inflationary pressures. If all profits are centralized at the parent, subsidiaries may lack access to capital for reinvestment in local markets.

considerably. Rather than merely funnelling earnings upward, a subsidiary can be logged as an asset on the parent's consolidated accounts. Internal transfers between subsidiaries and the parent can then be treated as discretionary transactions, rather than mandatory profit distributions. This flexibility liberates the corporate group from strict dependence on revenue extraction, allowing it to focus on exogenous factors such as regulatory regimes (taxation, reporting rules, capital controls), market conditions (exchange rates, investment incentives, sector growth), and political and legal risks in different jurisdictions (Birkinshaw and Morrison, 1995; Dowd et al., 2017; Forte, 2016, Greggi, 2019; Grubert and Mutti, 1991; US Department of the Treasury, 2016).

MNCs are not profit harvesting machines but asset harvesting machines – a point that will become clearer throughout this book. This means that not only is the scope of jurisdictional arbitrage being much greater than assumed, and this is my third point, but the motivating rationale for employing jurisdictional arbitrage is not simply about taxation or circumvention of this or that regulation. At core, jurisdictional arbitrage arises from deep-seated contradictions that we have inherited from the period of the Second Industrial Revolution – a period of rapid technological advance that witnessed profound transformation in production, manufacturing, communication, and transportation. However, this era also witnessed the emergence of modern borders. This was the era when key nations such as Germany and Italy emerged, while the United States solidified its identity as a unified state. Meanwhile, countries such as Britain and France drew sharper distinctions between the motherland and their colonies. It was a period, therefore, that produced the rigid and somewhat arbitrary fragmentation of the world's geographic space.

A system of states, founded on the principles of sovereignty, produced a fragmented regulatory landscape. Essential resources needed by the Second Industrial Revolution, such as raw materials, skilled labour, and market access, became unevenly distributed, located within institutional and political environments influenced by the historical and institutional legacies of wars and colonialism. It was during this period that the worlds of geopolitics and geoeconomics began to fall out of sync – not only spatially but also epistemologically. The world of states is a world of 'things', but advanced economies began a momentous process whereby they shifted gear into a forward-looking perspective, represented by the concept of intangible assets.

The corporate world is not simply making money from coordinating factors of production efficiently while producing goods the market desires. The corporate world is augmenting value based on the principles of futurity, and it does so by augmenting the value of its assets.

Unfortunately, this fragmented and misaligned spatial environment became entrenched, and this is my fourth point, two, perhaps three, decades after the core ideas of economics had already been established. Since then, economics – along with related fields that built upon the epistemological foundations of what became known as neoclassical economics, such as international business and political science – has struggled to fully account for the complexities of the real world. The preferred approach has been rather to begin with a theoretical proposition – a theory of markets where people are exchanging 'things' – and then treat the countless contradictions arising from the misalignment of geopolitics and geoeconomics, the world of things, and the economy of intangibles as intellectual puzzles to be solved. But seen from the perspective of jurisdictional arbitrage, the limitation of the approach become clear.

Put simply, if the global economy truly resembled the seamless, homogeneous, and borderless 'market' depicted in economic textbooks, arbitrage would not exist and MNCs would be merely profit-harvesting machines. Arbitrage occurs, then, in an intellectual space overlooked by economics. One way to resolve this conundrum is to dismiss arbitrage as an 'artificial' construct. The advantage of this approach is that economics can then sidestep the issue altogether, focusing solely on what it deems 'genuine' or not artificially constructed. Needless to say, this is not the approach I take in this book.

But the same system of states that increasing misaligned with the needs of business also produced unwittingly, and this is my fifth point, gaps that could be exploited by those very same businesses. In this sense, jurisdictional arbitrage is both a product of and a strategic response to geopolitical and geoeconomic misalignments of the late nineteenth century. Arbitrageurs are not merely navigating an inherited geopolitical and geoeconomic 'system' that are arbitrary – they actively seek to create their own regulatory spaces, islands of stability in what was essentially an out of sync environment. By strategically exploiting the gaps and inconsistencies produced by sovereignty, the newly minted MNCs learned to shape, up to a point, the rules of the game to suit their interests.

Why then do businesses seek to control the environment? The answer seems obvious. We all want to limit our dependence on things that are beyond our control. But the answer is more complicated when it comes to business. A business entity whose value is based on future performance must control the environment – or must show, perform, if you wish, that it can control the environment and hence its future. In this way, jurisdictional arbitrage represents more than a set of strategic manoeuvres. These practices are both performatives as much as they threaten the foundational balance between private enterprise and public responsibility. But as economists are fond of saying, there are no free lunches. Establishing and vetting arbitrage schemes involves significant costs, which can be justified by the scale of operations. The larger and wealthier the MNC, the greater its potential gains from implementing internal treasury operations or engaging high-cost professional legal, accounting, and financial services.

In turn, and this is my sixth point, this positions arbitrage as a previously unrecognized form of power, making it a subject of significant interest to political science and international political economy. In Chapter 9, I argue the power dynamics of jurisdictional arbitrage resemble the predator–prey dynamics found in nature. Businesses, as the 'prey', outmanoeuvre their 'predators', the states, by camouflaging themselves and using the states' own rules against them. Through this strategic adaptation, firms turn the constraints imposed by states into tools for their survival and advantage. To use another analogy, jurisdictional arbitrage acts as a canary in the coal mine, signalling a warning, in this case, how modern businesses transform challenges into solutions that, in turn, shape the fabric of contemporary life.

Behind these 'corporations' there are people, individuals making decisions, crafting strategies, and deliberately exploiting the complexities of legal and regulatory diversity for profit. Corporate actions, though executed under the guise of legal entities, ultimately reflect the choices, motivations, and agency of the individuals who lead and manage them. Executives, legal advisors, and financial experts serve as the architects and primary beneficiaries of a system designed by none other than themselves.

These people also act collectively, if unwittingly, undermining, and this is my seventh point, the implicit social contract between states, businesses, and citizens. The social contract that underpinned the rise of the regulatory state of the late nineteenth century was built on the expectation that businesses contribute to societal wealth, through taxation, job creation, and compliance with regulations, in exchange for the rights and privileges granted by states, such as access to markets, legal protections, and infrastructure. The ability to neutralize, or at least partially circumvent, the regulatory environments allows businesses to exploit the benefits provided by the state while avoiding some of the corresponding costs.

Arbitrage is closely tied, therefore, with broader issues of inequality and the emergence of what I call the *rule-based transgressor elite* – arguably the most powerful elite of our time. This group thrives on its ability to operate within the boundaries of legal frameworks while systematically exploiting their loopholes, leveraging arbitrage to amass wealth and power in ways that reinforce existing disparities and reshape global dynamics. Scientists often refer to theory of a 'microcosm' or 'microcosmic event', whereby a small-scale situation can encapsulate or reflect the characteristics of a larger system (Benton et al., 2007). In this book, I treat jurisdictional arbitrage as a microcosmic event. I do not aim to provide exhaustive research into the various forms of jurisdictional arbitrage schemes, nor do I offer a complete theory of modern corporate groups. Instead, I argue jurisdictional arbitrage schemes open a unique window into the functioning of corporate power within a world of states, illuminating how corporate groups navigate and influence the boundaries and frameworks of national jurisdictions.

Why MNCs Are Not What They Seem

At first glance, the title of this section may seem provocative, even counterintuitive. How can MNCs, arguably the most important business organization today, 'not exist'? The term 'multinational corporation' conjures up an image of a unified, centralized entity operating seamlessly across borders.[7] Yet the reality is far more complex, and it is far more complex for a reason.

---

[7] It is common to speak of MNCs as if they were singular organizations that think, behave, and act much like a person. We speak of firms 'wanting' to grow or survive, as if they have an innate biological drive, or ascribe them moral responsibilities and expect them to behave ethically, much like individuals. We speak of firms 'deciding', 'choosing', or 'strategizing', or alternatively as 'aggressive' 'ambitious', or 'risk-averse', as if they had a singular mind. We

In *Global Political Economy: Understanding the International Economic Order* (2011), Robert Gilpin recounts a story of a group of graduate students at Princeton University who asked their Economics professor to offer a course on MNCs. They were firmly rebuffed on the grounds that 'multinational corporations do not exist' (Gilpin, 2011, 33). Gilpin interprets the rebuff as a vivid demonstration of the absurd limitations of neoclassical theory.

But perhaps the unnamed professor in Gilpin's story had a point. A corporation is a licensed entity, granted existence by a sovereign authority. A corporation, by definition, cannot be multinational. Itzhak Hadari writes: 'The typical MNC is a cluster of separate legal entities in several jurisdictions, which exist only if the laws of each jurisdiction recognize them as legal entities. It is a business and economic creature, and the usage of that term is presently found *only* in those fields' (Hadari, 1973, 754; emphasis added).[8] Whereas we tend to speak of the MNC in the singular, the reality, at least as far as lawyers are concerned, is that there is no 'MNC' that can transact in markets, pay tax, or pay off politicians.[9] Lacking a formal legal personality, these business entities simply cannot perform any of the tasks generally assigned to them in the literature.

But before we conclude MNCs do not exist, let me modify the statement in a way that, in my view, deepens the puzzle. A single

---

describe firms as 'healthy', 'struggling', or even 'dying', attributing to them human-like conditions. The literature contains plenty of references to terms such as 'subsidiaries', 'affiliates', 'special purpose vehicles', 'joint ventures', and 'holding companies', but these are often framed as mere administrative supports, logistical tools rather than fundamental elements of the MNC's strategic architecture.

[8] Bartlett and Ghosal define MNCs as 'clusters of geographically dispersed and goal-disparate corporations that encompasses a parent company, one or several headquarters, and a multitude of national subsidiaries scattered across the globe ... Two or more corporations [are] linked by sufficient stock ownership to cause them to function as one, coordinated going concern' (Bartlett and Ghoshal, 2002, 6).

[9] The concept of 'MNC' remains unsurprisingly unsettled. Some prefer 'multi-national enterprise' over MNC, others 'transnational corporation' or 'global firm'. Alfred Chandler (2005) argues the term 'corporation' often carries specific legal and structural connotations, implying a formal, centralized organization. Well, that is not entirely correct. But Chandler's proposal to use the term 'enterprise' to imply a more flexible and dynamic entity that can adapt to different markets and regulatory environments does not really deal with the question of the various uses of the decentred legal organization of modern MNCs.

corporation can set up branches around the world and *can* then conceivably be described as an MNC. But it so happens that most modern MNCs – particularly the well-known household names – have opted for a different organizational modality. Hadari's (1973) concept of MNCs as 'clusters' of companies is not exactly true, either. Modern MNCs are not a mere assortment of independent entities; they are profoundly integrated, with a dual nature. I prefer to describe them as *centrally coordinated multi-corporate enterprises* (CCMCEs). These corporations are deliberately structured so they can function as a single, unified business in markets, coordinated at the highest level to achieve strategic cohesion across borders. Legally, however, they are structured as CCMCEs, or groups of independent companies, causing many to refer to them as a 'corporate group'.

The question is whether the organization of the MNC as a CCMCE truly matters – and, if it does, for whom. At first glance, the question might seem inconsequential; after all, if it were significant, surely it would have garnered more attention by now.[10] Under the influence of two brilliant economists, Roland Coase and James Buchanan, economics gradually evolved from about the 1960s to incorporate 'economics of choice' stressing the market is exchange of property titles (Buchanan, 1978). This perspective suggests that 'firms' internalize transactions that can be executed at a lower cost within the organization than through the market (Alchian and Demsetz, 1973; Demsetz, 1988; Fama, 1980; Jensen and Meckling, 1976). This approach reframes firms, including MNCs, as legal and economic constructs designed to optimize efficiency, rather than as cohesive, centralized entities. Harold Demsetz argues, for instance, that the core question in economics is why a 'firm-like' web of contracts tends to coalesce in markets (Demsetz, 1997). Firms, including MNCs, are viewed as 'no more than a web of contracts and other legal documents that tie together various parties to a specific company' (Cohen, 2007, 28).

[10] Economists are largely untroubled by the decentralized structure of MNCs, for two interconnected reasons. First, the concept of the firm in economics has long been treated as a 'theoretical construct' (Allen, 2005, 899) bearing little resemblance 'with its real-world namesake' (Demsetz, 1983, 377). The specific legal organization of firms, whether as limited companies, partnerships, or other structures, has long been viewed as relatively inconsequential.

Legal scholars question, however, why economists devote so much attention to contract, transaction, and property while ignoring a fundamental component in the creation and organization of business enterprises: entity law in the form of the laws of incorporation. There is evidence that the number of subsidiaries in the corporate group is rising. In an analysis they conducted for the US Fed, Dafna Avraham, Patricia Selvaggi, and James Vickery (Avraham et al., 2012) found the number of subsidiaries and affiliates owned by some of the largest US banking holding companies rose to an average of 3,400 in 2012, up from about 1,000 in 1990. Figures indicate an astounding proliferation over time. In 1985, Phillip Blumberg found that the 1,000 largest US industrial corporations had an average of forty-eight subsidiaries. In 2012, Stephen Cohen reported the entire group of MNCs had about 77,000 subsidiaries – and was surprised by this number. But by 2018, the top 100 alone were reported to have over 73,000 subsidiaries (Phillips et al., 2020). The trend shows no signs of stopping, let alone slowing down: the number of subsidiaries had risen by an average 8 per cent when my colleagues and I took a second look eighteen months later (Palan et al., 2021).

Why have 'firm-like' webs of contracts taken the form of an increasing number of subsidiaries and affiliates? There is nothing in the theory of the nexus of contracts – or indeed in any other economic theory – that begins to answer the question of why MNCs have such an extraordinary number of subsidiaries.

Business and management studies, in contrast, provide an answer – or so it seems. They argue subsidiaries play a critical role in enhancing operational efficiency, managing risk, and adapting to diverse markets (Desai, 2009; Zey, 1999; Zey and Camp, 1996; Zey and Swenson, 1998). However, these explanations require closer scrutiny. The term 'operational efficiency' is remarkably broad and can encompass a wide range of practices. While it might refer to streamlining supply chains or optimizing resource allocation, it can just as easily serve as a euphemism for practices such as regulatory arbitrage.

This raises important questions about the true drivers of subsidiary proliferation. Is it genuinely about improving business operations, or is it a strategic response to a global system riddled with regulatory and jurisdictional inconsistencies?

Another set of developments largely overlooked by the web of contract theories is the structural organization of foreign direct investment

(FDI). A significant portion of FDI is not direct at all; it is intermediated. Instead of a straightforward flow from a parent company to a subsidiary in a foreign country, investments are often routed through subsidiaries in third countries. The phenomenon of intermediated FDI accounts for a substantial share of global FDI flows. Put differently, the CCMCE is not a flat organizational structure but a three-dimensional one.

We are thus presented with four interrelated puzzles: why MNCs are organized as CCMCEs; why the rules of incorporation and entity law, central to the CCMCE structure, are so often overlooked; why the number of subsidiaries established as independent companies continues to rise; and why the organization of CCMCEs has become increasingly complex. Underlying these four puzzles is a fifth. How can we have a meaningful discussion about the organization of CCMCEs without comprehensive data and a clear understanding of how MNCs are structured?

Equity Mapping: A Methodological Approach to Uncovering Corporate Control

I was reminded of a story I heard at a conference many years ago about how the Chinese state prepared for the advent of the internet in the 1990s. Chinese officials had invited the CEO of a pioneering American internet company to a two-day event aimed at discussing the future of the internet in China. During the event, various officials presented their ideas and plans for both encouraging and regulating internet use. When it was the American CEO's turn to speak, he began his talk with a simple question to the audience: 'How many of you have ever used a computer?' Only two officials raised their hands. He followed up with, 'How many of you have ever surfed the internet?' The answer was none of them had. Chinese officials in the 1990s were making grand plans for the internet without having basic, hands-on experience with computers or the internet itself. They were relying on theoretical knowledge or abstract ideas about what the internet could be, without engaging with the technology first hand.

I was reminded of this story because one of the significant challenges in having a meaningful discussion about jurisdictional arbitrage is the void of information – an informational desert that obscures its true scale and mechanisms. Despite the rich and expanding body of literature on MNCs and their subsidiaries, we know surprisingly little about how these corporate groups are actually organized. At best, we are presented with schematic diagrams of operational planning – visuals populated with empty boxes labelled 'divisions' or 'organizations' – that offer no insight into the actual subsidiaries underpinning these structures. Subsidiaries are often viewed as merely functional entities, serving operational purposes, akin to limbs of a larger body. This perspective assumes their distribution within corporate chains is largely random, guided by immediate needs rather than strategic design. Why bother with the anatomy of corporate groups if 'physiology' is good enough?

The CORPLINK project upon which this book relies sought to learn how CCMCEs are legally structured and how intra-firm transfers take place.[11] The technique uses an algorithm to capture information from corporate filings and converts the ownership data of MNCs and their subsidiary organizations, as recorded in the Orbis database, into visualized 'maps' using a standard social network analysis (SNA) approach. These visualizations, which the CORPLINK project designated as equity maps (EMs), provide a detailed and accessible representation of the ownership and control structures within corporate groups.

As the computer processed the data and began generating these maps, the resulting images were both surprising and revealing. The structures of modern CCMCE were far more complex and intricate than assumed. The CORPLINK project produced more than 250 EMs of large corporate groups, systematically mapping the structures of the 100 largest non-state, non-financial companies in the world in 2018 (based on revenue). These EMs represent raw data on and visualization of corporate organizations, collected directly from primary sources, before any analysis or processing has been applied.

Figures I.1 to I.3 showcase examples of some of the EMs of three CCMCEs. These maps vividly depict the vast, multi-tiered networks formed by CCMCEs, illustrating the intricate connections between parent companies and their numerous subsidiaries distributed across multiple jurisdictions.

---

[11] I am immensely grateful to Richard Phillips who was involved in the project and who developed a technique of mapping the actual structure of CCMCEs, drawing on data from the Orbis database.

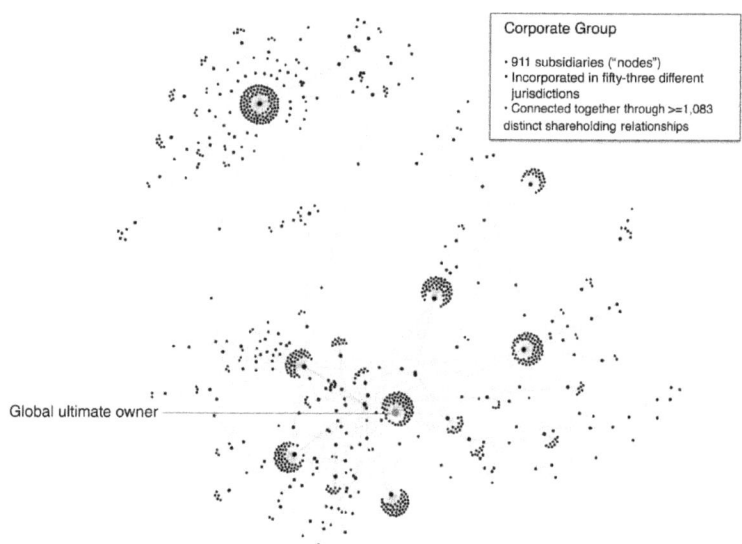

Figure I.1 Volkswagen equity map, *c.* mid 2018.
Source: Orbis database as analysed by the CORPLINK project

In each of these maps, a corporate subsidiary is depicted by a dot, with each dot representing a separate entity, often a corporation. Each of these corporate entities has its own managers, board of directors, and shareholders, and each is required to file annual reports in its respective jurisdiction. The group's global ultimate owner, typically a holding company, is depicted in red.

Subsidiaries that control other subsidiaries extend outward to form a chain, illustrating the hierarchical relationships within the group. Subsidiaries that do not control other entities are positioned closer to their parent company, often forming clusters around it. These clusters represent subsidiaries that are directly linked to their parent without holding further subsidiaries themselves.

Additionally, some subsidiaries are controlled through at least two separate subsidiaries or chains of subsidiaries, creating more complex ownership pathways. Palan et al. (2021) refer to these as 'splitters', where ownership is divided among multiple layers or paths within the group. In Figure I.2, the EM of Wells Fargo highlights these splitters ownership patterns in purple, showcasing the intricacies of its corporate structure.

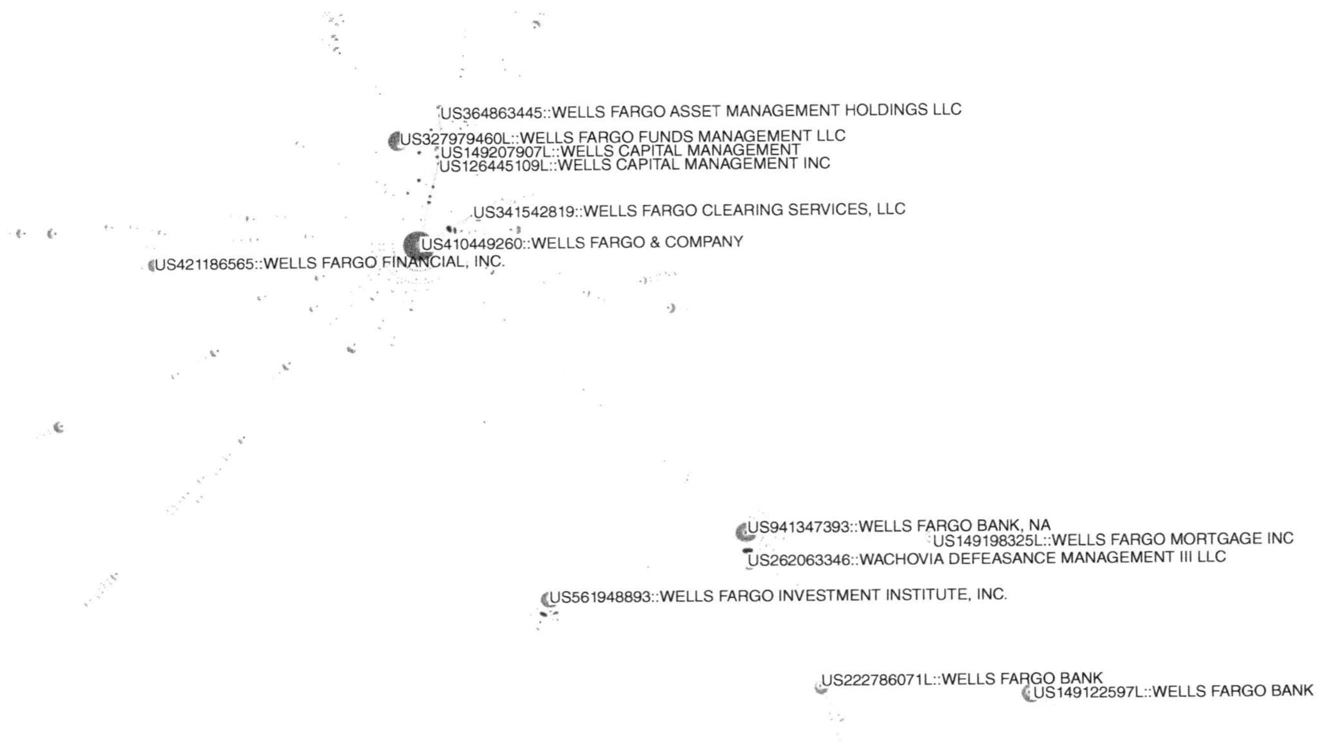

Figure I.2 Wells Fargo equity map, c. 2021.
Source Orbis data analysed by the CORPLINK project

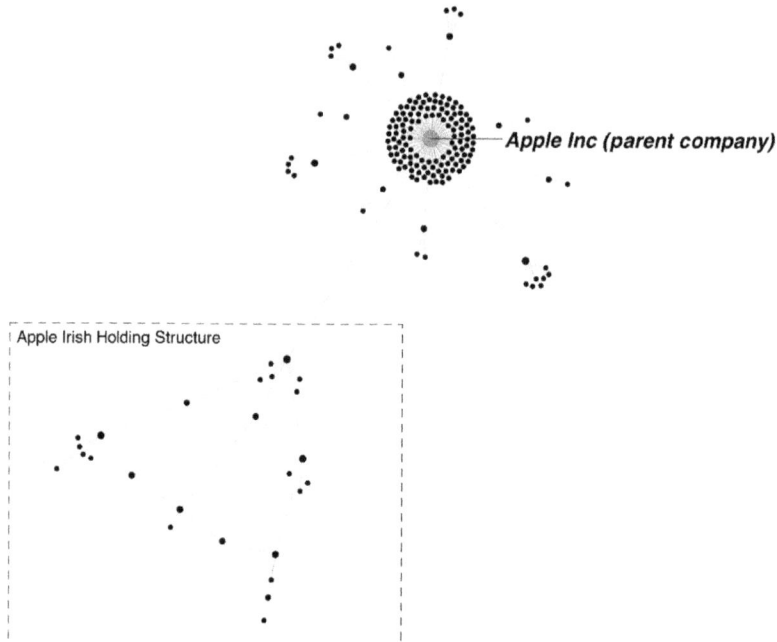

Figure I.3 Group structure of Apple Inc., highlighting Irish holding structure, c. January 2019.
Source: Orbis data analysed by CORPLINK project

Market Friction, Firms, and Jurisdictional Arbitrage

The debate about arbitrage is not particularly new. More than a century ago, US President Theodore Roosevelt sharply criticized lawyers for devising 'bold and ingenious schemes by which very wealthy clients, individuals or corporate, can evade the law which are made to regulate the interest of the public' (quoted in Fleischer, 2010, 230). Decades later, President John F. Kennedy voiced similar concerns, lamenting the behaviour of the MNCs of his era.[12] President Barack Obama, echoing Kennedy's concerns, observed: 'The tax system is

---

[12] 'More and more enterprises organized abroad by American firms have arranged their corporate structures – aided by artificial arrangements between parent and subsidiary... so as to exploit the multiplicity of foreign tax systems and international agreements in order to reduce sharply or eliminate completely their tax liabilities both at home and abroad' (Kennedy, 1964).

subject to gaming, as corporations manipulate complex tax rules to minimize taxes and, in some cases, shift profit actually earned in the United States to low-tax jurisdictions' (The White House and the Department of Treasury, 2012, 13).[13]

What tends to be missed, however, in the rather technical discussions about arbitrage is an underlying problem, the fundamental flaw that makes arbitrage both possible and desirable in the first place.[14] I discuss those broader historical conditions in Chapter 2. I trace the origins to the late nineteenth-century system of states and the fledgling American capitalism. Before the nineteenth century, state power was centralized, focusing on the monarch and the capital. State power tended to diminish with distance until it became tenuous in frontier regions in Europe such as Alsace-Lorraine or Trento. At its core, the modern state that was the product of the late nineteenth century established a system of rules that operated consistently, replacing fragmented and localized governance with a cohesive legal framework (Mann, 2008; Poulantzas, 1978).

At the same time, and for complex reasons explored in the next section, the market underwent significant transformations after the US Civil War, centred on the rise of the corporation and, equally importantly, the emergence of intangible property. Likely influenced by the vast scale of the US market, the first large modern corporate forms emerged, starting with railway companies, followed by energy and steel giants such as Rockefeller's Standard Oil and Morgan's creation of US Steel in 1902. Consumer-focused companies such as Heinz soon began to appear as well.

---

[13] It is interesting to observe how President Roosevelt's concern with the way the wealthy evade laws became a far narrower interest in tax avoidance over time. The narrowing of the debate was accompanied by the realization, expressed so well by President Obama, that despite the introduction of ever-more ambitious national and multilateral programmes to tackle 'abuse', the gaming of the tax system continued unabated. The preoccupation with tax avoidance is entirely understandable but can be misleading.

[14] At the core of the issue, there is a fundamental tension within the processes of internationalization and globalization, which has unfolded from the late nineteenth century onwards, within the framework of another distinct development: the rise of a discrete form of statehood and sovereignty. The unifications of Germany, Italy, and the United States after their respective wars joined the Netherlands, the United Kingdom, and France in forming territorially defined states characterized by horizontal distributions of power. By the late nineteenth century, these forces had shaped a distinctive form of political power and organization.

These corporations were vast logistical enterprises, mastering the challenges of production and manufacturing across great distances and involving large numbers of people. They also required immense amounts of capital and investment. Investment is a bet on the future earning capacity of an organization. The forward-looking perspective of investors became increasingly tied to the concept of intangibles, marking a pivotal innovation in the evolution of modern capitalism.

This specifically American type of corporate organization soon began to spill across borders, starting with companies such as the sewing machine manufacturer, Singer. The interplay between these two trends – the rise of corporations and the role of the state – unfolded in a particularly intriguing way.[15] Large corporate organizations, with their future-oriented investments, rely heavily on the stability provided by legal systems. However, reliance on state and the law highlights two fundamental challenges of internationalization in the context of a dissected sovereign system.

First, states are not particularly good at providing the 'rules of the game' that economists would consider approximating anything like 'Pareto optimality' – a state where resources cannot be reallocated to make someone better off without making someone else worse off. The institutional environment provided by the state and the law, Douglas North argues, sets the parameters for the contracting process by establishing incentives and constraints for both individuals and firms (North, 1982). Political systems, however, are not well designed to produce economically efficient working rules (Buchanan and Tollison, 1984; North, 1990; Stigler, 1971). Instead, states evolved within a distinct context shaped by conflicts and wars among the nobility, where the primary concerns were power, territorial control, and survival, not the optimization of economic outcomes. The legacy of these historical evolution

---

[15] States established legal frameworks within their territorial boundaries. As David Gerber explains, the law began to serve as 'a fabric of norms, practices, and understandings that structure the way markets operate, influence the outcomes they produce, and shape consequences for those affected by them' (Gerber, 2010). On the other hand, the law increasingly defined 'background' rights and obligations, enabling participants to assess the risks and opportunities of transactions and strategies. This provided stability for investments and created incentives that allowed competition to thrive. In this way, legal frameworks do not merely regulate markets but actively construct them, enhancing their productive capacity and shaping the economic landscape (Gerber, 2010, 418).

is a 'property rights structure that will maximize rents to the ruler (or ruling class) [and] produce economic growth' (North, 1982, 28).[16]

Second, legal systems are fragmented, and differing regulations and jurisdictions create obstacles to seamless operations. This problem is exacerbated because, as David Gerber notes, 'the laws that are applied to global markets are not themselves global – or even transnational! Instead, the *laws of individual states* govern *global markets*' (Gerber, 2010, 418; emphasis added). Consequently, the sort of rights and duties that are the backbone of market relationships are far less secure internationally, reliant on a system of bilateral agreements between states, and relatedly, there is no clear unifying fabric of laws and norms operating internationally.

What can business hope to achieve under such circumstances? Most of the literature focuses on two tactics adopted by the corporate sector. Business may try to relocate, to the extent it is possible, to jurisdictions with more favourable combinations of factors of production, political conditions, institutional stability, and regulatory environments. A great deal has been written about this option, especially policy advice such as the Washington Consensus, which advocates for governments, in return, to adopt business-friendly tax and regulatory regimes (Davies, 2016; Dicken, 2007; Kahan and Kamar, 2003; Stopford et al., 1991; Williamson, 1993).[17] But the tactic of relocation is limited by inherent factors such as the geographic distribution of resources and the size of specific markets. Furthermore, future political and institutional shifts are hard to predict, making this strategy vulnerable.

Relocation to preferable jurisdictions does not resolve the inherent limitations of the rules of the game of society as analysed by North (1990). Consequently, businesses often resort to a second, complementary tactic, seeking to influence the political process in each of the countries in which they trade in the hope of influencing governments to produce a regulatory environment that aligns better with their interests.

---

[16] The state can be 'a potential resource or threat to every industry in the society' (Stigler, 1971, 3). The field of the 'political economy' of regulation emerged based on the notion of 'rent-seeking' predatory bureaucracies of states and large corporations (Posner, 1974; Stigler, 1971).

[17] Some theorists argue that under such conditions, a phenomenon known as the Tiebout thesis occurs (Boadway and Tremblay, 2012). According to this view, competition forces state to improve their cost (e.g., taxation) and service offerings, leading to what is termed the Tiebout optimality. I return to the question in Chapter 1.

Much has been written about this strategy as well (Hill et al., 2013; Kim and Milner, 2019; Lee, 2024; Saittakari et al., 2023; Truman, 1971; Waterhouse, 2013). Naturally, the way businesses interact with politics is profoundly influenced by the nature of the political systems in their home or host countries. And while there is little doubt that businesses devote significant resources to lobbying, bribing, or even 'capturing' entire political systems, this approach is not without drawbacks either. Success can be tenuous, outcomes are uncertain, and there is always the risk of free riders – competitors who benefit from any favourable changes without incurring the costs of advocacy.

But there is a third option: engaging in arbitrage. This strategy entails establishing subsidiaries in third countries and channelling investments through them to circumvent undesirable rules or regulations, including taxation. At its core, this strategy seeks to combine the best of both worlds, ensuring the tangible aspects of a business – such as production, sales, or resource extraction – are placed where economic logic dictates, at least to the extent this is possible. In other words, in countries that, by a quirk of history, possess the essential factors businesses seek when internationalizing. The strategy is intended, at the same time, to ensure the legal and regulatory dimensions of transactions are insulated as much as possible from the same quirks of history.

This strategy is more cost-effective than the first two, as it does not require relocating production or manufacturing, incurring substantial expenses, or navigating political risks. Instead, it relies on an in-depth understanding of legal and accounting frameworks, coupled with the relatively low cost of establishing subsidiaries across jurisdictions. The strategy is also remarkably sophisticated. As I explain in Chapter 3, the strategy involves a decoupling of the physical from the legal, so that goods or services can be produced or exchanged in one country, but the legal exchange of property titles takes place elsewhere, in selected jurisdictions.

Erin O'Hare and Larry Ribstein refer to jurisdictional arbitrage as 'repackaging arbitrage' (O'Hara and Ribstein, 2009, 108). Using a kind of 'cut-and-paste' strategy, MNCs establish subsidiaries and affiliates in a manner that allows each entity to select a distinct regulatory dimension. Together, these subsidiaries, often situated across multiple jurisdictions, construct a tailored regulatory pathway for transactions. Because businesses are not constrained to choosing complete regulatory packages from any single jurisdiction but can cherry-pick advantageous elements from different systems, jurisdictional arbitrage does not inherently promote regulatory optimization. By exercising this option, companies can present a more attractive profile to investors, who are increasingly drawn to firms that demonstrate adaptability and forward-looking value in a complex global environment.

Table I.1 summarizes the core principles of jurisdictional arbitrage from a business perspective.

Table I.1 *The logic of jurisdictional arbitrage*

Aspect of Transaction	Economic Logic (Market Efficiency)	Regulatory Logic (Legal & Tax Framework)
Physical Exchange	Production and manufacturing are based in locations optimized for market conditions, such as low costs or strategic supply chains.	Regulatory and tax frameworks are applied based on physical presence.
Legal Registration	Production and manufacturing are relocated to jurisdictions offering better regulatory and tax environment	Registration occurs in jurisdictions with more favourable legal and tax conditions, reducing associated regulatory and tax burdens.
Jurisdictional Arbitrage	Physical and legal exchanges are decoupled to avoid higher regulatory costs in primary markets, allowing companies to focus on market efficiencies.	Legal and operational activities are separated across jurisdictions to maximize benefits from both economic and regulatory environments.
Common Treatment of Arbitrage	This has led to the proliferation of 'empty' shell companies and 'phantom' investments	These are artificial constructions.
Jurisdictional Arbitrage Thesis	Production and manufacturing are optimized in economically and regulatory favourable locations, achieving a balance of cost-efficiency and tax minimization.	Legal registration is shifted to jurisdictions with favourable tax and regulatory frameworks, minimizing compliance costs without physically moving operations.

'Accumulation' versus Intangible Property

If the logic of arbitrage makes economic sense – and, indeed, there is nothing inherently surprising about arbitrage from an economic standpoint – why has so little attention been devoted to jurisdictional arbitrage as a general phenomenon in economics or political science? The ignorance of arbitrage goes deep. Even one of my all-time favourites, a survey of the field of law and economics written by Nicholas Mercuro and Steven Medema, which covers a range of approaches, including transaction cost economics, public choice theory, new and old institutional economics, and postmodernist legal theory, does not mention the word 'arbitrage' a single time (Mercuro and Medema, 2020)! Why is that?

I now realize this must have to do with *timing*. By this, I mean the dominant theoretical frameworks we rely on today – whether drawn from neoclassical economics or Marxist thought – were formalized just before the emergence of a distinctly American form of capitalism. I highlight four key institutional transformations taking place in the United States, each of which has taken place a decade or more after the first wave of neoclassical theories. It is not surprising, therefore, that neither Marxism nor marginalism factored in those important changes.

The first important institutional transformation occurred when the US Supreme Court and UK House of Lords established the basic framework of the modern doctrine of corporate personality. In the United States, the concept of corporate personhood was reinforced by legal decisions and interpretations, including the *Santa Clara County v. Southern Pacific Railroad Co.* decision in 1886, when a corporation became 'an incorporate body that is able to act as if they were real persons for legal purposes' (Quentin, 2020). Corporations were granted the right of free speech under the First Amendment, and under the Fourteen Amendment can claim equal protection under the law and due process (Stern, 2017, 34; for a discussion, see Robé, 2020).[18]

In the United Kingdom, in the case of *Salomon v. Salomon & Co. Ltd.* (1897), the House of Lords affirmed a corporation is a separate legal entity, granting it the status of a 'legal person' with rights and obligations like those of an individual.[19] These two cases (and similar

---

[18] The individuals who serve as managers, workers, or shareholders can be replaced, but the legal person persists; this, of course, is the reason why investors invest in the company and not in individuals.

[19] As Dewy explained, once a corporation is created, it is real (Dewey, 1926, 655). There is considerable debate on the origins of this innovation, but

decisions in France, Germany, and elsewhere) established the contemporary interpretation of company law.[20]

Once incorporated, a company was considered a distinct legal entity, separate from its shareholders. The separation of the corporate entity from its shareholders creates what is known in legal jargon as a 'corporate veil' that protects shareholders from personal liability for the company's debt; hence, the shareholders' liability is limited to the amount unpaid on their shares. After these rulings, just as the state as an artificial legal person does not 'belong' to the monarchy, the corporation in Anglo-Saxon law does not belong to the principals, that is, the shareholders, and managers are no longer merely the agents of those shareholders.

The significance of modern entity law comes into sharp relief in the context of a second, important institutional mutation that took place first in the United States and was soon copied elsewhere. In a series of decisions between 1899 and 1892, the state of New Jersey enacted progressive corporate laws that allowed corporations to own stock in other corporations. The combination of the two sets of legal instruments gave rise to a new phenomenon, the corporate group or 'going concern'. The corporate group structure that emerged in the United States during this time diverged significantly from the European model.[21] The US model was characterized by the use of holding companies and subsidiaries – distinct legal entities interconnected

---

the general consensus is that the modern corporation emerged 'from a stew of medieval and early modern European business forms' (Wright, 2013, 20). It became a separate legal person, however, only in the late nineteenth century.

[20] Although the case did not explicitly grant corporations constitutional rights, the court's headnote suggested corporations were entitled to the protections of the Amendment, originally intended to protect the rights of individuals. In the United States, the concept of corporate personhood can be traced to a Supreme Court decision in 1819 in *Dartmouth College v. Woodward*. Yet well into the nineteenth century, most corporations in the United States were incorporated by special legislation. In 1892, Germany introduced Gesellschaft mit beschränkter Haftung, which allowed for a company with limited liability even if all shares were held by one person.

[21] There were scores of important corporate groups and industrial conglomerates in nineteenth-century European economies. For instance, the Rothschild banking dynasty was structured as a decentralized yet closely coordinated family enterprise, spanning multiple countries in Europe. The Krupp family adopted the joint-stock company model, but the different branches of the group were privately owned and managed directly by the family, thus allowing centralized decision-making.

directly or indirectly through equity ownership to the parent. In this framework, corporate groups in the United States were legally structured as clusters of independent companies, often with opaque and complex relationships among their various entities in the group.[22]

In a third and crucial innovation, in a series of landmark rulings by the US Supreme Court, the American legal system began to recognize a new form of property: intangible property. This category included from around the 1920s intellectual property (IP) such as patents and copyrights, trademarks, and more significantly – and most elusive of all – and surprisingly earlier, the concept of 'goodwill'. Goodwill was another product of the New Jersey amendment and refers to the premium paid when one company acquires another – which it could do following the New Jersey amendment. If the purchase price of an acquired company was over the fair market value of the target company's identifiable assets minus its liabilities, the excess can be attributed to factors such as brand reputation, customer loyalty, employee relationships, propriety technology, and overall competitive advantage. The excess value was written in the accounting books as 'goodwill' (Allan, 1889; Commons, 1919; Jaffé, 1924), Simply stated, goodwill is the value the market places on the capacity of various properties of the corporate group, including estimates of robustness of its corporate organization or even corporate culture, to generate future income.

It was a moment of no return. Intangible capital is often defined in economics by what it lacks – that is, as 'productive capital that lacks a physical presence' (Crouzet et al., 2022). But that is the wrong way of looking at it. The shift in valuation from fair value based on tangible property towards intangibles that took place from the late nineteenth

---

[22] One of the first strategic uses of the holding company concept by investors was to amplify control. In a straightforward example, a 50 per cent ownership stake in a company is sufficient to control 100 per cent of its decisions. However, through a cascading chain of holding companies, this control can be achieved with far less equity. For instance, a company might own 50 per cent of another company, which in turn owns 50 per cent of a third, which itself owns 50 per cent of a fourth, and so on. By the third layer of this structure, only 12.5 per cent of the original equity investment is required to control a significantly larger set of assets. This leveraging technique allows the consolidation of substantial economic power with minimal capital investment, facilitating the rise of sprawling corporate groups in the US economy. I return to this in Chapter 2.

century onwards encouraged companies to think strategically about how to structure operations, allocate resources, and position intangible assets. Modern corporate groups increasingly link income projections to market size and growth potential, moving away from traditional profit-based assessments (Modigliani and Miller, 1958). The value of intangibles, in turn, reflects several key factors. It encompasses the group's access to and control over larger markets and the capacity to stabilize its future by reducing reliance on external factors – political processes that are beyond the group's direct control – and its ability to safeguard IP and its goodwill within a world governed by sovereign states.

The valuation of companies in markets extends beyond taxation. For example, a company able to shield itself from liabilities, such as potential claims related to unknown risks (e.g., unforeseen asbestos use by subsidiaries in foreign markets) would likely have higher valuation of its goodwill. Similarly, a company with access to cheap capital, whether through financial innovation or by arbitraging restrictive financial regulations, would also enjoy a higher market valuation. And a company demonstrating an ability to minimize or, more importantly, control its global tax liabilities would be rewarded with enhanced market valuation as well.

The value of tangible property is seemingly tied to the physical asset; its materiality provides a clear basis for valuation. In contrast, the value of intangible property is inherently inseparable from the legal entity that holds it. A patent, trademark, or logo is intrinsically linked to the corporate organization that leverages, protects, and exploits it. In 2024, Coca-Cola's brand was valued at approximately US$106.45 billion, but give the logo to, say, Toyota, and its value would plummet. The corporation as an artificial legal person underscores the strategic significance of intangible assets within the broader framework of what Berle and Means called the 'corporate economy' (Berle and Means, 1948, 2).[23]

---

[23] Berle and Means argued corporations 'ceased to be merely legal devices through which the private business transaction of individuals may be carried on' (Berle and Means, 1948, 2). They became the core of a modern economy, a corporate economy – a subset of a market economy serving as a platform for the exchange of property rights. Berle and Means's work cannot be understood outside the context of the Great Depression that fundamentally altered the role of the state in capitalist economies. They felt concepts such as 'business civilizations' or 'the corporate economy' better captured the nature of capitalism that was then in crisis.

The traditional neoclassical models that focus on production and marginal cost do not adequately capture how the value of intangibles is created, stored, or traded. Assigning values such as 'goodwill' to a 'firm-like nexus of contracts' is inherently problematic. These concepts, which underpin much of modern firm theory, reflect a bygone era centred on tangible goods and the notion of a 'productionist' firm. Crucially, intangible property, unlike IP or data, has reoriented the economy towards valuation based on future potential rather than present assets alone.

However, there is much more to arbitraging. As I explain in Chapter 2, the early MNCs of the late nineteenth century were from inception organized according to the American corporate group model. They were never singular entities, and very soon after the introduction of the New Jersey amendments, they evolved into CCMCEs. They adopted the corporate group structure primarily to arbitrage incorporation laws and anti-trust regulations. Internationally, the CCMCE framework was adopted initially for a different reason: it offered an efficient and cost-effective method for establishing operations in foreign markets. Over time, the CCMCE model began to serve a second, equally significant, purpose: arbitrage. This evolution was closely tied to the management of intangibles, a factor that increasingly influenced the structure and strategy of multinational enterprises.

The three developments discussed here, the advent of the corporation as an artificial legal person, the right of those persons to hold stock in other artificial persons, and the innovation of intangible property, were closely intertwined therefore, both temporally and analytically, with a fourth development: the rise of the CCMCE. As discussed earlier, MNCs employed arbitraging as a key strategy for navigating political environments. For instance, Amazon's strategic focus has historically emphasized market expansion and customer acquisition over immediate profit maximization. Amazon is not alone. Many corporate groups value long-term scalability and future market dominance, emphasizing how growth potential and market share can drive future revenues and profitability.

Such strategies are far easier to implement because MNCs are not singular companies but organized as clusters of independent companies. The CCMCE structure allows companies to play different roles and reorganize their subsidiaries in ways that facilitate higher valuation of the group. The logic of arbitrage as it works through these four institutional developments is summarized in Table I.2.

Table I.2 *Arbitraging and intangibles*

Factor	Frictionless Market	Dissected Market	Tangible Assets	Intangible Assets	Firms as Productive Entities	Firms Augmenting Value in Market	Jurisdictional Arbitrage
Definition	Ideal market with no transaction costs	Market with barriers and regulatory divides	Physical assets such as machinery and property	IP, brand, research and development (R&D), 'goodwill'	Entities focused on production and output	Firms focused on enhancing market presence and value of goodwill	Strategic structuring to leverage regulatory, tax, and financial differences across regions
Transaction Costs	Minimal to none	High owing to regulatory and other barriers	Not applicable	Not applicable	Minimal focus on market friction	Actively navigates market structure and perception	Aimed at minimizing tax/regulatory costs, leading to diverse cross-border structures
Asset Mobility	High, assets can be freely transferred	Limited owing to legal and logistical barriers	Limited by physical location	High mobility across jurisdictions	Primarily involves fixed assets	Involves reputation and value-building strategies	Assets are positioned in regions that maximize tax efficiency and reduce regulatory burdens

Table I.2 (cont.)

Factor	Frictionless Market	Dissected Market	Tangible Assets	Intangible Assets	Firms as Productive Entities	Firms Augmenting Value in Market	Jurisdictional Arbitrage
Valuation	Transparent, driven by supply and demand	Less transparent owing to segmented regulations	Relatively straightforward and measurable	Challenging, involves subjective valuation	Tied closely to physical output	Tied to brand value and market influence	Subsidiaries as assets
Investment Impact	Investments increase efficiency	Investments navigate or mitigate barriers	Capital investments in infrastructure	Investments in innovation, R&D, brand	Investments expand productive capacity	Investments enhance firm's strategic market value	Investment choices align with tax, regulatory, and economic incentives across regions
Subsidiary Organization			Subsidiaries enable physical asset management based on local needs	Subsidiaries can hold intangible assets strategically across jurisdictions	Firms harvesting profits from subsidiaries	Firms used subsidiaries as assets	

CCMCEs, Jurisdictional Arbitrage, and the Question of Power

Since arbitrage is about the relationship between states and markets, it raises inevitably the question of power. The idea that MNCs have enormous power is well established. There is broad agreement that over the past three or four decades, the power pendulum has swung decidedly from the state towards the corporate sector (Hathaway, 2020; Stopford, Strange, and Henley, 1991; Waterhouse, 2013).

What, then, is the true source of a firm's power? Most answers focus on firms as singular entities, treating MNCs as monolithic actors.[24] Political scientists often assume that when MNCs engage in politics they do so as conventional political actors, operating within the rules of politics and leveraging traditional means such as financial resources to achieve their goals. In this view, MNCs are simply political entities with vast resources, and the question of their power becomes a matter of tactics.

My argument, however, is that instead of seeking to change regulations or influence governmental agendas, CCMCEs use jurisdictional arbitrage schemes as techniques of accommodation with existing legal frameworks. CCMCEs are using arbitrage not in order to persuade parent or host states to modify their regulatory environments, nor are they seeking to control the regulatory agenda or even persuade states to change their agendas. On the contrary, jurisdictional arbitrage is a power dynamic where the actors leverage existing rules to their advantage, creating a paradox where compliance becomes a tool for exercising power. Adherence to formalities allows CCMCEs to navigate and exploit inconsistencies or gaps in the regulatory framework. Arbitrage represents, therefore, a distinct form of power, arguably the primary technique wielded by CCMCEs in their interactions with states and the broader state system.

---

[24] John Kenneth Galbraith says power is 'the great black hole of economics' (Galbraith, 2007, xxxiv). Economics evolved as a theory without power. Economics without power centres on one set of relationships intentionally abstracted from the full gamut. It is called 'market', and it is a story of how 'all corporate and executive actions is subordinate to the pursuit of profits, and all such pursuit is subordinate, in turn, to the rule of the market' (Galbraith, 2007, xxxv). But power is always in the background. I return to the theme in Chapter 9.

What Is Known about Jurisdictional Arbitrage: A History of Missing Opportunities?

What, then, is known about jurisdictional arbitrage? And why does the literature often dismiss arbitrage as an artificial construct? Much of this stems from the historical narratives surrounding firms and corporations.

The traditional theory of the firm developed from Adam Smith's theory of the factory. It emphasized how firms produce and supply outputs. It resulted in a productionist-oriented perspective, whereby firms were seen primarily through the lens of production and manufacturing.[25] The conventional view of the market relationship was strongly influenced by the work of Alfred Marshall, who defined 'markets' as 'public exchange, mart or auction rooms, where the traders agree to meet and transact business' (Marshall, 2009, 270). For Marshall, 'traders' could be abstracted and theorized in the form of the 'representative firm'.[26] Firms were supply-side traders transforming inputs (e.g., labour, raw materials, capital) into outputs (goods or services) using available technology.[27]

This approach treated the firm as a 'black box', ignoring its internal workings, let alone paying attention to the purpose or functions of arbitrage.[28] In his seminal article 'On the Nature of the Firm', Roland Coase (1937) persuaded economists to abandon the simplified view. Coase

---

[25] Firms were viewed as 'production functions for transforming inputs into outputs according to the laws of technology' (Williamson, 2010, 676; see also Aigner et al., 1977; Aigner and Chu, 1968). The productionist perspective was also strongly associated with Marxist interpretations (Epstein, 2005; Froud et al., 2006). Edith Penrose (2009), by no means a Marxist, notes that something strange was taking place: at a certain point of growth, firms seemed to have 'metamorphosed' and began to behave more like investment funds. This behaviour pattern, she argues, could not be modelled by conventional microeconomics.

[26] Marginalist theory views firms as dynamic entities that engage in profit-maximizing behaviour based on subjective valuations and market conditions. The equilibrium firm is in a state of long-term equilibrium, where its revenues exactly match its costs, including normal profits.

[27] Neoclassical theory acknowledged the potential for distortions in the market caused by 'rent-seeking' behaviour of bureaucracies, states, or large corporations. But those rent-seeking organizations, extracting wealth without creating new value, were seen as merely disrupting the smooth functioning of competitive markets (Posner, 1974; Stigler, 1971). The investor did not play an important role in the thinking about firms.

[28] Harold Demsetz (1988) argues the neoclassical theory of the firm was designed to align with the broader framework of market theory, rather than a comprehensive stand-alone theory.

suggested firms exist to minimize transaction costs associated with market exchanges. Transaction costs referred to the costs of participating in the market, such as negotiating, enforcing contracts, and dealing with legal and other externalities. Tantalizingly, Coase's theory had the potential to open the door to a broader exploration of arbitrage – but it did not.

Coase argued firms operate within two distinct economies. Externally, they interact with the broader market economy, where goods, services, and resources are traded according to price signals. Here, the price mechanism serves as the organizing principle, allocating resources through supply and demand dynamics. Internally, firms establish an economy governed by a command-and-control structure. CEOs and managers direct resources and coordinate activities without the need for repeated bargaining, contracts, or external price-setting for every internal interaction.

The firm, as conceived by Coase, performs then an arbitrage function between these two economies. Firms leverage their internal economy to avoid the inefficiencies of the external market, while still interacting with the external market to acquire resources and sell products. As Coase saw it, firms internalize transactions for two primary reasons: to reduce certain costs associated with market transactions such as information gathering and to mitigate costs introduced by regulations. The first rationale, transaction costs, has garnered the lion's share of attention from economists, becoming a cornerstone of the economic theory of the firm.

The second rationale concerning the role of regulation has been largely overlooked and forgotten. Since so much has been written about the first, I will focus on the second.

In the fourth part of his original article published in 1937, Coase argued regulatory burdens, such as taxes, compliance costs, or government interventions, often incentivize firms to internalize more transactions or vertically integrate to escape market regulations: 'Transactions organized within a firm are often treated differently by Governments or other bodies with regulatory powers' (Coase, 1937, 391). He highlighted the case of sales taxes. His specific example is no longer relevant, but the principles he pointed out, namely that firms have incentives to internalize not just to reduce transaction costs but also to minimize regulatory burdens, remains salient.[29] Indeed, he

---

[29] At the time, jurisdictions might have imposed sales taxes on transactions conducted between divisions or subsidiaries within the same firm. By

argued, 'Regulation would bring into existence firms which otherwise would have no raison d'être' (Coase, 1937, 391).

Over time, the trajectory of the interpretation of the theory of transaction cost theory has shifted. The contemporary focus is no longer on Coase's broader considerations but emphasizes the problem of contractual weaknesses, such as incomplete contracts, enforcement difficulties, and information asymmetries (Allen, 2005; Barzel, 2003; Rindfleisch, 2020; Williamson, 2010; Williamson and Winter, 1993).[30] Coase's analysis was targeted at national firms, but what many people forget is that his original article was published well before the concept of the MNC as a distinct field of research emerged in the 1960s.

When MNCs expand, they do more than simply enter new markets; they also extend their internal economies across borders. The arbitraging of the two economies identified by Coase – the internal and the external – has been internationalized as well. Internalized economies, known as intra-firm trade, now operate on a global scale and account for a significant portion of global commerce. According to some estimates (Borga and Zeile, n.d.; Lanz and Miroudot, 2011; Ylönen and

---

internalizing transactions, firms could avoid these costs and streamline operations. Over time, governments recognized the inefficiencies and unintended burdens created by these types of taxes. To address this, many countries introduced exemptions or discounts for internal transfers, ensuring sales taxes were applied only at the final point of sale, when goods or services were sold to external customers.

[30] In the 1960s, a new interpretation of Coase's transaction cost theory began to develop. Harold Demsetz argued Coase's distinction between market and bureaucratic-led exchanges was a red herring. The key question is not why large firms exist but why 'firm-like nexuses' coalesce in markets. In collaboration with Armen Alchian, he said:

It is common to see the firm characterized by the power to settle issues by fiat, by authority, or by disciplinary action superior to that available in the conventional market. This is delusion. The firm does not own all its inputs. It has no power of fiat, no authority, no disciplinary action any different in the slightest degree from ordinary market contracting between any two people. (Alchian and Demsetz, 1972, 778)

In this view, the firm is essentially a legal construct, a collection of contracts that bind together various parties, such as employees, suppliers, shareholders, and managers. It is a nexus through which exchanges operate at transaction costs lower than those for market exchanges (Micheler, 2021, 11). The relationships are seen through the lens of agency theory (Fama, 1980; Jensen and Meckling, 1976). The MNC consists of a nexus of transactions that operates across borders. This theory is also known as contract theory.

Teivainen, 2018), approximately one-third of global trade consists of intra-firm transactions. This internal economy of intra-firm trade is, as I go on to show, the primary arena where jurisdictional arbitraging schemes are conceived and executed.

In support of the proposition that subsidiaries are independent legal persons, governments introduced strict rules on investment and transfers among subsidiaries, such as the arm's length principle (Avi-Yonah, 1995; Eden et al., 2001; Wittendorff, 2010). The principle stipulates transactions among affiliated entities – whether located in the same country or other jurisdictions – must be conducted as if they were independent parties. While firms aim to internalize transactions to reduce costs and maintain control, they often find themselves constrained by the need to apply market-like logic within their own internal networks. This creates an internal economy that functions with elements of market pricing, contracts, and competitive pressures, despite being housed within a single corporate 'organization'. So if MNCs cannot avoid the complexities of the market within their own boundaries, what benefits do they gain from engaging in large-scale intra-firm trade?

The logical answer points to the increasing importance of arbitrage. From a Coasian perspective, the large and expanding internal economy of the firm evolved not merely to bypass external markets but also to arbitrage certain types of regulations. As I explore more fully later, this core function – or potential interpretation – of Coase's theory has been overlooked for a variety of reasons.[31]

Another common mistake is to subsume regulatory costs under the broader umbrella of transaction costs, thus obscuring critical distinctions (Marjosola, 2021). In Chapter 1, I challenge this conflation, arguing regulatory costs must be treated as conceptually distinct from transaction costs. By making this distinction, we can develop a theory of the limits of arbitrage, a framework that has remained elusive as long as these concepts are treated interchangeably.

---

[31] One conceptual issue is the frequent conflation of financial arbitrage with regulatory and jurisdictional arbitrage. While these forms of arbitrage share similar characteristics, they are, as I argue in Chapter 1, diametrically opposed in their impact. This confusion has contributed to a widespread misinterpretation of the Modigliani and Miller theorem (Modigliani and Miller, 1958), with many thinking it inherently undermines the need for a theory of arbitrage.

The field of International Business (IB), which is shaped by economic theory, tends to discuss MNCs as singular as well. The origins of IB can be traced to a question posed by Hymer (1982): Why would companies pursue FDI, assuming the risks of unfamiliar and often volatile foreign markets? Soon thereafter, an interest in 'multinational corporations' gathered traction, and the new field of IB was born, developed by scholars such as John Dunning and Raymond Vernon (Dunning, 1988; Dunning and Lundan, 2008; Vernon, 1981, 2013) who relied heavily on historical evidence.

The development of IB was a theoretical breakthrough, as it created a framework for understanding MNCs. However, this achievement was overshadowed by a significant epistemological oversight: MNCs were initially assumed to function like domestic firms, simply operating on an international scale. The IB literature provides plausible yet overly general and abstract answers to the question of why MNCs have so many subsidiaries and why they are spread around the world. A common explanation is the overarching concept of 'operational flexibility' – a term frequently invoked but seldom unpacked in detail (Andrews et al., 2022, 2023, Birkinshaw and Morrison, 1995; Desai, 2009; Fagre and Wells, 1982). IB focuses on how MNCs overcome economic risks in highly competitive and political volatile markets, such as exchange rate volatility, differences in consumer demand, and competition in foreign markets, managing asymmetric information, market failures, and transaction costs while exploiting their firm-specific advantages (e.g., technology or branding).

There is no doubt that many subsidiaries are established, as scholars have demonstrated so well, for operational flexibility. It is a strong and valid explanation, addressing the practical need for adaptability in production, marketing, and logistics. However, *it is not the only answer*. Setting up an investment involves more than deciding what will be produced or marketed. It also requires careful consideration of taxation, regulation, and the protection of investment from political or economic instability. Naturally, these two goals often intertwine, with sophisticated corporate planners seeking to seamlessly blend regulatory arbitrage strategies into their broader operational frameworks.

The most developed body of literature on jurisdictional arbitrage is that on taxation. Studies often focus on specific case studies or legal frameworks, providing detailed analyses of arbitrage strategies and their implications. Examples include transfer pricing, treaty shopping, and hybrid mismatch arrangements (Beer et al., 2020a; Desai and Dharmapala, 2009; Eden, 1998, 2009; Greggi, 2019; Grubert and Mutti, 1991; Loretz et al., 2017a; Wittendorff, 2010). The literature stresses jurisdictional arbitrage schemes are often deeply embedded in the architecture of corporate groups, making it challenging to identify and isolate them from an external perspective. Internally, these practices are often well understood by management teams but hidden from external stakeholders, regulators, and even shareholders. Firms deliberately obscure those practices, claiming the operational logic and the structural design of corporate groups are proprietary knowledge.

Opacity is the operational word here (Lambooy et al., 2013). While such strategies are ostensibly legal, the complexity of corporate arrangements – such as multi-tiered subsidiary networks, hybrid entities, and interwoven financing arrangements – makes it challenging to identify where, how, and to what extent arbitrage is taking place. The problem of opacity has given rise, in turn, to a literature that seeks to classify and typologize arbitraging schemes. A notable contributor to this literature is the Organisation for Economic Co-operation and Development (OECD), which has developed broad typologies of these schemes in its Base Erosion and Profit Shifting reports (Avi-Yonah, 2019; Crivelli et al., 2015; OECD, 2013). These works tend to discuss isolated instances of regulatory or tax loopholes, however, rather than framing them within a broader theory of arbitrage.

It is unfortunate that much of the tax and regulatory arbitrage literature fails to make explicit connections to the fields of law and accounting. Economics and IB tend to view MNCs through the lens of contract theory of the firm, but contract theory is considered by a majority of legal scholars to be simply incorrect (Blumberg, 1993; Ferran, 1999; Orts, 2013a; Robé, 2011).[32] A doctrinal confusion is further obscured because of the tendency to confuse 'firm', which is an analytical category, with 'corporation', which is a legal concept.[33]

---

[32] Seeing the company as a 'single nexus' under which rights and obligations are held together through contracts, or contract theory, dates back to the nineteenth century (Micheler, 2021, 2). Eilís Ma Ferran says the dominant theory of the firm, 'contract theory', 'struggles to explain convincingly the basic fact of separate legal personality' (Ferran, 1999, 11).

[33] One distinction is that 'corporation is a legal instrument, with a separate legal personality' used to legally structure the firm, while a firm is an organized

Contract theory, argues Eva Micheler (2021), is not wrong per se; it simply harkens back to the older doctrine of corporation prior to the US Supreme Court rulings of the late nineteenth century.

On the surface, the debate between economists and legal scholars about the nature of the firm seems pedantic or purely theoretical. It is not. The legal literature asks questions that economists and IB then attempt to answer. What is the rationale behind the incredible complexity of corporate group structures? Why are corporate groups organized as clusters of independent companies? Why do states fail to decree against such structures? Is arbitrage pervasive in these organizations or not? Economists like to say there is no free lunch, and jurisdictional arbitrage certainly comes with its own set of opportunities and constraints.

One stream of legal and business studies is more practical and targeted at managers and professionals – the use of entity law in strategy (Eicke, 2009a; Karayan et al., 2002). A second stream is entity law and arbitrage. A great deal has been written about the abuse of entity law, particularly the legal fiction that each subsidiary within a corporate group is an independent legal person (Avi-Yonah, 2019; Beer et al., 2020a; Blumberg, 1993; Ferran, 1999; Greenfield, 2008; Muchlinski, 2001; Robé, 2016). At a more granular level, arbitraging schemes rely on exploiting jurisdictional divergences in areas such as entity classification laws (e.g., partnerships versus corporations), tax residency rules, and the like. This includes the 'play-acting' of independence, where entities are legally constructed to appear autonomous while remaining functionally interconnected (Dine, 2012a; Kerber, 1999; O'Hara and Ribstein, 2009; Palan and Phillips, 2022).

The legal and accounting literature also suggests jurisdictional arbitrage extends far beyond simple tax or regulatory exploitation, emphasizing the critical role of entity law and corporate legal organization in facilitating these practices (Blair, 2002; Blumberg, 1993; Micheler, 2021; Muchlinski, 2001; Robé, 2011). Entity law, the treatment of each subsidiary as an independent legal person, allows corporate management to decide on lines of control of their subsidiaries. This literature tends to stress the importance of the enablers, the roles played

---

economic activity (Robé, 2011, 3). Another implication of contract theory was the idea that corporations are not appropriate units of taxation (Arlen and Weiss, 1995; Biondi, 2017).

by specialized legal and accounting teams that are either embedded within the corporate group or provide consultancy services and carefully design structures to maximize arbitrage opportunities (Mitchell, 2008; Sikka, 2003; Sikka and Hampton, 2005; West, 2018). These specialized teams understand the opportunities for arbitrage created by legal divergence but rarely articulate them as part of a broader theoretical framework. Instead, they focus on navigating specific rules and systems, implicitly embedding an understanding of arbitrage into their analyses. The strategic use of these mechanisms is often codified internally in documents and models, but this information is not made available to external stakeholders.

Lawyers and accountants excel at dissecting the operational and structural mechanisms of jurisdictional arbitrage, but few if any step back to examine how these practices fit within the broader historical and systemic evolution of capitalism. Jean-Philippe Robé's *Property, Power, and Politics* (2020) develops a comprehensive analysis of the interplay between property rights, corporate organization, and social power. Robé situates his work within the broader context of global capitalism and focuses on the evolving concept of property as a key factor in the distribution of social and political power. He emphasizes property is not just a passive asset but a social relation that grants power to its holders. In the modern era, this means those who control corporate property – large multinational firms – wield enormous influence over both economic and political systems. The legal frameworks that organize corporate ownership and control are crucial to understanding how power is distributed. Robé's work is closely associated with the CORPLINK project, especially its aim to provide a theory of global power by examining the legal evolution of property and the corporate form. This approach is highly relevant to understanding jurisdictional arbitrage and its role in reshaping global power dynamics.

In *The Architecture of Markets*, Neil Fligstein (1993) argues firms must use institutional strategies to control their competitive environments, shaping market structures in ways that favour long-term survival and success. Fligstein alludes, in fact, to arbitrage as a form of control in the US context:

Corporate activities could be strictly limited by state action, but as interstate commerce expanded, states lost their ability to control corporations from a different state. Managers and entrepreneurs of the largest interstate firms became capable of dictating the rules by which they did business (Fligstein, 1993, 23).

Similarly, Kimberly Hoang's *Spiderweb Capitalism* (2022) provides a detailed study of how Vietnamese capital utilizes corporate shells and subsidiaries to navigate a challenging regulatory and economic environment. This perspective shifts the focus away from seeing corporations as monolithic entities and towards understanding the decisions, actions, and strategies of the individuals who direct and manage corporate activities. These individuals – managers, executives, board members, and investors – use their positions within the corporate form to exert influence and maintain control over market conditions, regulations, and competitive dynamics.

In fact, there have been many opportunities to conceptualize arbitrage as more than a series of isolated, artificially constructed phenomena. What consistently stands in the way is the lack of a theory – or rather, the absence of a framework robust enough to situate arbitrage within a broader systemic understanding. The broader theoretical framework I develop in this book is inspired by the work of Thorstein Veblen and John R. Commons.

What This Book Is About

The central argument of this book is that jurisdictional arbitrage schemes arise from the tension between historical forces and forward-looking imperatives. While powerful business actors push for global market integration, this process takes place within a fragmented political landscape, where each authority operates according to its own domestic priorities, vested interests, and unique institutional frameworks, rules, and laws. The tension between the weight of the past and the demands of a future-oriented economy where value is speculative necessitates the creation of schemes that are 'past-proof'. These schemes aim to minimize disruptions from the past, embodied in states and their regulatory frameworks, ensuring historical constraints interfere as little as possible with projections of future value.

These schemes exploit the gaps, loopholes, and omissions in the laws of one country to arbitrage the laws and regulations of another. In this book, I present findings from the analysis of corporate EMs derived from the CORPLINK project. The bulk of the book explores the techniques and schemes of arbitrage, focusing on the underlying logic that connects the CCMCE model to the separation of actual exchanges from their legal registration. Specifically, I examine the intricacies of tax arbitrage, liability arbitrage, and corporate reporting arbitrage, uncovering how these strategies are employed within the modern corporate landscape. I also explore why Europe, despite the European Commission's explicit objectives, has emerged as the central node in global corporate arbitrage. Additionally, I examine whether the United States government has developed sophisticated arbitrage strategies as a geopolitical tool to leverage other states.

A study of jurisdictional arbitrage is inherently a study of power in the modern world. The book concludes with a question that my friend and mentor Susan Strange often posed: *Qui bono?* Who benefits, and who loses, from arbitrage? This final inquiry seeks to unravel the broader implications of these practices for global governance, economic equity, and power dynamics.

The Technique of Equity Mapping

Surprisingly, little is known about the internal legal structures of MNCs, or, as Lewellen and Robinson describe it, 'the way subsidiaries are arranged within ownership structures' (Lewellen and Robinson, 2013, 3). One field that has traditionally attempted to map the internal organization of firms is due diligence.

The concept of a singular, unified MNC holds limited practical relevance for due diligence, as it offers no foundation for substantiating claims of improper fund allocation. Investigating corporate bankruptcies requires a granular mapping of how funds were allocated, by whom, and whether these allocations adhered to economic principles or involved fraudulent activity.

To achieve this, investigators must deconstruct the corporate group into its constituent entities – individual subsidiaries and affiliates – and meticulously analyse the historical trade and financial transfers among them. This detailed process enables the tracing of fund flows and the identification of potential misconduct, often concealed within the complexity of the corporate structure.

Due diligence firms have, therefore, developed equity mapping techniques to analyse the complex structures of corporate organizations. Traditionally, these efforts have relied on publicly available subsidiary filings as well as court-sanctioned access to internal data and communications within corporate groups. Investigators use this information to manually reconstruct the corporate group structure. Databases such as Orbis are often utilized to piece together and correlate fragmented corporate structures, providing a clearer picture of the relationships and financial flows within a group.

Given the inherent complexity of corporate groups, due diligence firms have often adopted the 80/20 principle (Brossart, 2010; Gole and Hilger, 2009; Howson, 2017; Peppitt, 2008; Rosenbloom, 2002). This approach operates on the premise that 20 per cent of subsidiaries account for 80 per cent of the group's activities. By focusing on these critical entities, investigators can concentrate their efforts where significant operations and financial flows are most likely to be uncovered, enabling a more efficient and effective analysis of the corporate structure

Investigators also often petition courts to grant access to what is known among corporate lawyers as the corporate 'step papers'. These documents are typically organized as detailed PowerPoint presentations or documents prepared collaboratively by consultancy firms or Big Four accounting firms and corporate legal teams to provide corporate managers with a clear and concise rationale for structuring an investment in a particular way.

Corporate lawyers frequently use step papers to draft Advanced Pricing Agreements (APAs), *ex ante* dispute settlement mechanisms negotiated behind closed doors with tax administrations of various countries (Eden and Byrnes, 2018). Step papers outline the sequential steps required to execute the planned transaction and include a detailed analysis designed to optimize the structure across multiple dimensions relevant to the organization, such as tax implications, legal compliance, and regulatory considerations. They serve as a critical resource for understanding the strategic intent behind complex corporate arrangements.

Step papers are also used to commission a second opinion on the legality and soundness of the proposed structure; typically, managers would seek external review from an accounting or legal firm or an investment bank. These outside advisors are tasked with identifying potential weaknesses in the organization's structure and, where necessary, fine-tuning it. This process ensures the investment becomes even more 'tax neutral' and avoids potential regulatory pitfalls.

A treasure trove of such step papers came to light during the LuxLeaks scandal, in which over 300 APAs were leaked to the press from the

Luxembourg office of the accounting firm PricewaterhouseCoopers (PwC). These leaks exposed the tax planning arrangements negotiated by PwC on behalf of major MNCs in Luxembourg. The LuxLeaks were brought to light by an important organization known as the International Consortium of Investigative Journalists (ICIJ). From time to time, the ICIJ receives data from whistleblowers exposing individual or corporate abuses, such as the well-known Panama Papers and Paradise Papers. Once these data leaks are obtained, the ICIJ meticulously analyses the information, often uncovering systemic misconduct or tax avoidance schemes involving powerful actors. Importantly, the ICIJ makes these data available to academics for further analysis.

In a remarkable article, 'The State Administration of International Tax Avoidance', Omri Marian (2017) identifies and analyses a pattern of corporate tax abuse facilitated through Luxembourg, based on information provided by the ICIJ LuxLeaks papers. By meticulously dissecting these corporate tax arrangements, Marian sheds light on the extent to which tax avoidance practices are structured and in some cases state-supported, providing a clearer understanding of how MNCs manipulate international tax systems to their advantage.

Step papers are a treasure trove of strategic corporate planning, but they remain closely guarded secrets. In fact, knowledge of their existence is not widely shared outside certain legal and financial circles.[34] They are rarely discussed in the public domain, yet they highlight the intricate behind-the-scenes efforts MNCs make to ensure compliance, while also exploiting legal frameworks to their advantage through sophisticated tax planning and regulatory arbitrage.

The use of publicly available information not only for due diligence purposes but also to reconstruct corporate organizations for academic investigation is a relatively new development. A notable pioneer in the field of corporate mapping is the Berlin-based company OpenOil; in collaboration with the open data platform OpenCorporates.com, it has undertaken groundbreaking studies to illuminate the inner workings of corporate groups. One of OpenOil's most striking achievements was the creation of a detailed schematic map of BP's global equity ownership chains. This map uncovered a sprawling corporate structure consisting of 1,280 affiliates spread across eighty-four

---

[34] We learned about step papers from our colleague and collaborator on the CORPLINK project, Jean-Philippe Robé.

countries, organized into a complex hierarchy extending twelve tiers deep – otherwise stated, there were twelve layers of affiliates holding stakes in other affiliates (OpenOil, 2018). OpenOil kindly helped the CORPLINK project develop the technique of corporate mapping.

Another organization, OpenCorporates.com, has taken the idea further and created the first map of the corporate structures of seven of the world's largest banks. These maps were a landmark achievement, offering an unprecedented view into the vast networks of corporate affiliates that underpin these financial institutions. They gave a good idea of the number of subsidiaries in different countries but could not show a clear line of control among subsidiaries, which, as I go on to show, is a critical component of any arbitraging scheme.

The CORPLINK study developed these techniques of equity mapping further, drawing on data from Orbis database produced by Bureau van Dijk, a leading and comprehensive source of global ownership data. The Orbis database aggregates and standardizes data from over 170 sources and provides a great deal of information on corporations, including company names, addresses, industry classifications, and contact details. It has information on corporate hierarchies and beneficial ownership and provides standardized financial statements, including balance sheets, income statements, and cash flow statements. Sometimes Orbis has data on past and pending merger and acquisition deals and data on sanctions, Politically Exposed Persons, and adverse media, thus assisting in compliance checks and risk management.

The Orbis data is arguably the best available, but it is far from perfect. The limitations are well documented (Cobham et al., 2015; Cobham and Janský, 2018; Ribeiro et al., 2010; TAXUD, 2018). The data coverage is not complete, and there are gaps, particularly in developing countries. There are also issues of translation, say, from Chinese to English, something that Wei and Palan discovered in an analysis of the four largest Chinese banking conglomerates (Wei and Palan, 2023). But Orbis is improving all the time.

As far as this study is concerned, a detailed corporate map that achieves, say, 90 per cent accuracy would be sufficient to capture the broad patterns of relationships within the firm that we were looking for. The key was to generate a sufficiently detailed and reliable view of corporate group structures to make meaningful comparisons, yielding insights into the complexities of MNCs and their use of jurisdictional arbitrage, within the inherent data constraints.

The main issue with Orbis from our perspective was that ownership data are supplied in an Excel-like 'data dump' format, containing shareholder information that is often inconsistent or incomplete. For example, one company might claim majority ownership by another, but the exact percentage of ownership is not disclosed. In other cases, more accurate descriptions of minority shareholding are given, but they are not consistent across the dataset. This inconsistency meant the data required extensive cleaning before they could be used effectively. To extract the most reliable and accurate data possible, they were subjected to a series of verification steps, using triangulation techniques to cross-check and validate the information. To the best of our knowledge, no other mapping exercise has taken such a rigorous approach to cleaning and verifying ownership data on this scale.

The CORPLINK project developed an algorithm that captures information from corporate filings and converts the ownership data of MNCs and their subsidiary organizations, as recorded in the Orbis database, into visualized 'maps' using a standard SNA approach. These visualizations, or EMs as in Figures I.1–I.3, provide a detailed and accessible representation of the ownership and control structures within corporate groups, allowing CORPLINK to develop the comparative studies of corporate organization and planning presented in this book.

1 | Decoding Jurisdictional Arbitrage
Strategies, Implications, and Global Dynamics

Introduction

When King William III of England imposed a window tax in 1696, windows began to disappear in the realm. Pope Paul III's introduction of the salt tax in 1540 yielded the famous Tuscan bread without salt. It was not William III's intention to eliminate windows in the realm, nor was the pope particularly concerned about the amount of salt in bread. The windows and salt disappeared because taxpayers decided to 'arbitrage' the new taxes by altering their behaviour.

The practice of arbitraging rules is likely as ancient as the rules themselves. Financial arbitrage was known among the Greeks, and trading arbitrage was practised by the Romans (Poitras, 2021). The first known use of arbitrage in its modern meaning appears in Mathieu de la Porte's 1704 treatise *La science des négociants et teneurs de livres*. The etymology of arbitrage traces back to the Latin *arbitrari*, meaning 'to give judgement', and *arbitrium*, meaning 'judgement' or 'decision'. This linguistic origin reflects the essence of arbitrage as a practice of making judgements or decisions to take advantage of opportunities (Poitras, 2021, 97).

Although arbitrage has a long and well-known history, a theory of jurisdictional arbitrage is yet to emerge. In this chapter, I propose a synthetic framework for studying jurisdictional arbitrage, drawing on insights from five seminal works: Victor Fleischer's *Regulatory Arbitrage*, Annalise Riles's *Managing Regulatory Arbitrage: A Conflict of Laws Approach*, Frank Partnoy's *The Law of Two Prices: Regulatory Arbitrage Revisited*, Katharina Pistor's *The Code of Capital*, and Erin O'Hara and Larry E. Ribstein's *The Law Market*. Before turning to these authors, I begin by distinguishing between the various types of arbitrage.

Unpacking Arbitrage: The Five Key Types of Strategic Manoeuvring

The first step in developing a theory of arbitrage is recognizing that arbitrage is not monolithic – there are various types, each with its own characteristics and dynamics. The most common reference in economics is to financial arbitrage, the act of exploiting price differences in different markets to make a profit.[1] This process is key to what is known in economics as the 'law of one price' (Miljkovic, 1999). The theory is that arbitrageurs help to eliminate price discrepancies by buying in lower-priced markets and selling in higher-priced ones. The law of one price holds that identical goods or assets should have the same price in different markets, once costs such as transportation and transaction fees are accounted for.

In this classical form, arbitrage, or more specifically financial arbitrage, is considered central to the functioning of financial markets and market efficiency. Over time, the concept of arbitrage has come to describe other strategies or techniques capitalizing on differences between systems, whether those systems are financial, legal, regulatory, or even geographic. Whereas in financial arbitrage traders exploit price differences between markets or financial instruments, the term tax arbitrage is used to describe how firms or individuals exploit differences in tax rates between jurisdictions to minimize tax liabilities.[2]

Tax arbitrage is commonly considered to have the opposite effect to financial arbitrage, as it creates market distortions. A paper by Joseph Stiglitz, 'The General Theory of Tax Avoidance', is often cited as a foundational work in understanding the economics of tax arbitrage (Stiglitz, 1985). Despite the title, the paper does not provide a unified framework for understanding all forms of tax avoidance, Nevertheless, Stiglitz makes several key contributions to understanding

---

[1] This can involve buying a security or currency in one market and selling it simultaneously in another market where the price is higher, thereby capitalizing on the temporary price differential. For example, the US dollar may be traded in various locations, such as London, New York, and Tokyo, each with slightly different exchange rates at any given moment.

[2] Cross border tax arbitrage is sometimes described as international tax arbitrage (ITA). ITA 'refers to a situation in which … taxpayers rely on conflicts or differences between two countries' tax rules to structure a transaction … with the goal of obtaining tax benefits' (Marian, 2017, 222).

the macroeconomic impacts of tax avoidance, particularly by emphasizing that tax avoidance is not economically neutral and has significant implications for both tax revenue and broader economic stability. As he says, 'It is often difficult to ascertain who really benefits from many tax avoidance schemes' (Stiglitz, 1985, 325).

Stiglitz's analysis sparked empirical research into the magnitude of tax avoidance, especially by multinational corporations (MNCs). Hines and Rice (1994) discovered that more than a quarter of US foreign investment were located in offshore tax havens, and nearly a third of the foreign profits of US firms were reported in these low-tax jurisdictions. Other economists and economic geographers subsequently developed innovative triangulation techniques, employing diverse sets of data to estimate national and global corporate tax avoidance (Alstadsæter et al., 2018; Garcia-Bernardo et al., 2019a; Haberly and Wójcik, 2015a; Zucman, 2015).

The discovery of the shadow banking system following the financial crisis of 2007–2008 expanded the use of the term arbitrage to cover the idea of regulatory arbitrage in the financial system (Nesvetailova, 2017; Partnoy, 2009). It turned out that innovation in finance is often driven less by market competition and more by efforts to arbitrage banking and financial regulations. Regulatory arbitrage involves exploiting discrepancies in regulatory frameworks, and it appears beyond financial systems. Similar arbitraging techniques began to proliferate during the twentieth century in line with the expansion of the regulatory state (Glaeser and Shleifer, 2003; Majone, 1994).

Law operates as a system of explicit rules, but it is inherently limited in its ability to address every scenario. The resulting gaps and ambiguities create opportunities for arbitrage, as actors exploit loopholes or unregulated aspects of the law to their advantage. This notion is at the heart of Victor Fleischer's theory of 'regulatory arbitrage', a form of 'regulatory gamesmanship' that exploits the intrinsically limited ability of legal systems to attach 'formal labels that track the economics of the transaction with sufficient precision' (Fleischer, 2010, 228). Since any regulation can be potentially arbitraged, the concept of regulatory arbitrage encompasses a range of practices aimed at optimizing business operations, minimizing compliance costs, or circumventing regulatory constraints or arbitraging reporting and liability rules across different regulatory domains (Fleischer, 2010; Friedrich and Thiemann, 2021; Gloukhovtsev et al., 2018; Riles, 2013).

Regulatory arbitrage is often used to describe both domestic and international forms of arbitrage (Avi-Yonah, 2020; Coendet, 2021; Friedrich, 2021; Langenbucher, 2021; Quentin, 2020). However, I propose reserving the term for domestic contexts, to distinguish it from a much larger and more complex subfield: jurisdictional arbitrage. Jurisdictional arbitrage refers to any form of arbitrage that exploits the intricate landscape of multiple sovereign states, each with distinct legal and regulatory frameworks. It is probably an inevitability that any market fragmented among sovereign authorities will be subject to jurisdictional arbitrage practices (Avi-Yonah, 2017; Burke, 2012; Dine, 2012a; Kerber, 1999; Palan and Phillips, 2022; Panayi, 2015, 2009).

One interpretation of the dynamics involving financial and regulatory arbitrage (which includes jurisdictional arbitrage) revolves around two types of assets: financial and intangibles. Financial arbitrage takes place within the financial system, primarily among financial assets, ensuring that debt instruments are aligned in pricing. This type of arbitrage primarily concerns portfolio investments on a global scale. Regulatory arbitrage, on the other hand, typically operates in the realm of intangibles, as understood by Commons (see discussion in the Preface). This involves navigating through various regulatory landscapes to maximize the benefits, as we will see, derived from intangible assets.

Law and Its Limits: Structural Constraints and Legal Boundaries

Every discussion of regulatory arbitrage begins with the law, as the legal framework establishes the rules, boundaries, and disparities that arbitrage seeks to exploit. The law, writes Sebastian Orts, 'supplies the social technology by which business enterprises are constructed and maintained' (Orts, 2013, 1). 'The law itself', writes Rolf Eicke, 'is the main driver [of arbitrage], since it creates planning opportunities with its wordings, its systematic inconsistencies and in particular with its omissions' (Eicke, 2009, 11).

Fleischer (2010) argues that the arbitrageur does not aim to alter rules or regulations. Instead, the arbitrageur leverages the precise language of the law, skilfully navigating the regulatory framework to serve its own interests. In common law countries, it is generally the case that 'actions which do not cross the – verbal – lines drawn by legal rules are, naturally, not prohibited' (Fleischer, 2010, 228). Lawyers exploit ambiguities in the law to craft transactions that formally comply with the letter of the law but violate its spirit. They comply 'with the letter of a law while violating its very spirit in order to obtain a regulatory advantage' (Fleischer, 2010, 229). But as Katja Langenbucher observes, 'Behaviour which complies with the wording, but not with the spirit of a rule will often be perceived as *non honestum* (dishonest)' (Langenbucher, 2021, 95).

Viewed in this way, regulatory arbitrage is both a form of 'manipulation' and 'pervasive' (Fleischer, 2010, 228).[3] Fleischer's characterization of regulatory arbitrage as 'manipulation' has met with significant resistance. Managers and lawyers contend that economic transactions inherently offer multiple structuring options, making the choice of structure a necessary aspect of business. Why should legal and financial advisors structure transactions in a way that increases costs for their clients? Why is a more costly investment or more heavily regulated investment necessarily more ethical than an efficient one? Lawyers are tasked with translating management's intentions into legal terms, while accountants must convey the financial implications of these decisions in the company's accounts. Legislators establish rules in broad terms, while courts refine and interpret these laws in specific cases.

Arbitraging is controversial. Some view arbitrage as techniques of transgression that tend to operate by stealth: the aim is to subvert rules, laws, or taxation, not by changing those rules, but by rendering the subject of law partially or fully invisible to the regulator.[4]

---

[3] Although financial instruments such as complex derivatives are also legal instruments, they transform into effective marketable instruments once they are standardized. This standardization process, which aims to regularize their structure and trading practices, actually stands in contrast to the goals of regulatory arbitrage. The standardization process reduces the opportunities for arbitrage, effectively minimizing the inconsistencies that arbitrageurs capitalize on.

[4] In Chapter 9, I will revisit the theme of law and visibility, as I contend that arbitrage functions as a form of power that operates through techniques of camouflaging. This perspective suggests that arbitrageurs not only exploit discrepancies in markets but also utilize methods of concealment and obfuscation to manipulate or hide their actions. This discussion will delve into how these practices influence legal frameworks and the visibility of such activities, shaping both market behaviours and regulatory responses.

But others argue that arbitrageurs are performing a public duty, brutally exposing mistakes, awkward wording, or otherwise unanticipated loopholes left by the legislature; hence, some may argue, the effect in the aggregate is to improve governance and legislation (Friedrich, 2021).

The broader consensus is that the arbitrageur are exploiting what is known as a second-mover advantage.[5] Governments lay out precise rules, and 'the taxpayer is allowed to choose from this menu the transactional form most likely to reduce their tax bill' (Schizer, 1999, 1349). Internationally, the arbitrageur acts on the same principle of the second-mover advantage. If a country decides to restrict foreign ownership of a domestic asset to no more than, say, 30 per cent, an arbitrageur may construct a 'split' ownership structure to appear as if two different companies are complying with the law on foreign ownership. In reality, they are not. If a country defines the tax residency of a corporate entity not on the basis of the location of registration but on the basis of the type and intensity of activities performed by the corporate entity in the country, an arbitrageur will comply with the law by creating a semblance of activity simply to comply with the law.

The Economics of Arbitrage: Mechanisms, Incentives, and Implications

Fleischer alludes to a distinction that is often made between core economic principles and the regulatory environment. The distinction has played a crucial role in the thinking of arbitrage as a non-essential component of the economics of the firm. Core principles, such as supply and demand, utility maximization, and cost minimization, are seen as universal and enduring across time and space. In contrast, the regulatory environment is viewed as contingent, specific to a given institutional context and subject to change.

---

[5] The concept of 'second mover advantage' refers in management studies to the benefits a company might gain by following and not leading in a particular market. This strategy contrasts with the 'first mover advantage', where being the first to enter a market can provide significant competitive benefits. Second movers can learn from the experiences of first movers, including their successes and mistakes, and can enter the market with a more refined product or strategy. The term 'second mover advantage' has been adapted by corporate lawyers to interpret the strategies employed in regulatory arbitrage.

In their book *Strategic Corporate Tax Planning*, Karayan et al. (2002) recast the distinction not as one between core economic principles and peripheral regulatory solutions but as one between strategy and application. This reframing is significant because it shifts the focus from the impression that regulatory arbitrage has no economic consequences, emphasizing instead how firms leverage tax and regulatory planning as a strategic tool. Karayan et al. introduce the SAVANT (Strategy, Anticipation, Value Added, Negotiations, and Transformation) principle of planning, a structured framework for effective tax strategy, explaining it as follows:

> To add maximum value to each transaction, decision makers need to stay focused on the firm's *strategic* plan, *anticipating* tax impacts across time for all parties affected by the transaction. Managers *add value* by considering these impacts when *negotiating* the most advantageous arrangement, thereby *transforming* the tax treatment of items to the most favorable status. (Karayan et al., 2002, xvi; emphasis in original)

It is difficult to imagine that every transaction would be subjected to such rigorous evaluation, given the volume and complexity of global business operations. The administrative burden and the intricate, multi-jurisdictional nature of many transactions make comprehensive application of SAVANT a daunting task. The insights from Karayan and colleagues emphasize that the dimension of planning and structuring transactions plays a critical role in 'adding value'. The key question this raises is: To whom does this added value accrue, and how is it achieved?

Traditional economic theory tends to focus on factors such as supply and demand, market equilibrium, and the efficiency of resource allocation, but it typically pays less attention to how the actual structuring of transactions can add value. This aspect is more prominently addressed in fields such as corporate finance and strategic management, and particularly in legal and regulatory studies where the nuances of transaction design are critical.

The Conflict of Laws: Navigating Jurisdictional Tensions

Closely tied to the question of law is the issue of legal diversity. Countries have distinct legal systems, resulting in a variety of rules and regulations globally. Diversity is coupled with conflicts of law – questions about which jurisdiction's rules should govern particular aspects of a transaction (Atkinson, 2009; O'Hara and Ribstein, 2009; Panayi, 2015; Riles, 2013). Arbitrage thrives on this diversity, exploiting both the inconsistencies in legal frameworks and the ambiguities inherent in conflicts of law. In this context, jurisdictional arbitrage takes on a supplementary meaning: it not only capitalizes on the wording of the law but also leverages jurisdictional limitations and conflicts to its advantage (Gerber, 2010; Panayi, 2015; Riles, 2013).

This concept lies at the heart of Erin O'Hara and Larry Ribstein's (2009) theory of the 'law market'. O'Hara and Ribstein argue the principle of the internal affairs doctrine that dominates in the United States. Under this principle, rules governing key aspects of corporate law – such as corporate governance, fiduciary duties, and shareholder rights – are determined by the state in which the corporation is chartered, regardless of where it conducts its operations (Greenfield, 2008, 108). As businesses can easily relocate operations across state lines, state-level autonomy fosters a dynamic and competitive legal landscape. The result is a law market wherein corporations practise shopping 'for law, just as they do for other goods' (O'Hara and Ribstein, 2009, 2).

Shopping for law is not unique to corporate law but arises, O'Hara and Ribstein argue, from general law market dynamics. US courts generally uphold the choice-of-law rule in matters of internal governance, enabling corporations to select the legal framework of any state, independent of their geographic operations. Internationally, conflicts of law comprise rules that determine which jurisdiction's laws apply when parties, transactions, actions, or events intersect across multiple jurisdictions. When commercial transactions operate across borders – whether between states within the United States or internationally – each jurisdiction has a right to apply laws as it wishes. Under such circumstances, an international law market is an inevitable outcome of a globalized economy split among numerous sovereign entities.

We may deduce from O'Hare and Ribstein that internalization of markets under the auspice of the state system has 'turbocharged' the demand for law shopping across jurisdictions, as entities seek favourable legal environments within a fragmented, yet interconnected, international market (Avi-Yonah and Panayi, 2010; Broe, 2008; Nakamoto et al., 2019; van Os and Knottnerus, 2011). In turn, these dynamics foster an international regulatory competition (Fischel,

1981; Mendoza and Tesar, 2005). Countries adjust their regulatory standards or tax rates to attract international business. As nations vie for corporate presence, some lower their standards so far that they initiate a 'race to the bottom' in regulatory enforcement.

Annelise Riles and the Art of Disentangling the Transaction

In its classical form, financial arbitrage is regarded as a fundamental mechanism that ensures the smooth functioning of financial markets (Varian, 1987). Arbitrageurs operate across markets and financial centres, helping to synchronize prices and ensure consistency, even when assets are traded in different currencies or are subject to varying regulatory environments. In doing so, they become agents of market correction, quickly capitalizing on opportunities when prices deviate from their fair value. This not only brings prices back in line; it also increases liquidity and enhances price discovery, as market participants adjust their positions based on the actions of arbitrageurs. In theory, arbitrageurs contribute to the overall stability and transparency of financial markets (Fama, 1980; Ross, 1976).[6]

For Annalise Riles, arbitraging is more than a technical or legalistic exercise. Instead, she treats arbitraging as a way of thinking, a mindset that involves recognizing the underlying connections and commonalities between transactions or systems that may seem unrelated or distinct. Her work provides a more philosophical and theoretical approach to arbitrage, framing it as an 'art of association', where the aim is to find hidden functional similarities between transactions, laws, or systems that appear different on the surface. She notes 'how remarkably sophisticated arbitrage is as a mode of thinking', suggesting traders seek out 'hidden functional similarities across what may look on the surface as different transactions: a basket of stocks and an index, or the rules of one legal system and those of another' (Riles, 2013, 70).

Riles lifts the lid on the more complex and sophisticated mechanisms at play. Whereas financial arbitrage is the 'art of association', jurisdictional arbitrage can be seen, in the context of the law market,

---

[6] Plenty of evidence shows the law of one price does not really work (Ardeni, 1989), yet the concept of the market used in economics is predicated on the idea that identical goods must have identical prices, and these are the product of demand and supply dynamics.

as the 'art of dissociation'. This takes us back to the fundamentals of the concept of the market. In economics, the market tends to refer to the abstract mechanisms of supply and demand or the actual places and processes where exchanges occur. A free market is a platform for the exchange of property titles between voluntary participants. The ownership of a good is transferred from the seller to the buyer through contractual agreements, but it is often forgotten that this concept of the market implies that market transactions occur simultaneously in two realms: the physical and the legal. A tangible aspect of the transaction is the actual delivery and receipt of goods or the provision of services, and an intangible aspect is the legal recognition and protection of the transaction. The dual nature of transactions is fundamental to how markets operate. If transactions are legally documented, there is clarity about ownership and accountability, reducing the likelihood of disputes and making them easier to resolve if they occur (Mattei, 1997; Mercuro and Medema, 2020; Orts, 2013a).

A common assumption is that the tangible exchange of goods or services and the intangible legal exchange occur simultaneously, both temporally and spatially, and hence are correlated. For instance, when I purchase my morning coffee, the legal payment is registered with a receipt at the same moment and in the same place where I receive the coffee. Within a national market economy, it is not unreasonable to assume the legal replication of a transaction such as an exchange of property titles is automatic, instantaneous, and largely unproblematic.

But in a market dissected among sovereign authorities, the location of the tangible aspect of the exchange can be divorced from the location of the registration of the transaction. The separation of the two acts hitherto perceived as one allows firms to place the tangible elements of a transaction in one jurisdiction while registering in another. This is the core 'art of dissociation' of arbitrage that Riles alludes to. Strict adherence to the letter of law, including identifying gaps or loopholes in the law of one country or another, allows the two dimensions of transactions to be dislocated spatially along different law jurisdictions. The dissociation of the two acts of the transaction allows companies to place certain assets, particularly intangibles, in low tax, low regulated environments, while charging other subsidiaries of the same group that are in high tax or heavily regulated environments for the use of those assets. Thus the arbitrageur is able to arbitrage, that is avoid, taxation in high tax countries.

Partnoy's Law of Two Prices and Pistor's Theory of Legal Wrapping: The Interplay of Finance and Law

Frank Partnoy's *The Law of Two Prices: Regulatory Arbitrage Revisited* (2018) shifts the direction of the discussion from the techniques of arbitrage to the economic consequences of jurisdictional arbitrage. Whereas financial arbitrage produces the law of one price, he argues, regulatory arbitrage has the opposite effect:

> In a competitive market with low transaction costs and low barriers to trade, financial arbitrage will lead to equivalent goods having the same price and the law of one price will hold, but regulatory arbitrage will not generate the same result in a competitive market with low transaction costs and barriers to trade. Instead, one group of goods will continue to enjoy the benefits associated with regulation, whereas the other economically equivalent group of goods will continue to incur regulatory costs. (Partnoy, 2018, 1019)

Partnoy's law of two prices states that when two identical or similar goods, services, or assets are subject to different regulatory regimes or market conditions, they can have diverging prices.[7]

Why, then, are similar assets or transactions priced differently across markets? In *The Code of Capital*, Katharina Pistor (2019) offers an important correction to the common perception of the relationship between economics and law. Her insight seems to be (although she does not use the metaphor) that just as particles acquire mass through their interaction with the Higgs field, so too assets acquire value from their interaction with the legal, institutional, and political environment. The concept of capital 'is made from two ingredients: an asset, and the legal code' (2019, 2). The 'code of capital' refers to the legal

---

[7] Partnoy writes:

> The difference between the effects of financial and regulatory arbitrage is illustrated by shares that are subject to a regulatory cost. Someone who wants to buy a share of stock might instead enter into a "derivative" position that is economically equivalent to the share but is not subject to the regulatory cost. The overall cost of the share would include the price of the share plus the regulatory cost, whereas the overall cost of the economically equivalent derivative would not include the regulatory cost. The difference between the price of the share and the price of the derivative would be a "wedge" that would persist as long as the difference in regulatory cost persisted. (Partnoy, 2018, 1019)

> The derivative market operating through offshore financial centres is an illustration of the law of two prices.

frameworks – such as property rights, contracts, collateral laws, and corporate law – applied to an asset to transform it into a wealth-generating entity. A piece of land, for instance, becomes capital when it is protected by property laws that define ownership, allow transfer of the land, and provide recourse through the courts in case of disputes. Without the legal structure, an asset not only lacks the necessary protections and entitlements to fully function as capital but also has no meaning or value. Once an asset is legally 'coded' by national laws, regulations, or contracts, it becomes capable of generating wealth for its holder.

Assets, or what economists call 'factors', Pistor shows, have no intrinsic value independent of the legal, regulatory, and political framework. The implications are profound. As strange as it may sound, similar assets can have different prices based purely on location. Jurisdictions can be thought of as a series of Higgs field equivalents, each of which imprints its own value on assets.

With the help of Pistor's theory, we can understand Partnoy's insight about the law of two prices. It is well understood that production and manufacturing costs differ significantly across countries, and the divergence is due to factors such as labour costs, regulatory environments, and access to raw materials. MNCs leverage the divergences in labour and capital across regions. They strategically spread their production activities along global supply chains, optimizing efficiency and cost-effectiveness (Gereffi et al., 2005; Gereffi and Korzeniewicz, 1994). By leveraging the comparative advantages of different regions – whether these advantages be cheaper labour, favourable tax policies, or more lenient regulatory frameworks – these corporations reduce overall production costs and improve profit margins. The global distribution of production also allows them to be more agile in responding to market demands and shifts in trade policies.[8]

---

[8] Perhaps a good starting point is an historical convention, trade theory. Trade theory was shaped in the 1920s by the seminal contribution of two Swedish economists, Eli Hechsher and his student Bertil Ohlin (H-O). They posited that countries are 'bundles' of factors (land, labour, capital), and the exchange of commodities internationally is therefore indirect factor arbitrage (Leamer, 1995). International trade transfers ensure, in the words of Paul Samuelson, that 'otherwise immobile factors of production move from locations where these factors are abundant to locations where they are scarce' (Samuelson, 1948, 23), with MNCs acting as agents of this indirect factor arbitrage.

But MNCs further refine their operations by taking advantage of regulatory divergence and the law market. Rather than rely entirely on the existing regulatory framework of states, they disentangle them, employing Riles's 'art of dissociation', so that production and manufacturing travel in one set of jurisdictions, and the legal and regulatory applications travel in another, through a series of those Higgsfield-equivalent country laws, regulations, institutions, and politics. By doing so, MNCs entrench the law of two prices.

The result is that MNCs no longer view countries solely as collections of factors of production as assumed in traditional trade theory (Leamer, 1995); they view countries as bundles of institutions and regulations.

My colleagues Len Seabrooke and Duncan Wigan use the concept of a global wealth chain to describe the strategic organization of value and wealth across jurisdictions (Seabrooke and Wigan, 2017). Although their framing highlights important aspects of these processes, I find it insufficient to capture the full scope of techniques employed by MNCs. To my mind, there are no distinct or separate chains in operation. Instead, we see a strategic and integrated engagement with regulatory wrappers, where the goal is not merely to move wealth or resources through discrete pathways, but also to ensure each segment of the production process operates within the optimal regulatory environment.

No Free Lunch: The Dynamics of Simple and Complex Transactions

The preceding discussion challenges the common perception of jurisdictional arbitrage as a fringe activity or niche financial manoeuvre. Instead, it appears to be pervasive across markets and is a core strategic tool for MNCs. This raises an important question: Are there any limitations to arbitrage? The literature identifies adversarial reputational risks that may inhibit firms from engaging in arbitrage (Duhoon and Singh, 2023; Dyreng et al., 2016, 2012, 2010), but are there economic limitations on arbitrage?

Frank Partnoy's (2018) distinction between simple and complex transactions offers an insightful framework within which to theorize the economic limitations of jurisdictional arbitrage, even though the framework was intended for financial arbitrage contexts. Partnoy poses two hypothetical transactions: 'Suppose there are two economically equivalent transactions, Simple and Complex. Simple is subject to a regulatory cost of Penalty, but Complex is not. The expected return of Simple will be less than the expected return of Complex because of Penalty' (Partnoy, 2018, 1030).

We can analyse these two hypothetical transactions in the context of transaction cost theory. 'Simple' transactions represent those where the underlying financial or economic principles are well understood and the mechanisms are transparent. In these cases, arbitrage opportunities are typically short-lived because market participants quickly recognize and correct inefficiencies. Jurisdictional arbitrage in simple transactions, such as basic tax avoidance by relocating profits, might meet with swift regulatory responses. Once regulators are aware of the loopholes being exploited, they will act to close the gaps, reducing or eliminating the arbitrage opportunity.

Simple transactions typically involve straightforward regulatory requirements, minimal legal complexities, and lower compliance costs. They can often be managed without the need for extensive legal or financial structures. Firms opting for simple transactions rely on standardized procedures, well-understood legal frameworks, and fewer intermediary structures, resulting in lower legal advice costs and faster implementation.

'Complex' transactions involve more intricate structures and less transparent mechanisms, making it harder for regulators to detect and address arbitrage. They involve cross-border subsidiaries, sophisticated legal structures, and various compliance challenges that inherently increase transaction costs. These transactions are also harder for regulators to understand and respond to, allowing firms to retain arbitrage opportunities longer.

Arbitraging is a precise and expensive business requiring highly specialized expertise. The complexity of international regulations, tax structures, and legal systems calls for specialized legal and financial advice, the involvement of multiple intermediaries, and higher upfront costs (e.g., to set up subsidiaries across multiple jurisdictions, structure complex deals, or navigate multiple legal systems), although these costs often result in long-term regulatory savings through tax avoidance strategies, regulatory arbitrage, and other methods of exploiting differences between jurisdictions. To manage the higher transaction costs, firms engaging in complex transactions must adopt robust governance frameworks, for example, setting up specialized teams, creating internal processes for compliance monitoring, and establishing institutional arrangements to ensure complexity does not result in inefficiency.

For complex transactions to be profitable, firms must establish institutional arrangements to manage and reduce the high transaction costs. Achieving this often requires economies of scale, whereby a larger firm can absorb costs more efficiently than its smaller competitors. Complex transactions incur significant fixed costs, such as setting up legal frameworks, establishing subsidiaries, and maintaining compliance systems across multiple jurisdictions. Large firms can spread these fixed costs over more transactions, reducing the average cost per transaction. For example, a global company with many subsidiaries can amortize the cost of setting up and maintaining a global tax strategy or compliance network.

Larger firms have the resources to hire specialized legal, financial, and compliance teams. The larger the firm, the more widely those costs are spread. In-house expertise becomes increasingly affordable as the firm scales, allowing it to manage high transaction costs more effectively than smaller firms, which might need to outsource these functions at a higher per-unit cost. Larger firms can streamline their internal processes to handle complex transactions, from managing cross-border legal issues to coordinating multi-jurisdictional subsidiaries. They also benefit from increased bargaining power with service providers such as banks, auditors, and law firms. Their scale allows them to negotiate better terms and lower fees for the services required to manage complex transactions, thus reducing costs.

I am not arguing that the decision to opt for simple versus complex transactions (or for simple versus jurisdictional arbitrage schemes) comes down exclusively to a question of economic costs. The evidence suggests other considerations play a role, such as reputation, shareholder composition, or even religiosity. Even so, the economic cost is likely to be central to any decision. Simply stated, there is a trade-off between upfront transaction costs and the potential long-term benefits of complex transactions, and firms will opt for complex transactions presumably only when the regulatory savings or competitive advantages gained from arbitrage outweigh the initial legal and compliance costs.

The hypothetical framework of simple and complex transactions suggests that the larger and more international firms become, the greater their incentive will be to arbitrage national rules. Some evidence supports this suggestion. As businesses began to internationalize, they found it necessary to set up dedicated planning units comprising lawyers, accountants, and other financial professionals to help structure investments in ways that would ensure their compliance with myriad local laws while simultaneously seeking to minimize regulatory costs, including taxation (Bankman, 2004).[9] Today, specialized units of lawyers and accountants, known as corporate treasury operations, are set up to structure investment to ensure it complies with local laws. In addition to lawyers and accountants, these units often include experts in financial instruments, such as futures and derivatives, legal instruments that evolved as techniques for manipulating time and space (CFA, 1998; Donohoe, 2015; Schizer, 1999).

The Tiebout Efficiency Hypothesis: Market Competition in Public Governance

The theory of competitive arbitrage has been embraced by some economists to support the idea of regulatory competition, building on the foundational work of Charles Tiebout. Writing about competition among municipalities in the Los Angeles area, Tiebout (1956) posits that householders are attracted to municipalities that successfully balance tax and public services. In the market, competition encourages innovation and better services at lower costs. By the same token, Tiebout suggests municipalities that offer a desired mix of tax and services thrive, and those that do not fail, because wealthy, tax-paying residents will exit them, Competition will cause municipalities to do exactly what markets normally do – they will pursue optimization. The pursuit of optimization will incentivize municipalities to balance cost and services more efficiently, thus optimizing their offering.

Tiebout's theory of regulatory equilibrium has been used by some economists to claim fiscal competition, of the sort provided by tax havens, should incentivize efficient regulation. Firms are attracted to jurisdictions offering an efficient mix of services and regulations, including taxation, and abandon those that do not. In doing so, firms incentivize jurisdictions to counter-offer, and the latter must do so by

---

[9] These divisions or branches are often located within the organization, but they can include external groups of advisors, typically selected from leading investment banks, legal firms, or accounting firms (CFA, 1998; Donohoe, 2015; Schizer, 1999).

increasing the efficiency of provisions. The idea, implicit mostly, is that markets will find a way to counter market distortions, thereby limiting the 'natural' predatory tendencies of states. This theory has led some economists to root for tax havens (Hong and Smart, 2010; Rose and Spiegel, 2007), and it was an official policy of the United States for a short time (Avi-Yonah, 2005).

The application of Tiebout's theory to fiscal competition among states is predicated on the erroneous assumption that MNCs must choose among jurisdictions – that is, they must weigh regulations as costs versus services offered by states. They weigh the pros and cons of diverging jurisdictions and settle for the 'best offer'. But as O'Hare and Ribstein (2009) show, jurisdictional arbitrage does not necessitate moving or even having to choose among full bundles of regulations. On the contrary, the beauty of jurisdictional arbitrage (if this is the right term) is that it allows the arbitrageur to choose among elements of legal environments and combine them to create a preferred regulatory environment.

In essence, jurisdictional arbitrage allows firms to gain the benefits of favourable legal, regulatory, or tax environments without the need to physically relocate significant portions of their business to those jurisdictions. Paradoxically, the techniques of jurisdictional arbitrage can arbitrage the Tiebout model, exploiting the very premise on which it is based. In the Tiebout hypothesis, individuals and firms are thought to 'vote with their feet' by choosing jurisdictions with the optimal mix of public goods and tax rates, essentially allowing for a market-based sorting mechanism where governments compete to attract businesses. While Tiebout's model assumes such mobility leads to efficiency in the provision of public goods, jurisdictional arbitrage takes this a step further by enabling firms to exploit differences between jurisdictions without necessarily moving their actual operations.

The divergence among regulatory regimes entrenches price disparities and regulatory inconsistencies across borders, but rather than encouraging price convergence, jurisdictional arbitrage places increasing pressure on regulatory bodies.

Conclusion

Jurisdictional arbitrage is a variant on the practices known as regulatory arbitrage, or the practice of exploiting discrepancies in laws and

Conclusion

regulations across different legal jurisdictions or regulatory regimes. Such schemes or structures exploit the law's inherent limitation to codify transactions, combining this with the limitations exposed by conflicts of law principles. In effect, conflicts of law create legal myopia, limiting the reach of one jurisdiction and regulatory authority. The sophisticated arbitrageur exploits these two factors to disentangle the two sides of transactions, the tangible and the legal, to reroute the legal registrations of a transaction in one set of preferred jurisdictions while routing the physical aspect of the trade in another. In doing so, the arbitrageur is taking advantage of different legal 'wrappers' to exploit the law of two prices. The arbitrageur does so to optimize the regulatory environment surrounding a deal, specifically the national rules and regulations impacting it.

These highly sophisticated strategies are likely to be core components of a business strategy, allowing firms to reduce costs, optimize profits, and gain competitive advantages. Larger firms, with their vast resources and sophisticated legal, financial, and advisory teams, are particularly well positioned to engage in complex arbitrage activities. Their global reach allows them to compare and exploit differences between jurisdictions at a scale that smaller, domestic firms cannot match.

2 | The Advent of the Centrally Coordinated Multi-corporate Enterprise

Introduction

In 1867, the Singer Manufacturing Company of New York, a leading manufacturer of sewing machines, established a manufacturing facility in Glasgow, Scotland. In 1882, Singer expanded to a much larger plant in Kilbowie, Scotland. Singer is considered to be the first multinational corporation (MNC) of modern times (Bostock and Jones, 1994; Stern, 2017; Wilkins, 2005).[1] Singer and other fledgling MNCs had to navigate an entirely different type of market – one divided and regulated by sovereign national states, each with an exclusive authority over a defined geographic territory.

In this chapter, I discuss how early MNCs adapted to the changing economic landscape of the late nineteenth and early twentieth centuries, specifically how and why they adopted the form of the centrally coordinated multi-corporate enterprise (CCMCE).[2] I stress the

---

[1] Singer was not the first MNC; that title is often credited to either the Muscovy Company (1555) or the Turkey Company (1583). Similar chartered companies evolved in France and the Netherlands as well. Some were enormous enterprises even by today's standards. The Dutch East India Company's market capitalization reached approximately 78 million Dutch guilders in the early seventeenth century. Adjusted for inflation and economic context, some estimates suggest this would be equivalent to around US$7.9 trillion today! Otherwise, these companies have little in common with modern MNCs. They were royal chartered companies, organized as corporations of merchants, each of whom traded its own account but was subjected to a rigid set of common rules. Crucially, these royal charters of earlier centuries tended to operate in colonies or territories that were outside the formal European state system (Wright, 2013, 20).

[2] Alfred Chandler (Chandler, 1993) describes the new type of corporate organizations that developed in the late nineteenth century in the United States as multi-divisional corporate structures. Railway companies, or rather franchises, employed logistical experts from the army to develop manufacturing on a large scale and operate over great distances. They adopted the army's organizational structure so they could operate with greater ease on the move, conquering time and space.

importance of the institution of the artificial legal person and the attendant concept of the corporation as a legal person. The resulting CCMCEs, as I explain in Chapter 3, were perfectly aligned to exploit the increasingly sophisticated techniques of jurisdictional arbitrage discussed in Chapter 1.

The Rise of a Discrete State System in the Nineteenth Century

Corporations are ultimately licensed by states, and it is only by understanding how these states have evolved that we can begin to grasp how the corporate world operates within the framework of nation-states.

The field of international relations traces the origins of the modern state and the modern state system to the treaties signed at the end of the Thirty Years War in Osnabrück and Münster, known collectively as the Peace of Westphalia (1648). While it is true that the Peace of Westphalia marked a turning point in European political history, the principal actors involved in the treaties – the Holy Roman Emperor, the King of France, and their respective allies – were not nation-states in the modern meaning of the term. The European political authority of the late seventeenth century was characterized by a system of frontiers rather than clearly defined borders. These fuzzy boundaries often overlapped with diverging and conflicting layers of political authority. Nobles, cities, church authorities, and other regional powers frequently crossed them, creating a complex and fluid geopolitical map (Donnan and Wilson, 2021).

The accepted wisdom during the post-Renaissance period in Europe was that diversity within state boundaries was a challenge to governance. The larger and more diverse a state's population, the more difficult it was to govern effectively. Over the course of three centuries (seventeenth, eighteenth, and nineteenth), rulers in Europe sought to homogenize their territories, forging national identities. This historical process of centralization and homogenization was rationalized in the emerging political discourse, often referred to as the 'reason of state' (Botero, 1956 [1598]).[3]

---

[3] Sometimes extreme measures were taken, such as the expulsion of the Moors and the Jews from Spain in 1492, followed by the Huguenots from France. Each expulsion had enormous consequences; for instance, the rise of London

As states consolidated their territorial power, they began to replace the fragmented frontier system with more clearly defined boundaries. The shift from frontiers to boundaries was supported by a variety of technologies of power, including cartographical representations (Biggs, 1999). Beyond practical tools, maps were also used as techniques of homogenization, helping to accentuate a new spatial perception of separation between territories (Biggs, 1999, 385).[4] A process of territorial discretization – drawing a parallel with discrete numbers – culminated in the rise of what Michael Mann calls the 'infrastructural state' during the late nineteenth century (Mann, 2008). This modern state had the capacity to penetrate its society and enforce governance across its territory. Nicos Poulantzas describes the modern political conception of space as 'continuous, homogeneous, symmetrical, reversible, and open' (Poulantzas, 1978, 99).

A crucial development accompanying the evolution of the discrete state form was the parallel evolution of law. During that period, state increasingly began to be viewed as an artificial legal person (Dewey, 1926), a concept with roots in Roman law. Roman jurists developed the notion of the *universitas*, a collective entity that could own property and engage in legal activities distinct from its individual members (Kurki, 2019). The Catholic Church adopted these ideas to create its own legal status as a separate entity (Robé, 2016). Medieval guilds, religious institutions, and trading companies were early forms of legal associations possessing certain rights akin to those of individuals. They were often chartered by monarchs or parliaments but were not considered fully independent legal persons in the modern sense. It was only during the nineteenth century that the state as a legal person evolved within domestic legal systems. States began to be viewed and to view themselves as separate, independent entities with their own legal rights, obligations, and responsibilities.[5] They adopted a legal

---

and Amsterdam as financial centres following the expulsion of Jewish bankers from Iberia, and the rise of Geneva as a financial centre with the influx of Huguenots.

[4] The timing of the rationalization of legal systems of the new national states is not easy to pinpoint. The Gilded Age, typically considered to be 1869–1896, is seen as the period of the creation of the modern United States. The unification of Germany in 1871 marked the official beginning of the German Empire under Otto von Bismarck.

[5] The concept of legal personhood has roots in Roman law, where certain entities, such as municipalities or collegia, were recognized as having legal

personality, so that they could sue and be sued by members of their own populations.

Once a state embraced a clear, territorial conception of its authority and its identity as a legal entity, it had to define its own legal status. The notion of the state as a legal person hinges on a critical distinction between state and its government – the government seen as merely the entity that manages or exercises control over and in the name of the state. While the government consists of individuals who wield authority on the state's behalf, the state remains a distinct and autonomous entity from government. But as governments in advanced countries increasingly acted in law on behalf of the state, it became essential to define the nature of the entities subject to governance in the name of the state.

The state as a legal person articulated, in turn, using a shared legal framework, who or what fell under its jurisdiction. In a fascinating historical process, states began to draw, therefore, a clear distinction between those within their jurisdiction and those outside it. The differentiation extended to the movement of people, goods, and money, each requiring new legal classifications and frameworks. As states solidified their territorial boundaries, they also began to assign legal status to various actors and activities within their domain.

The French Revolution is generally considered to mark the beginning of an historical process in which individuals came to be recognized as 'citizens' – discrete legal persons endowed with specific rights

---

personality. The idea gained prominence in medieval Europe. Canon law recognized the *persona ficta* doctrine, allowing monasteries to have a separate legal existence from individual monks who took vows of poverty. The concept was extended to other entities such as towns and universities, which were granted charters by the government or pope. They could own property, enter contracts, sue and be sued independently of their members. The Common Law tradition contributed to the development of legal principles recognizing the state as a legal entity. Constitutional developments, including the Magna Carta (1215) and subsequent legal instruments, shaped the legal framework within which the state operated, The Glorious Revolution of 1688, the Bill of Rights (1689), and the Act of Settlement (1701), further contributed to defining the powers and limitations of the state. Similarly, the French Revolution (1789) and subsequent revolutionary changes had a profound impact on the legal and political structure of France. The Napoleonic Code (1804), a comprehensive legal code that sought to unify and modernize French law, addressed various legal aspects, including the recognition of the state as a legal entity. It also introduced the concept of the commercial legal person. The concept was adopted elsewhere during the nineteenth century.

and responsibilities vis-à-vis the state. While the practice of issuing birth certificates can be traced to at least the early sixteenth century in England, it was not until the early twentieth century that permanent state agencies were established to maintain comprehensive national citizen registries. Citizens were increasingly granted freedom of movement within national boundaries, allowing them to act as economic agents with the ability to make choices within the state's territorial framework. Their legal status empowered them to engage in contracts, own property, and participate actively in a market economy that was becoming ever more regulated by centralized state legal systems (Robertson, 2010).

By the early twentieth century, many countries had begun issuing passports to their citizens, allowing them to travel to other states – a relatively new concept at the time.[6] Children were given legal status, recognized as citizens-in-waiting, dependent on their parents until they reached adulthood and assumed their own rights and responsibilities as full citizens. Over time, the state's role in registering and regulating other entities also expanded. In many advanced countries, certain categories of animals and pets became subject to state registration and legal protection, and the state began to require the registration of vehicles of all kinds – whether for transport, agriculture, construction, or other uses. These vehicles were assigned legal identities through registration numbers, displayed as evidence of their compliance with state regulations, in the form of number plates, flags, or other identifying marks. This principle extended to all ocean-going vessels, ships, yachts, aircraft, and even stationary oil rigs, all of which are now required to carry a flag representing their state of registration. However, in a twist of legal innovation, many fly the flags of states with little connection to their actual operations, a practice known as flags of convenience.

Goods and commodities became subject to regulations that defined what could be imported or exported, while financial flows were governed by a growing body of laws related to taxation, tariffs, and trade. Legal systems assigned new meanings to these 'moving parts', creating

---

[6] Before passports became common, travellers often carried letters of introduction or safe conduct passes. Issued by monarchs, nobles, or other authorities, these documents vouched for the traveller's identity and requested safe passage (Robertson, 2010; Surak, 2023).

a system of denomination that controlled movement and interactions within and across state boundaries. Today, every economic transaction, every single contract – whether implicit or explicit – within the vast network of trillions of contractual relationships that underpin the global economy is located and ultimately sanctioned by a state. The modern market, with its immense complexity, is not simply an abstract system of exchanges but is deeply embedded in the legal frameworks provided by states.

Advent of the Commercial Artificial Legal Person

The spatial discretization of the nation-state as it transformed itself into an artificial legal person involved the denomination of commercial entities as artificial legal persons as well. The concept of the commercial legal person also has a long history, intertwined with the evolution of associations and states. The nineteenth century saw a significant transformation in this regard, as the leading industrial nations began to codify laws that granted corporations full legal personality, enabling them to act as independent entities within a legal framework (Hannah, 2013; Jones, 2002; Post et al., 2002; Williamson and Winter, 1993). The recognition of commercial entities as legal persons meant they could own property in their own right (i.e., separate from individual shareholders), enter contracts, and sue or be sued independently of the individuals who owned or managed them (Blumberg, 1993, 1985; Muchlinski, 2001; Orts, 2013; Robertson, 1995).

It was not until 1844 that English law allowed the incorporation of a company through registration (Ferran, 1999, 8). The Joint Stock Companies Act was a pivotal piece of legislation that enabled companies to be incorporated through a simpler process of registration, without needing a royal charter or a parliamentary Act. A joint stock company allowed multiple shareholders to own portions of a company, with their ownership represented by shares. The Act also required companies to maintain public records of their incorporation and operations, marking the first step in creating a regulated environment for corporate activity. A decade later, in the Limited Liability Act of 1855, shareholders' liability for company debts was limited to the amount they had invested in the company (Davoudi et al., 2018).

The notion of the corporation as a legal person evolved gradually through these legislative reforms. In France, this development had begun earlier, with the establishment of the Napoleonic code that consisted, among other items, of a general law of incorporation in 1796. The same legal framework recognized the state itself as an artificial legal person. The subsequent evolution of modern incorporation law in France closely mirrored that of the Anglo-Saxon world. The introduction of limited liability in France in *Loi sur les sociétés*, on 24 July 1867, allowed shareholders to limit their personal liability to the amount of their investment, fostering greater risk-taking and entrepreneurial activity (Robé, 2020).

Germany followed suit, introducing similar principles in its company law reforms in 1896. The limited liability company became a foundational element of industrial capitalism, allowing businesses to scale operations while mitigating personal financial risk for investors.[7] By the late nineteenth century, as the result of a series of legal reforms and judicial interpretations in both England and the United States, the corporation had firmly established itself as a legal person within Anglo-Saxon jurisprudence.

The *Santa Clara County v. Southern Pacific Railroad Company* case of 1886 is considered a landmark decision in US legal history for its role in establishing the legal concept of corporate personhood. The Supreme Court does not directly address the question of corporate personhood in the text of the decision, but the headnote, prepared by the court reporter, indicates the justices believed the Fourteenth Amendment's protections applied to corporations. The court's ruling is commonly interpreted to have implicitly recognized corporations as persons under the Equal Protection Clause of the Fourteenth Amendment, extending certain constitutional rights to corporations (Commons, 1934).

The idea of corporate personhood had been evolving in US jurisprudence long before *Santa Clara*, however. For example, in *Louisville, Cincinnati & Charleston Railroad Co. v. Letson* (1844), the court ruled a corporation could be considered a citizen of the state in which it

---

[7] In the early twentieth century, legal reforms in China aimed at modernizing the legal system, including the introduction of legal concepts influenced by Western legal traditions. After a hiatus, the Company Law of the People's Republic of China, enacted in 1993, played a significant role in defining and regulating artificial legal persons, particularly business entities. The law recognized various forms of business organizations, including limited liability companies and joint-stock companies, as legal persons.

was incorporated, for the purposes of determining federal jurisdiction. Shortly after *Santa Clara*, in *Pembina Consolidated Silver Mining Co. v. Pennsylvania* (1888), the Supreme Court reaffirmed corporations are persons for the purposes of the Fourteenth Amendment's Due Process and Equal Protection Clauses. These court rulings laid the groundwork for corporations to claim constitutional rights previously reserved for individuals, including the ability to enter contracts, own property, and engage in litigation, allowing corporations to function as legal persons within the framework of US law (Baars and Spicer, 2017; Commons, 1934; Hannah, 2013; Wilkins, 2005; Williston, 1888).

Salomon v. A. Salomon & Co. Ltd. (1897) is considered a landmark decision in English law (Ferran, 1999; Jones, 2002, 1981). Salomon was a majority shareholder in a leather and shoe manufacturer, a family business. After incorporation, the company purchased the business from Salomon. The company later failed, and creditors sought to recover their debts by holding Salomon personally liable. The creditors argued the company was a sham, and Salomon, as the primary shareholder and controller, should be responsible for its debts. The House of Lords ruled in favour of Salomon, affirming the principle that a duly incorporated company is a separate legal entity from its shareholders. In other words, once a company is legally incorporated, it becomes a separate legal person, distinct from the individuals who own or manage it.

The implications were that once a corporate artificial legal person is established, it is distinct from the people who hold shares in the enterprise or the people who manage them. As Elis Ferran points out, 'Managers or shareholders ... acquire the contractual rights and undertake the contractual liabilities that are involved in the running of the business', but they do not own the corporation (Ferran, 1999, 13). As an artificial legal person, the corporation is no longer reducible to fundamental units such as contracts. The corporation transcends, in other words, its managers, employees, or investors, all of whom could be replaced without altering the nature of the corporate legal person.[8]

---

[8] In American jurisprudence, a corporation is recognized as a legal entity separate from its owners, giving it certain rights and responsibilities under the law. 'Corporation' is used in Australia, Canada, and many other countries, but the United Kingdom uses the concept of the company to convey a similar legal structure. In France, Société anonyme (SA) describes a public limited company, whereas Société à responsabilité limitée (SARL) is more or less

Even a single-shareholder small business cannot treat the corporate balance sheet as its own private account. Slavery has been banished in modern society, so the enslavement of 'artificial legal persons' is gone as well.

This principle is known as the corporate veil. Shareholders are not personally liable for the company's debts beyond the value of their shares (Blumberg, 1985). In the English case, Salomon could not be personally liable for the debts of the company, even though he was its primary shareholder and had control over the company's affairs. Moreover, corporations were no longer narrowly defined by their original purposes but could evolve and diversify over time. The close association between the company and its shareholders as owners was broken, and like any person, it was subject to taxation (Micheler, 2021).[9]

Beyond these specifications in English, European, and American law, corporations now have human rights obligations under customary international law, as reflected in instruments such as the United Nations (UN) Guiding Principles on Business and Human Rights and emphasized in the G20 High Level Principles on the Liability of Legal Persons for Corruption. Corporate liability can be criminal, civil, or administrative, depending on a country's legal system, and key conventions such as the UN Convention Against Corruption and the OECD Anti-Bribery Convention require member states to establish the liability of legal persons for corruption offences (Wright, 2013).

Did New Jersey Change the World?

About the same time as the doctrine of the corporation as legal person became entrenched, another development took place in the United States that irrevocably altered the relationship between corporations and 'firms'. Between 1899 and 1892, the state of New Jersey introduced

---

similar to the UK concept of the private limited company. There are differences among countries in the way commercial associations come about and operate within the territorial boundaries of the licensing authorities – but they all have one thing in common: they are licensed by a sovereign authority to transact in its territory. Countries seldom allow a commercial entity to be truly 'multinational'; that is, they do not recognize a sharing of the rights and duties of a corporation by two sovereign authorities.

[9] The 1901 statute of the state of Delaware specifies that even the smallest of businesses controlled entirely by a single shareholder cannot treat the corporate balance sheet as its own private account.

a series of amendments to its incorporation laws, commonly known as the holding company rules, allowing corporations to own stock in other corporations (Alef, 2009; Grandy, 1989).[10]

There is some debate about the originality of the so-called New Jersey Rules. New Jersey had no ambitions to change the world. It liberalized its incorporation laws in a bid to attract business from its richer neighbour, New York State. In fact, joint stock companies were allowed to own stocks in specific industries such as insurance in New York in the 1850s (Davies, 1969). The concept of the holding company was also well established in Europe during the nineteenth century, but holding companies were set up in Europe largely by banks (Paquier, 2001).

If there is some debate about the degree of innovation introduced by New Jersey, there is less debate about its implications for the development of modern corporations. The American type of corporate groups was created, as trusts were replaced by holding companies that controlled other companies that came to be known as subsidiaries. In 1933, the US Securities Act defined a company as a subsidiary if more than 50 per cent of its voting shares were owned by another company. Since states in the United States had discretion in determining their own incorporation laws, they could determine the laws designed to attract business to their territories, such as the capital size of firms, the ability to operate across state lines, and the authority to merge and hold stock in other corporations (Grandy, 1989, 685).

New Jersey's liberal statutes were designed specifically to attract corporate holding companies and corporate headquarters to New Jersey. Companies quickly learned to set up holding companies in New Jersey and later Delaware to take advantage of the more favourable corporate laws. Standard Oil Trust led the way by incorporating as Standard Oil Company of New Jersey in 1889, and over

---

[10] By the 1880s, industrial corporations had joined railroads in operating across state lines, but in the United States, the governing authority defining the internal relations of firms remained at the state level (Grandy, 1989, 684). New Jersey found itself in a financial squeeze after the Civil War and was seeking revenues. For the previous twenty-five years, railroads funded the overwhelming majority of the state (Grandy, 1989, 678), so officials initially responded to the post-war political and fiscal crisis by turning to the railroads. After a decade of fruitless attempts to raise railroad taxes, the state passed a reasonably effective statute in 1884 that broadened the base of railroad taxation and raised the rates.

the next fifteen years, smaller competitors adopted a similar structure. By the end of the nineteenth century, giant corporate groups ruled the US economy. Over one-third of all manufactured goods produced in the United States was made by 1 per cent of US manufacturers, a handful of railroads controlled inter-regional ground transportation, and two companies operated the nation's long-distance communications. They were all organized as corporate groups (Grandy, 1989; Yablon, 2006).

New Jersey actively promoted itself as a business-friendly environment, where companies could enjoy lower taxes, fewer restrictions on corporate behaviour, and more flexibility in their organizational structure. The subsidiaries of New Jersey-based holding companies were often located in other states where the company's market was, and they operated under the specific regulatory environment of those states. While each subsidiary had to comply with the local regulations, such as labour laws, environmental regulations, or taxation, these laws were often less burdensome because they were limited to the subsidiary and did not apply to the entire corporate group. A New Jersey holding company shielded the parent entity from the stricter regulations that might apply to the subsidiaries if they were directly controlled by the same entity based in those other states, making it easier for corporations to centralize control without facing regulatory scrutiny as a single entity in each state where they operated.

New Jersey's success in attracting corporate headquarters and parent companies was copied by other states, including Delaware and later Nevada and South Carolina (Arsht, 1976; Dyreng et al., 2013).[11] A new game began to evolve, 'chartermongering', defined as 'the active solicitation of corporation charters for the purpose of bolstering state revenues' (Grandy, 1989, 677). This represented the origins of the law market that O'Hare and Ribstein talk about. At the time, observers were concerned about the possibility of a 'race to the bottom' being created by incorporation law (Barzuza, 2011).

New Jersey continued to liberalize its laws from 1888 to 1896, as did its competitors, but in the early twentieth century, New Jersey

---

[11] There are some broad similarities between some of the best-known international arbitraging schemes and US domestic schemes. As I see it, American companies and their lawyers may have adapted domestic schemes to international circumstances. European, Japanese, Chinese, and other corporate groups then adopted these adjusted American schemes.

amended its corporate laws to introduce more stringent regulations (Grandy, 1989). In 1902, the state of Delaware stole a march over New Jersey by granting business planners and investors broad latitude to privately order the rules of the internal firm and limit or even eliminate the fiduciary duties of managers (Manesh, 2011). If there was a race, the winner was undoubtedly Delaware. Companies flocked to Delaware. As Kent Greenfield laments, today, with less than a third of 1 per cent of the US population, Delaware 'gets to set the rules of corporate governance' for six out of ten of the nation's largest corporations (Greenfield, 2008, 2).[12]

New Jersey and the Emergence of the Corporate Group

The context for the Jersey amendments was a rising dissonance between the development of business and the law of incorporation in the United States. From around the 1870s, major corporations across industries began to form horizontal combinations. Initially, these took the form of trade associations or cartels, where industry players came together in informal agreements to manage their market. Vertical combinations began to evolve as well. One of the first and most important of these was Carnegie Steel, formed in 1872 as J. Edgar Thomson Steel Works. By the 1880s, many of these combinations adopted the format of a trust. In the trust arrangement, competing companies exchanged their stock for trust certificates, granting the trustees control over the participating firms. The largest and most profitable of these was the Standard Oil trust, organized in 1882 (Berle, 1950; Petrin and Choudhury, 2018; Wright, 2013).

Over time, concerns over the growing power of big business led Congress to take legislative action. The first major attempt to curb corporate dominance came with the Sherman Antitrust Act of 1890, which aimed to restrict monopolistic practices and promote fair competition. However, despite its passage, enforcement of the Sherman Act remained weak in its early years, as courts often interpreted it in ways that favoured business interests (Collins, 2012). It was not until the early twentieth century, under Theodore Roosevelt's 'trust-busting' policies, that anti-trust enforcement gained real momentum.

---

[12] New Jersey abandoned the game of competitive legislation to attract corporate headquarters or parent companies in 1911 (Yablon, 2006).

But at around the same time, partly driven by the discussions that preceded the Sherman Act, New Jersey became the first of many states to permit a company to buy stock in its competitors without a special Act of the state legislature. The New Jersey holding company innovation may have come partly in response to the Sherman Antitrust Act (1890), whereas the Clayton Antitrust Act (1914) was introduced later partly as a response to the abuses of the New Jersey holding company model. The concentration of capital in the United States developed earlier, but in New Jersey the corporate group organization settled around the concept of the corporation (Kreider, 1933).

After New Jersey, companies could adopt a formal relationship as one company could own a stake in another. A question that emerged in the context of such formal mergers was why some companies paid more than what was considered market value when purchasing another. For instance, during the formation of the largest trust at the time, the US Steel Trust in 1901, Andrew Carnegie received US$300 million for a company that, according to fair value accounting, was only worth US$70 million (Allen, 1979). The argument was that the newly merged enterprise would significantly enhance its future earning capacity, far exceeding what each company could achieve independently. As a result, investors were willing to pay a premium for the merger. This substantial discrepancy created a new type of an asset, an intangible asset (see discussion in Preface) and written in the accounting book as 'goodwill' (Allan, 1889; Commons, 1919; Cooper, 2007; Jaffé, 1924).

Years later, Adolf Berle, a lawyer and economist who advised the Roosevelt administration and a follower of Veblen and Commons (Hill, 1967), linked the emerging group structure in the United States to the question of the concentration of capital and arbitrage. Berle noted how: 'The legal doctrine of corporate personality was built around the idea of a sovereign grant of certain attributes of personality to a definable group, engaged in an enterprise [but due to the New Jersey amendment] the divergence between corporate theory and the underlying economic facts has occasioned a variety of problems' (Berle, 1947, 344).

Specifically, the advent of the group structure created a situation whereby 'a single large-scale business [was] conducted, not by a single corporation, but by a constellation of corporations controlled by a central holding company, the various sector being separately incorporated' (Berle, 1947, 343–344). The results were that 'corporate personality did not correspond to the actual enterprise, but merely to a *fragment of the enterprise*' (Berle, 1947, 348, my emphasis). Since regulation could be applied only to a fragment of the enterprise, investors exploited the regulatory lacunae to arbitrage, among others, anti-trust rules. This development, as Berle noted, was 'far from the original conception of a corporation' (Berle, 1947, 348).

The beauty of the parent–subsidiary corporate structure was that it allowed companies to present their operations in a way that minimized exposure to more restrictive regulations in certain states, while still benefiting from access to markets and resources in those jurisdictions. Essentially, the motivation for the adoption of the US holding company structure was not just to improve operational efficiency, as often assumed, but also to engage in regulatory arbitrage, taking advantage of differences in state-level regulations to maximize control and profits while minimizing regulatory oversight.

Berle recognized, in other words, that the parent–subsidiary model that emerged in the United States may in fact have benefited from something that can be described as a *structural regulatory myopia* and the law market that was discussed in Chapter 1. The corporate group structure that emerged in the United States was designed to arbitrage a regulatory environment predicated on the principles of IAD.

For Berle, the holding company structure served, in addition, as a tool for leveraging control: a pyramidal corporate structure emerged, allowing investors to extend control over significantly larger assets with relatively modest initial capital, by stacking ownership and leveraging the control of a series of holding companies. The dispersion of control along different subsidiaries, each formally a separate and independent company, made it difficult for regulators to counter the tactic and allowed investors to gain control over significant amounts of capital and resources, while spreading risk and investment across multiple companies. A stylized version of this structure is depicted in Figure 2.1.

The pyramidal corporate structure presented in Figure 2.1 is a simplified variant of the technique of corporate control that was used to construct large conglomerates. In reality, even greater leverage could be achieved through the sale of bonds or other forms of debt at different level of the corporate holding. By issuing bonds, companies could raise large amounts of capital without diluting their ownership stakes or control, allowing them to continue to extend their influence over subsidiaries and assets far beyond their initial investment.

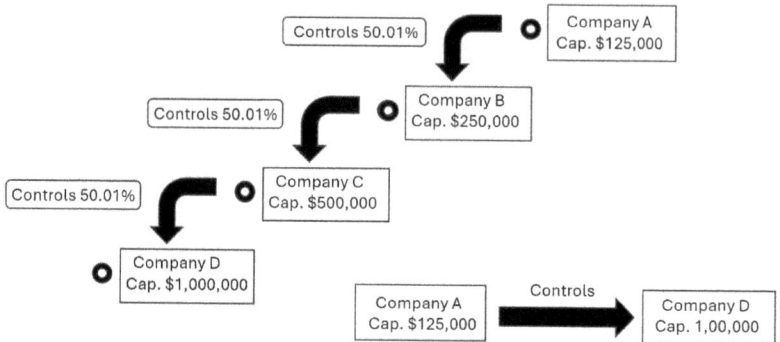

Figure 2.1 A pyramidal holding company structure.
The conclusion: Company A, with a total capital investment of US$125,000, indirectly controls Company D, which is capitalized at US$1 million, by holding majority ownership (50.01 per cent) in a chain of companies.

It appears that for Berle, the corporate group structure emerging in the United States was driven from the outset by arbitrage. When the United Fruit Company was created in 1899 from a merger of the Boston Fruit Company and Minor Cooper Keith's railway and banana companies in Costa Rica, it set up a New Jersey-based holding company, writes the historian James Martin, because this 'revolutionary corporate mechanism allowed for a more highly capitalized, farther reaching combination than ever before' (Martin, 2018, 20). The New Jersey or Delaware holding companies and subsidiaries were set up, therefore, to exploit regulatory advantages offered by the two states.

The pyramidal structure became a common tactic in early twentieth-century corporate America to amass economic power. Investors exercised control over large business empires with relatively little personal investment, enabling them to dominate markets or industries without needing to fully own the underlying companies. J. P Morgan was the master planner who developed the concept of highly leveraged business enterprises organized through a pyramidal holding structure. Lewis Corey estimates that by the 1920s the house of Morgan controlled in this way about 24 per cent of US corporate value and the Rockefellers another 18 per cent (Corey, 1930). The structure was designed to avoid accountability, as control was exercised indirectly through multiple layers of ownership. Each layer could obscure who was truly in control and complicate regulatory oversight.

The Invention of Intangible Property

The story of the rise of the CCMCE would not be complete without acknowledging another often ignored, albeit more important, development that profoundly changed the nature of the corporation. In a series of seminal rulings, largely aimed at resolving disputes between railway companies and state governments, US courts began to recognize a new category of property: intangible property (Commons, 1934). Cases accumulated as American states sought to regulate the prices charged by railway companies for the transport of goods and people within their borders. States argued unchecked prices could harm local economies, but railway companies fought back, claiming price controls would negatively impact their financial stability.

In adjudicating these disputes, the courts accepted that price controls proposed by states affected not only the current but also the future earnings of those railway companies. The courts also accepted that those anticipated future profits were a critical part of the financial valuation of these railway companies, reflected in the value of the companies' shares. In effect, the market viewed these prospective income streams as part of railway companies' original investment calculations and thus treated them as a kind of property that belonged to those companies.

At the time, such a concept of property – ownership over future income – did not exist formally in law (Jaffé, 1924). Property was traditionally defined, as we saw in the Preface, in terms of tangible assets, such as land, equipment, or physical infrastructure. However, US courts recognized the figure of the investor – practically non-existent in neoclassical economics – as an important stakeholder and adopted an investor's perspective as a legitimate concern. By recognizing the potential loss of future income streams owing to state-imposed price controls, the courts accepted the principle that those future earnings could be treated as a form of property, intangible property. This was a significant shift in legal thinking, as it allowed for the idea that future income, though not yet realized, had a present value that could be capitalized upon and protected under law (Allan, 1889; Commons, 1934, 1919).

Corporations as legal persons now could potentially own something amounting to more than physical assets. They owned intangible assets. These intangible assets were anything that could generate future income streams, a concept that gradually extended to include more elements such as trademarks, logos, and more nebulous values, such as entrepreneurial acumen, management expertise, and organizational culture. These qualities reflect the internal strengths of a corporation, such as leadership effectiveness, innovative potential, and corporate values, that contribute to long-term financial performance.

The principles of valuing intangible assets were also applied to post-New Jersey corporate groups in the context of corporate mergers and acquisitions. During these transactions, courts and businesses recognized the value of a would-be purchased company was not solely based on its physical assets; its value also included its intangible aspects, such as its established customer base, brand reputation, and potential for future profitability. This nebulous value was written in the accounting books as 'goodwill'. Rooted in English Common Law, the concept of goodwill refers to the value that exceeds the book value of a company's assets and liabilities. It represents the market's estimation of a company's reputation, customer loyalty, and other intangible strengths that ensure future income streams. In the early twentieth century, goodwill came to encapsulate intangible values that did not have a direct physical form but were nevertheless crucial in determining the overall value of a business. Courts used the concept to ensure intangible elements, such as entrepreneurial spirit or organizational culture, were factored into the financial statements of corporate groups.

The introduction of intangibles fundamentally reshaped the corporate world, transforming how businesses were structured, valued, and financed. Among other things, the concept of intangible property produced new types of companies. By the early twentieth century, there were complaints about companies pejoratively labelled *patent trolls* (Golden, 2006). These companies, or rather corporate groups, did not produce anything but used a portfolio of patents solely to collect licensing fees or settlements. George Selden is frequently cited as an early example of a patent troll (Byers, 1940). In 1895, Selden was granted US patent 549,160 for a 'liquid hydrocarbon engine of the compression type'. Selden, who never built a car, used his patent on the automobile to collect royalties from other automobile companies. He held back from manufacturing until he lost a case.

The accepted wisdom in economics had been that commercial organizations are set up to maximize profits. But with the introduction of the concept of intangible property, corporate strategy shifted and was no longer focused purely on production costs. In this way of thinking, corporate strategy extends beyond traditional operational efficiency or profit maximization to include maximizing intangible assets such as brand reputation, innovation, customer loyalty, organizational culture, and goodwill, all of which play critical roles in determining a firm's overall worth. Today, as I mention in the Preface, according to the latest estimates, about 90 per cent of the SNP500 value consists of intangible assets.

Surprisingly, even today the concept of intangibles does not play an important role in contemporary thinking about firms. The concept was introduced implicitly in the field of corporate finance by Modigliani and Miller. Modigliani and Miller's famous theorem was predicated on the idea that factoring Knightian uncertainty renders the concept of 'profit maximization ... a random variable and as such its maximization no longer has an operational meaning' (Modigliani and Miller, 1958, 263). Instead, they argued, 'any investment project and its concomitant financing plan must pass only the following test: will the project, as financed, *raise the market value* of the firm's shares?' (Modigliani and Miller, 1958, 264; emphasis added). Since the largest portion of the value of firms in market, as we saw in the preface is intangible, Modigliani and Miller effectively, but not explicitly, speak of intangibles. But that left us with a problem. Intangibles are considered, as I argued earlier, to be part of the financial investment logic of corporate groups, not as part of the strategic behaviour of companies.

Corporate Groups and the Accounting Concept of a 'Going Concern'

By the late nineteenth century, it was obvious that New Jersey's amendments and Delaware's incorporation rules were having profound implications on the development of American capitalism. US courts began to grapple with the challenges posed by these complex corporate structures and different stakeholders and began to refer to these groups as 'going concerns', a term John R. Commons says was 'taken over from the customs of business' (Commons, 1924, 8).

Courts' recognition of the concept of the going concern was crucial because it allowed corporate groups to be treated in certain litigations as functionally integrated. But the implications went further. Going concern conveys the idea of a commercial entity that may be made of diverse legal persons, acting in unison, an entity with its own history, acting in the present, and, most crucially, forward-looking. The past represents the entity's history, including its reputation, legacy, and previous financial performance. The present reflects its current state: its operations, financial health, and market position. The future is the most significant aspect in terms of going concern status: investors and managers expect the entity will continue to operate and generate returns.

The emergence of corporate groups was challenging not only for lawyers but also for accountants. Litigators and investors were not particularly interested in the precise format of the legal organization of each subsidiary or affiliate of a corporate group. Investors were interested in the performance of the group as a whole and its future. The emergence of the corporate group structure also had a profound impact, therefore, on accounting practices. The performance of the group, rather than individual subsidiaries, became the focal point for investors and managers, and the concepts of intangible assets and goodwill played a crucial role in understanding value, suggesting a group's value was often greater than the sum of its parts. But how is it possible to account for a whole that is more than the sum of its parts?

The legal situation was that each subsidiary, or holding company, is a separate legal entity, subject to its own financial reporting and legal obligations. But in reality, these subsidiaries, affiliates, or holding companies were part of a single business enterprise controlled by the parent company. Professional associations of accountants began advocating for changes in accounting practices to reflect the new realities of corporate organizations. These professional bodies, such as the Institute of Chartered Accountants in England and Wales, played a key role in shaping modern accounting standards around the concept of the going concern (Walker, 2006, 10).

The concept of the going concern, argues Robert Sterling, began to be used by accounting as a way of translating the 'firm's model' that economists had in mind into accounting (Sterling, 1968, 481). But something was lost in translation: 'Exactly what accountants mean when they speak of a going concern is difficult to determine' (Sterling, 1968, 489). In practical terms, from an accounting perspective, the attempt to treat a group of separate companies as a single 'firm' is fraught with conceptual and analytical difficulties. This is not helped by the fact that accounting is used not only by the firm for internal purposes or by the investors but also by the regulators, including for inland revenues. Regulators are interested in the present performance of the group, for instance, in the amount of tax to be paid. Managers and investors are interested in the performance of the group, not least any indicators about future performance. They may be forward-looking, but then, investors do not want to pay tax for anticipated future income that may not materialize. For example, a firm may buy a piece of machinery expecting it to yield income over the next ten years, but there is always the risk that market conditions, technological changes, or operational issues will prevent that income from being realized. Accounting must provide, therefore, estimates that reflect both potential future income and potential losses or underperformance.

In practical terms, this requires the use of techniques such as depreciation to spread the cost of an asset over its useful life, while also preparing for contingencies, such as asset impairment, changes in market conditions, or shifts in demand. The preferred solution was to create different sets of accounting books, each one serving different purposes. The accountants set up a system of management accounting. This system is primarily designed for internal use by managers. Management accounting is different from consolidated accounting, which is designed for external reporting, particularly for shareholders and other stakeholders. It captures, or is supposed to capture, the performance of the corporate group. Tax accounting is different again.

To complicate matters further, another issue pertinent to the discussion of the corporate group is diverging interpretations of the concept of 'profit' across various professional fields. Accountants, economists, and lawyers each define and calculate profit in distinct ways, leading to varying results even when assessing the same group. Accountants typically follow strict guidelines that prioritize tangible assets and historical costs. Economists might focus more on broader economic impacts, opportunity costs, and market dynamics. Lawyers, on the other hand, could interpret profit through the lens of legal frameworks and implications, often landing on a figure that sits somewhere between the other two calculations.

The result is that the same corporate group produces different accounting books, but also that it is able, up to a point, to interpret these books in a variety of ways. This divergence not only complicates financial assessments but also provides, as to be expected by now, many opportunities to arbitrage rules of disclosure. I return to this topic in Chapter 7.

The Rise of the CCMCE

Singer and other fledgling MNCs operated in a world where the legal rules of incorporation were specified by each state. But Singer wished to operate in another market beyond its home environment, which was in effect another discrete legal system with its own set of rules. There were no norms or blueprints for cross-border operations that would allow the reconciliation of two systems of law. Crucially, Singer possessed twenty-two crucial patents that were recognized in the United States but not elsewhere (Davies, 1969). As intangible value played such an important and growing role for American companies, the challenge of securing those intangibles abroad was not to be trifled with. In the United Kingdom, for instance, the concept of intellectual property laws was still evolving.[13] The challenge that American companies faced was how to craft a corporate legal structure that could support cross-border expansion of firms without losing their vital intangible assets. This was left to the lawyers and accountants to resolve.

Although the literature on the subject is surprisingly scant, some evidence suggests the fledging multinationals experimented initially with a variety of legal solutions to this conundrum. Some had tended to rely on intermediaries in foreign markets, such as export commission houses, to conduct international business. These intermediaries were responsible for facilitating exports and managing the logistics of foreign sales and manufacturing on behalf of the parent company (Mayo, 1979).

As an aside, it is worth noting that British companies operating primarily within the empire were often organized as mercantile groups. These firms were referred to as 'principals', while the intermediaries they used in different parts of the empire were known as agents (Russell, 1873). This terminology was later adopted by Ronald Coase in his seminal work (*The Nature of the Firm*, 1937). Over time, these

---

[13] In the United Kingdom, the Trade Marks Registration Act of 1875 established a system for registering trademarks, and the Patents, Designs, and Trade Marks Act of 1883 modernized the patent system. Under the Paris Convention for the Protection of Industrial Property, signed in 1883, foreign patent applicants were treated like domestic ones. The Berne Convention for the Protection of Literary and Artistic Works was signed in 1886.

discussions became central to the modern theory of the firm and were formalized as the *agency problem* (Fama, 1980.)

Returning to our topic. This method of using agents proved ultimately unsatisfactory because it did not foster strong or independent demand in foreign markets. Intermediaries often lacked the deep local market knowledge and commitment to develop sustained relationships with customers, limiting the growth of the firm's international presence (Berk, 2004; Wilkins, 2005).[14]

As companies sought more effective ways to expand abroad, they began to explore other strategies, such as sending their own agents or establishing foreign branches. Singer, for instance, sent two of its employees with British citizenship to the United Kingdom to serve as general agents for the company. These agents applied for UK patents in their names, and they played a key role in developing a new corporate organization in the United Kingdom based on a network of sub-agents (Davies, 1969). The result was that although Singer is typically seen as the first modern 'multinational', there were effectively two Singers, one based in the United States and another in the United Kingdom. The UK Singer was a separate legal entity controlled by local sub-agents who lived and worked in the United Kingdom.

The early experience of multinational firms with foreign agents and foreign branches was fraught with challenges and complications. Agents could, and often did, switch allegiances. They were independent operators, often acting on behalf of multiple companies, possibly leading to conflicts of interest. Because foreign agents operated independently, companies had limited control over how their brands and products were represented in those markets. One of the major drawbacks of operating through foreign branches was that companies could be treated as foreign entities for the purposes of tariff regulation. This meant the goods shipped from the parent company to the branch were subject to import tariffs, significantly raising costs and reducing the competitiveness of products in the foreign market. The parent company and the branch shared a joint account, and the parent company was legally liable for the debts and obligations of the branch.

---

[14] Early MNCs were cautious and preferred to target countries with similar legal systems. Over time, as MNCs gained experience and globalization progressed, they became more adaptable and began to operate in a broader range of countries with diverse legal systems.

As the concept of the corporate group and 'going concern' began to develop in the United States following the New Jersey amendments, a new solution emerged. Not by intention, as far as I can tell, but rather because of a lacuna. There were few legal restrictions on foreign ownership of companies in most European countries during this period. Some countries had bilateral treaties that facilitated cross-border investment and protected foreign investors' rights. This way or that, it appears that European countries were comfortable with the idea of foreign ownership of their corporations (Arsht, 1976; Cheffins, 2015; Yablon, 2006).[15]

As a result, by the end of the nineteenth century, companies that had previously relied on foreign agents or branches to manage their international operations began replacing those agents with local entities governed by host states' laws. They overwhelmingly preferred to either buy or set up a 'corporation' in a host state, although the corporate form was generally subject to far more extensive legal regulations, often more so than partnerships or sole traders (Ferran, 1999). By the early twentieth century, there is evidence that not only American but also international businesses were increasingly adopting the American parent–subsidiary model, replacing the older systems of agents and branches with more reliable and legally sound structures.

The proliferation of the American type of corporate group internationally, or as I call it the CCMCE model, offered MNCs an effective way to solve many of the compliance issues bedevilling the earlier models. Under the principle of the corporate veil as established in the Salomon case in the United Kingdom, a controlling shareholder is not the 'owner' of the corporation. In the same way, a parent corporation does not 'own' a subsidiary located abroad. It merely has a controlling stake in it. The legal nicety, sometimes referred to as a legal fiction (Greenfield, 2008), of treating subsidiaries as separate legal persons was immensely important in shaping the development of the modern MNC. Under this arrangement, the parent company located in one

---

[15] For a discussion on whether the New Jersey amendment was original, see Freedland (1955). Freedland argues New York had allowed cross-company shareholding among insurance companies since 1854. He agrees, however, that New Jersey universalized the rules and made cross-company shareholding the norm.

country either purchases or sets up a local company in a host country, positioning itself as the majority shareholder.

This also solved the difficult issue of intangible property. The corporate organization, the parent, could either 'sell' to the local subsidiary or assign to it rights over patents, trademarks, or other intangibles (the assigning of intangible property to a local subsidiary is often written in the accounting book as 'capital injection' because the parent is providing the subsidiary with an asset that has a financial value. This may be registered in national accounting as 'foreign direct investment', but in fact no money is transferred from one country to another). As an ostensibly separate and independent legal person, the subsidiary can apply for local patents or trademarks in the host country, but in contrast to agents or intermediaries, the subsidiary is controlled by the parent, and hence the parent's interest is protected.

There are other advantages to the model. Because subsidiaries are treated as local companies, the parent has no formal responsibility for the subsidiary's debts or legal obligations. In fact, one of the most attractive features of the parent/subsidiary model is the legal separation of the parent company from the subsidiary – a particularly attractive feature in the risky world of state politics and regulations. Moreover, as an independent legal person, the subsidiary can choose from a range of financing options, including raising funds from local financial markets, thus securing local financing without relying on capital from the parent company. This arrangement makes the subsidiary 'best suited to raising large amounts of business finance and to limiting and diversifying financial risks' (Ferran, 1999, 3).

The emerging CCMCE model allowed companies to manage foreign subsidiaries with limited liability and greater control, setting the stage for modern corporate structures. Companies could easily expand by acquiring and controlling other firms through share ownership. The parent company's liability was limited to its investment in the subsidiary, shielding the parent from direct financial and legal exposure. Subsidiaries could operate independently and raise capital from local markets, reducing the financial burden on the parent company. This facility came into play in the late 1950s with the emerging Euromarket in London. US companies were subject to strict financial regulations, but their foreign subsidiaries could raise funds in the Euromarket.

CCMCEs in a European Context

The history of the CCMCE did not end there. Although European states did not directly copy New Jersey's amendments, they were influenced by the corporate practices that emerged from the United States. Over time, the rise of MNCs (in reality, CCMCEs) led to calls for the reform of European legal frameworks to adapt and remain competitive in a globalizing economy. In response, several European countries reformed their corporate laws to allow greater flexibility in ownership structures and the creation of corporate groups. This included the ability for corporations to own shares in other companies, establish subsidiaries, and benefit from limited liability in much the same way US companies had under the New Jersey framework. European countries began to adopt the company holding structure as well, allowing firms to own and control subsidiaries while benefiting from limited liability protections. But this process took a very long time,

In Germany, holding company laws were formalized through the concept of *Konzernrecht* (corporate group law) as part of the 1965 German Stock Corporation Act (Aktiengesetz) which governed relationships between parent companies and their subsidiaries. This legal framework allowed German companies to expand domestically and internationally using the holding company structure, mirroring the advantages seen in the US system. Unlike other jurisdictions, German corporate group law requires a controlling agreement (Beherrschungsvertrag) for certain types of corporate group structures. In France and the United Kingdom, similar legal frameworks emerged, facilitating the growth of corporate groups that could manage diverse subsidiaries across multiple markets. In the United Kingdom, the Companies Act 2006 formally defined a 'holding company' in section 1159.

The CCMCE model of organization solved compliance issues, access to local markets, and protection of property and transaction (in countries offering such protection). Many suggest the legal subversion of groups into subsidiaries and affiliates proved useful because the separation of holding companies from subsidiaries introduced a cap on potential losses following particularly risky activities and encouraged investors to invest in the shares of a holding company. Many of today's subsidiaries and affiliates are doing essentially the same job: as 'special purpose vehicles', they can be invested in or traded independently of the performance of the parent corporation.

CCMCEs and Arbitrage

It appears the proliferation of the CCMCE mode of organization was driven, at least initially, not by arbitrage. But the system of sovereignty and sovereign equality encouraged the same dynamics already witnessed in the United States – the law market, regulatory myopia, and arbitrage. This proved particularly important as regulations and taxation began to rise during the twentieth century. It did not take long for CCMCEs to exploit divergence in national systems of taxation, in particular, divergence in nominal corporate tax rates.

The condition of competitive states in a federated polity such as the United States may have encouraged competitive arbitrage in incorporation rules, but competition in a global market divided among national regulatory authorities, many of which had little or no stake in the game, proved fiercer. In this context, not only the rules of corporate governance but also all rules become subject to the sovereign. Rules are defined by states on the assumption that rules cover a particular territory. Rules, regulations, and norms, the substance of a state, evolve parochially, predicated on the assumption that each state is a separate and independent sovereign authority, akin to a solitary planet travelling in the vastness of space. Each country sets its laws and will only cooperate with other countries on a bilateral basis – rarely on a multilateral basis. Each regulatory authority is enabled but also constrained by a higher set of rules, the basic ordering of the world according to the system of sovereignty and sovereign equality, and is able to regulate and control activities registered in its territory.

As in the case of the law market in the United States, the option of arbitraging national rules encouraged the development of 'pull jurisdictions' worldwide. These pull jurisdictions emulated the New Jersey and Delawares, but with a difference. They adopted what I refer to as a *licence-fee-based model* of development rather than a *tax-based model*. Their revenue depended on the volume of companies, each paying licence fees, rather than on taxation. They tended to be either countries that were traditionally trading nations, such as the United Kingdom, the Netherlands, and Switzerland, or their former or current colonies and territories, such as Singapore and Cyprus (Palan, 2010; Palan et al., 2013).

With the development of the group structure, the notion of the MNC as a single, centralized organization with a unified central brain was increasingly viewed as an over-simplification. Many MNCs operate with a significant degree of decentralization. Different regional offices or subsidiaries often have considerable autonomy in decision-making to adapt to local markets and conditions. Many scholars argue a more accurate metaphor for a modern MNC is that of a complex ecosystem or a network of interconnected nodes, each with some degree of autonomy but also interdependent. The ecological metaphor emphasizes interdependence and adaptability within a network.

Cayman's history as an offshore financial centre (OFC) began, as New Jersey or Delaware before it, with the enactment of its 1960 Company Law (Freyer and Morriss, 2013). Initially, Cayman simply copied the laws of its neighbours, Bahamas and Barbados. Like them, it amended its company laws many times to attract foreign capital, as did Ireland, the Netherlands, Singapore, and other OFCs (Dizkırıcı, 2012; Helliar and Dunne, 2004; Polak et al., 2011; Stewart, 2005). The race to the bottom witnessed in the United States in the early twentieth century became international.

Over time, these countries appeared to be attracting an inordinate amount of investment, routing through subsidiaries that often seemed to do nothing else but serve as investment conduits (Garcia-Bernardo et al., 2017; Mintz, 2004). Conduit countries are jurisdictions that primarily owing to their tax laws, bank secrecy, or corporate governance rules attract large capital inflows and outflows, even though net capital flows are small (Mintz, 2004).

The CCMCE model proved, perhaps unwittingly at first, perfectly designed to take advantage of gaps in rules and the international regulatory myopia. In 1902, for instance, the American Tobacco Company sought to avoid British protective tariffs by acquiring shares in local British companies. It encountered resistance and eventually opted for a joint venture with the British Imperial Tobacco Company by setting up the British-American Tobacco company (BAT) (Cox and Cox, 2000). BAT typified the experimentation common to the first phase of internationalization. In this phase, managers begin to appreciate the advantages of acquiring or setting up a foreign subsidiary compared with using local intermediaries or setting up branches in a foreign country.

The interaction of the doctrine of entity law with the concepts of sovereignty meant countries got to 'see' only the portion of cross-border business transactions that happened to reside in their 'territories' – or worse, the portion of transaction that the going concern decided to register in their territories. Under such circumstances, it became fairly easy to apply the technique of regulatory arbitrage in jurisdictional form, as jurisdictional arbitrage.

Conclusion: There Is No Such Thing as an MNC

From the outset, modern MNCs were organized not as singular organizations, but as CCMCEs. Whereas the American version of the parent–subsidiary model of organization evolved from the outset to arbitrage incorporation rules, internationally the CCMCE model was developed originally, I believe, not only or primarily because to arbitrage rules but also because it offered certain advantages over agents or branches. It was a pragmatic solution.

At the same time, however, the solution exacerbated a trend observed in the United States – an emerging gap between the legal corporation and the business organization, or the firm. Under these circumstances, the power pendulum began to swing decidedly towards corporate groups. Authorities knew, of course, that the CCMCEs were operating under one management, but they had regulatory control only over the entities that were registered in their territories. Not surprisingly, as we will see in Chapter 3, those CCMCEs leveraged their legal organisation and began to arbitrage national rules.

3 | Tools of Trade

Introduction

The argument so far can be summarized as follows. Economic transactions involve the exchange of goods and services, which simultaneously entail the exchange of property titles. Jurisdictional arbitrage is the strategic practice of decoupling the physical exchange of goods and services from the legal registration of those transactions, allowing firms to exploit regulatory and tax differentials across jurisdictions. Firms organized as centrally coordinated multi-corporate enterprises (CCMCEs) are optimally designed to enact such decoupling. They strategically position subsidiaries and affiliates across multiple jurisdictions, leveraging regulatory and tax differentials to separate the physical exchange of goods and services from their legal and financial registration.

This process is orchestrated at the institutional level by a specialized second-tier management structure, primarily composed of the chief financial officer, legal teams, and accounting departments. A first tier management, senior executives, strategists, and financial decision-makers define the company's long-term objectives, including market entry strategies, investment allocation, and risk assessments. This is where theories such as transaction cost economics (TCE) or institutional theory could come into play, helping to determine whether direct investment, partnerships, or contractual arrangements are optimal.

The second tier management of multinational corporations (MNCs) is composed of legal and financial professionals, known broadly as business planners (Manesh, 2011) or 'transaction cost engineers' (Fleischer, 2010, 231) are then tasked with structuring the business entity in compliance with corporate, tax, and investment laws, while accountants ensure financial reporting aligns with local regulations and international standards.

The purpose of this chapter is to further clarify how CCMCEs affect the dislocation of the physical from the legal. What, in other words,

The Concept of Corporate Planning

Table 3.1 *CCMCEs and the object of jurisdictional arbitrage*

Concept	Explanation
Economic Transaction	Situated in time and space, involving the exchange of goods and services, represented as the transfer of property titles.
Value Determination	Asset or property title values are influenced by their location, which includes legal and regulatory dimensions, such as taxation.
Role of MNCs	Specialize in cross-border transactions of goods and services, navigating varying regulatory frameworks that affect asset valuation and regulations.
Jurisdictional Arbitrage	Strategy to navigate disparities in regulation for strategic advantages by aligning operational structures with favourable jurisdictions.
Objective of Arbitrage	Ensure goods are exchanged under favourable economic terms while recording legal and financial transactions in beneficial regulatory jurisdictions.
CCMCE Model	Organizational structure of MNC as CCMCE enables dissociation of goods/services exchange from regulatory frameworks.
Strategic Outcomes	Maximize economic efficiency, minimize regulatory burdens, and bridge economic and regulatory dimensions of cross-border transactions.

are the tools of the trade employed by corporate planners – the lawyers, accountants, and financiers – who are responsible for translating management's strategic vision into a feasible economic structure?

Table 3.1 summarizes the argument so far.

The Concept of Corporate Planning

Jean-Philippe Robé says that discussions of corporate planning have tended to concentrate on current tax avoidance strategies, often at the expense of a thorough understanding of what planning is about.[1] Planning involves not only maximizing the value of transactions at the

---

[1] In private discussions. Tax planning can be defined as the ability of well-advised taxpayers to attain better tax treatment by restructuring their transactions (Schizer, 1999, 1344).

present time but also, crucially, he argues, involves preparing the corporate organization for future risks and uncertainties.

This is a fundamental point: corporate structuring is inherently forward-looking, crafted to anticipate and adapt to evolving regulatory, financial, political, and strategic landscapes. Planners seek to account for both known unknowns – risks that are identifiable but unpredictable in detail – and unknown unknowns, the unforeseen disruptions that can reshape entire markets. This comprehensive approach to corporate planning often results in what may seem like an excess number of subsidiaries, many of which appear to serve no immediate or obvious purpose. These so-called shell corporations, seemingly inactive, are often misinterpreted as mere instruments of opacity. In fact, these entities are often established as a form of insurance, prepared to address potential contingencies or opportunities that may never materialize.

For instance, when it comes to capital gains taxation, tax obligations are typically triggered only upon realization – that is, when an asset is sold or transferred. Rather than waiting until the point of sale to address these tax implications, the planners may opt to establish dedicated holding subsidiaries long in advance – sometimes decades before any actual transaction takes place. These holding subsidiaries may lie dormant for a long period of time, perhaps decades, appearing to be doing nothing in particular. The true purpose of these subsidiaries may become apparent only in key moments, such as an asset sale or a tax event.

Shell companies serve, in fact, different purposes. One type of an shell company may not be shell at all. I borrow the concept of the 'fossil' to describe this category of apparent shell subsidiary from Johnny West of OpenOil.[2] Fossil subsidiaries often stem from projects that were intended but never executed, such as exploratory ventures in the oil and gas industry. An oil company, for example, might set up a subsidiary to conduct exploration in a new region. If the exploration yields no viable resources, the entity may remain on the books as an inactive shell (Song, 2014). These fossil shells may remain active on paper either because dissolving them could lead to unnecessary costs or complications, or perhaps management is still hopeful the

---

[2] The OpenOil organization has graciously assisted the CORPLINK project in developing the technique of corporate equity mapping. During these sessions, the concept of fossil subsidiaries was thoroughly explored.

investment may come alive in the future. Certain jurisdictions require complex procedures for liquidating entities, leading some companies to opt for dormancy over dissolution (Pressey and Mathews, 2003). As a result, companies may find it more efficient to leave the fossils inactive than to formally close them. Additionally, an inactive subsidiary might be kept on the books for balance sheet purposes, providing optionality or offsetting certain costs in financial reporting.

A fossil may also prove to be a strategic asset in the future. It may 'flip' at some point and begin to play a role as a financial conduit (Mintz, 2004), facilitating the flow of capital between subsidiaries. A fossil that begins acting as a conduit is likely to generate less concern from regulators than a newly formed subsidiary that serves a new venture. The fact that some subsidiaries may appear dormant or operate as shells or conduits does not imply, therefore, that they lack a function within the organization. In fact, although they seem inactive, some shell or phantom subsidiaries form the backbone of long-term tax or regulatory planning strategies (Peters, 2004).[3]

Three Strategies of Subsidiary Control

When establishing a business entity abroad, an MNC faces a series of critical decisions. Despite the apparent complexity, these choices ultimately boil down to three fundamental options, with all other variations being mere adaptations or combinations of these core strategies. Consequently, however complex a CCMCE may appear, the actual complexity is a combination and aggregation of these three basic options.

Option 1: The parent sets up as many subsidiaries as it desires but controls them directly. In this model, presented in Figure 3.1, a parent company A, located in country A, sets up a fully or partially owned subsidiary C in country C. This model of direct control provides the parent company with a straightforward means of managing its foreign subsidiaries.

This direct ownership model can be viewed as a natural extension of the simple transaction structures discussed in Chapter 1. By minimizing

---

[3] The OECD (2025, 108) defines a shell company as 'a firm incorporated or organized or registered in the economy but [it] does not take part in the economic operations (other than pass-through capacity)'.

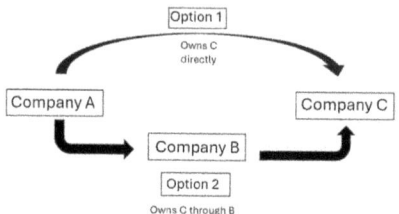

Figure 3.1 Direct and indirect ownership patterns.

the number of intermediary entities and maintaining direct oversight, this approach is closely aligned with TCE, as it reduces the layers of management, reporting, and regulatory complexity that might arise in more fragmented structures.

Studies of foreign direct investment (FDI) often operate under the premise that is often incorrect that MNCs prefer the simple structure, treating more complex structures such as multi-tiered ownership chains or offshore intermediaries as artificial deviations from this baseline. This perspective contributes to an analytical bias, where complex structures are regarded as distortions rather than strategic adaptations to regulatory, tax, or operational realities.

Option 2: The parent company sets up an intermediary subsidiary in a third country. The intermediary often acts as a conduit.[4] The second option may be repeated many times, creating a cascading structure or ownership chain as in Figure 3.2

Option 3: The third option involves a splitter arrangement that is a variant of an intermediary ownership, whereby the parent company divides control of a lower-tier subsidiary through two or more separate intermediary subsidiaries or chains of subsidiaries (Figure 3.2).

At every point, there will be inevitably a non-optionality outcome: a subsidiary that is located at the end of the chain. As I go on to show, end-of-chain subsidiaries is an important, if often unrecognized, category.

A CCMCE can be understood, therefore, as a *fractal* structure. Like fractals in nature, which repeat a similar pattern at different scales,

---

[4] A conduit subsidiary is defined as an intermediary company established to channel income between a parent company and other subsidiaries, typically in different countries. Some countries specialize as locations of intermediary subsidiaries; these are called conduit jurisdictions (Mintz, 2004).

Three Strategies of Subsidiary Control   95

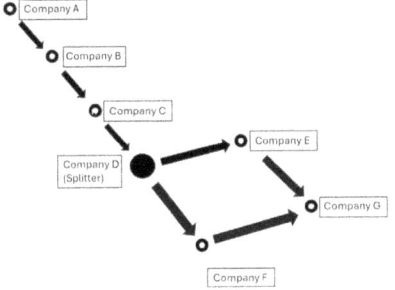

Figure 3.2 Schematic representation of a split ownership structure.

CCMCEs essentially replicate these core organizational principles, direct, indirect, and splitters, across various levels and locations.

That is not to say that there are many more options and permutations, not covered in this book. The parent company must decide, for instance, on the location and choice of company type. Each country provides various options for business associations, and each with a distinct regulatory and tax implications. For example, Germany offers several types of business entities: limited liability company (GmbH), limited liability entrepreneurial company, stock corporation (AG), and partnership limited by shares (KGaA). The parent company must decide on the financing structures for its subsidiaries, contractual agreements, compliance, and reporting strategies. Each of these choices can significantly influence the overall effectiveness of the arbitrage strategies employed by the parent company.

In addition to these options, the parent company must decide whether it wishes to act as 'active' or a 'passive' investor in subsidiaries. If it chooses to act as an active investor, it assumes a hands-on role in managing and guiding the subsidiary. If it chooses to act as a passive investor, it owns a stake in a company that outwardly would be described as a subsidiary, but without actively participating in its day-to-day management or operational decisions. Chains of intermediaries or splitters allow the CCMCE to make those decisions along the entire range of the chain. The permutations are endless.

Table 3.2 conceptualizes complex corporate multi-chain entities (CCMCEs) as fractal ownership structures, categorizing levels of control and management involvement across different configurations to assess their implications for transaction costs and opportunities for jurisdictional arbitrage.

Table 3.2 CCMCEs as fractal structures in the light of the theory of simple and complex transactions

Controlling Structure	Definition	Active Investment	Passive Investment	Simple Transaction	Complex Transaction
Direct Control	Subsidiary controlled directly by parent.	Parent actively manages subsidiary operations.	Parent acts as an investor without operational involvement.	Low transaction costs/limited arbitrage.	N/A
Indirect Control	Subsidiary controlled through an intermediary.	Intermediary actively manages subsidiary operations.	Intermediary 'acts' as an investor without operational involvement.	N/A	Medium transaction costs/greater scope for arbitrage.
Splitter	Control split through at least two intermediaries.	At least one intermediary actively manages a subsidiary.	At least one intermediary acts as investor without operational involvement.	N/A	Medium to high transaction costs/ even greater scope for arbitrage.
Corporate Chain	Hierarchical structure of entities from the parent company down to end-of-chain subsidiaries.	Choice of active and passive management of subsidiaries in chain.	Choice of active and passive management of subsidiaries in chain.	N/A	High transaction costs/maximum arbitrage
End of Chain	Subsidiary at end of chain.	Has no choice in the matter.	Has no choice in the matter.	Low transaction costs/limited arbitrage	N/A

Direct and Intermediary Controlled Subsidiaries

In a direct controlled approach, the parent company establishes a straightforward ownership and operational oversight. Although I call this option simple (see Chapter 1), even these apparently simple structures involve incredible layers of complexity. Transactions among parent and subsidiary in a directly controlled structure are subject to the following set of regulations:

1. host country's rules and regulations;
2. home country rules and regulations;
3. bilateral trade and investment treaties between host and home country;
4. multilateral trade and investment treaties to which the two countries are signatory.

In his book titled *Tax Planning and Holding Companies*, Rolf Eicke argues, 'Holding companies are a great opportunity and suitable vehicle for implementing, controlling, and adjusting tax reduction strategies' (Eicke, 2009, 1). Eicke further clarifies that at an intermediate level, holding companies or corporate subsidiaries are the key to tax planning (Eicke, 2009, 63); the reason being that intermediary entities in a third country complicate the pattern of investment.

In an intermediary situation, the investment is effectively split and treated legally as two sets separate, if not unrelated, investments. Under such a structure, the intermediary subsidiary in a third country plays the role of the host country to the 'first' investment (which may register on FDI data as the target investment country). At this state, the intermediary 'flips' and acts as 'home' country for the second investment, which the FDI data may treat as separate and independent (Carmassi and Herring, 2016; Chen et al., 2017). That is why countries such as the Cayman Islands are often registered as a large beneficiary of FDI investment as well as a large originator of FDI. The introduction of an intermediary, whether by design or not, entirely changes, therefore, the regulatory treatment of investment as it passes through the intermediary. As one investment consists now of two separate sets of investment, inevitably, the investment is subject, as we saw in Chapter 1, to higher transaction costs.[5]

---

[5] An agency theory perspective offers an alternative reading of the role of subsidiaries. In a corporate setting, principals (shareholders or corporate

If a single intermediary jurisdiction fails to meet all regulatory or tax optimization requirements set by management, the MNC may opt to leverage its CCMCE structure to establish a chain of subsidiaries spanning multiple jurisdictions. Such multi-layered structures consist legally of sets of discrete home–host relationships. So, for instance, the introduction of two intermediaries in different countries turns an investment into three sets of separate investments and so on. In such structures, typically, the first intermediary country in the chain is chosen because its laws and regulations may help disrupt a specific regulatory constraint, while additional subsidiaries in other jurisdictions are used to neutralize other regulatory or tax burdens and so on. Such structures require extensive knowledge, strategic planning, and financial creativity, as they significantly increase transaction costs while enhancing regulatory and tax efficiency.

To give one example of a potential use of such an intermediary subsidiary in a third country: in the early 1960s in the United States, the Kennedy administration innovated the concept of the controlled foreign company (CFC), whereby certain foreign subsidiaries were required to report their activities to US tax authorities (Lokken, 2005).

The CFC rules represented an ingenious response to systemic blind spots created by the principle of sovereign equality discussed in Chapter 2. While the United States lacked direct jurisdiction over foreign subsidiaries, it could enforce certain reporting requirements on domestic companies that served as parents regarding their foreign

> headquarters) delegate authority to agents (subsidiary managers), who are responsible for making operational decisions. However, there is a natural misalignment of interests between principals and agents, often leading to agency costs. These costs include expenses for monitoring agent actions, structuring incentives, and safeguarding against managers pursuing their own interests over the organization's. The choice between a simple (direct ownership) structure and a complex (intermediary-based) structure in an MNC reflects a balancing act in managing relationships, incentives, and monitoring between the principal and the agents. In addition, by using intermediary entities in jurisdictions that provide legal protections or tax efficiencies, the parent company can standardize contracts, incentive structures, and reporting practices across jurisdictions, lowering the need for customized agreements and detailed direct oversight at every level. Complex structures can also help prevent asset diversion or unauthorized actions by subsidiaries by centralizing key resources (e.g., intellectual property (IP), brand rights, or financing) in intermediary subsidiaries with stricter controls, limiting the operational subsidiaries' autonomy and reducing the risk of misaligned incentives.

holdings. CFC rules were intended to give the US Internal Revenue Service (IRS) an unprecedented access to a great deal of information on the scope and mode of taxpayer operations at home and abroad (Engel, 2000; Lokken, 2005; Meussen, 2007). Firms had to provide the IRS with balance sheets and operating results for all related and foreign entities, including the minutes of corporate meetings, names of domestic taxpayers and related foreign entities, copies of all foreign tax returns, and organizational charts showing the relationship of all domestic and foreign entities, including stock ownership percentages (Blumberg, 1993; Cheng, 2010; Hespe, 2013).

When a MNC sets up an intermediary subsidiary (B) in a third country, it may be able to arbitrage CFC rules. The parent company (A) treats the intermediary (B) as its CFC, meaning B's income could be subject to taxation under A's CFC rules. However, once B establishes another subsidiary (C) in a third country, C becomes CFC of the new entity (B). If designed properly, B can act as a 'blocker' (discussed later) meaning that C's profits are subject to B's country's CFC rules, rather than A's (Mattingly, 2020; Taylor, 2010).[6]

Another approach to arbitrage draws on a system of attribution of CFCs. To qualify as a CFC, the US parent must typically own more than 50 per cent of the stock (by vote or value) in the subsidiary. A CCMCE might opt to split ownership of one of its subsidiaries to avoid CFC status for specific subsidiaries. This approach is one of the potential use of the 'splitter' structure. At the same time, an American MNC may opt to maintain transparent ownership thresholds so that losses from lower-tier CFCs are attributed upward through the chain to an upper-tier CFC and ultimately to US shareholders. This structure is often used to transfer tax credits to the United States, thus helping the American parent reduce taxation there (for discussion, see Phillips et al., 2021).

In another classic example of what is known as treaty shopping, a CCMCE strategically establishes an intermediary subsidiary (B) in Country B to leverage a double taxation agreement (DTA) that its home country (A) does not have with the target country (C). This

---

[6] For instance, a parent company (A) in the US sets up an intermediary subsidiary (B) in the Netherlands that controls ultimate investment (C) in a tax haven (e.g., Bermuda). Instead of A being taxed directly on C's income, because C is technically controlled by B, B's CFC rules apply instead of A's, potentially shielding profits from immediate taxation (see Garcia-Bernardo et al., 2017; Mintz, 2004; van 't Riet and Lejour, 2018).

enables the parent company to expand its effective DTA network, even though Country A itself lacks a treaty with Country C (Broe, 2008; Nakamoto et al., 2019; Rodriguez, 2008; van Os and Knottnerus, 2011; van 't Riet and Lejour, 2018).

By employing complex chains of subsidiaries across multiple legal and financial environments, the CCMCE constructs a layered corporate framework, where each jurisdiction plays a distinct role in optimizing different aspects of the investment. The concept of structural myopia discussed in Chapter 2 ensures that countries struggle to track the full profit journey, leading to gaps that allow MNCs to optimize tax outcomes; the reason being that tax authorities 'see' only part of the structure, preventing them from recognizing the full impact of cross-border tax arbitrage. This approach enables firms to arbitrage regulatory differences, shielding assets, minimizing tax liabilities, and maximizing financial flexibility, often beyond the reach of a single jurisdiction's oversight.[7]

The Splitter Option (Option 3)

Splitters are types of intermediaries that can either emerge organically or randomly when different divisions or subsidiaries of the same corporate group independently choose to establish a joint venture or a collaborative structure.

In large CCMCEs, divisions often function with considerable autonomy, each responsible for its own strategic growth, market expansion, and partnerships. As a result, certain joint ventures or partnerships may emerge within the organization without direct involvement from corporate headquarters, leading to overlap in ownership and financial commitments. In such a case, a splitter may emerge organically or randomly.

Split ownership can be used, however, for arbitraging purposes. For example, most corporate disclosure rules require reporting when a company holds a controlling interest in a subsidiary. Typically, this threshold is 50.01 per cent or more. Instead of holding a single majority stake

---

[7] For instance, Jurisdiction B might offer favourable tax treatment for IP, making it ideal for holding IP assets. Jurisdiction C might have favourable rules for capital gains on asset sales, making it suitable for holding physical or financial assets. Jurisdiction D might provide a robust legal framework for dispute resolution, useful if the MNC anticipates the need for arbitration or legal protections.

(e.g., 51 per cent) in one subsidiary, a parent company may opt to split ownership through two or more subsidiaries, each holding stock in a lower subsidiary just below the threshold (e.g., 49.99 per cent). Because no single entity holds a controlling interest, corporate disclosure obligations may not be triggered. This method is particularly useful in jurisdictions where corporate transparency laws are tied directly to majority control rather than broader financial or strategic influence.

Split ownership can also be used to circumvent ultimate beneficial ownership (UBO) reporting rules. UBO regulations are designed to uncover the true owners behind complex corporate structures by requiring disclosure when a single entity or individual holds 25 per cent or more of a company. Instead of having one entity or person own 25 per cent or more in a company, ownership is distributed strategically among multiple entities or individuals, each holding just below the threshold (e.g., 24.99 per cent). This fragmented ownership can be used to obscure ownership, keeping the true beneficiaries hidden. This is particularly effective when combined with multi-jurisdictional structuring, where different regulatory regimes apply.

Beyond disclosure avoidance, split ownership can be used to manipulate tax liabilities. For instance, by distributing ownership stakes across multiple jurisdictions, companies can route income through low-tax subsidiaries that remain invisible under CFC rules (because those normally relate to subsidiaries). In countries where tax treaties provide lower withholding tax rates for minority shareholders, splitting ownership can qualify for lower rates on dividends, royalties, and interest payments. In addition, some jurisdictions classify minority-owned entities differently for tax purposes, allowing income to be treated as non-taxable or deferred.

The splitter arrangement can be, therefore, a powerful tool for arbitraging national rules that impose restrictions on foreign ownership. By structuring ownership across multiple entities, each with a minority stake, MNCs can bypass domestic ownership caps and regulatory control thresholds. As I show in Chapter 6, the splitter arrangement is often used to arbitrage liability rules as well.

End-of-Chain Subsidiaries

The organization of the CCMCE implies every chain must have an end-of-chain subsidiary, the entities at the terminus of corporate control structures. Owing to their location, end-of-chain subsidiaries lack the flexibility to engage in rule arbitrage in the same way as intermediate or holding entities. They are bound by local tax and compliance rules specific to their operations, leaving them limited flexibility. This means that, generally speaking, end-of-chain subsidiaries are not engaged in arbitrage. Arbitrage opportunities generally occur once profits are transferred upwards, often through intermediate entities, and holding companies in favourable jurisdictions can engage in tax optimization.

This is a key distinction in understanding the role of end-of-chain subsidiaries in offshore financial centres (OFCs). An important study by Garcia-Bernardo et al. (2017) distinguishes between two types of OFCs: conduits and sinks. Conduit jurisdictions, including the Netherlands, Ireland, Luxembourg, Switzerland, and Singapore, are both major recipients and significant sources of FDI. This unusual pattern of capital flows suggests these jurisdictions are home to intermediary subsidiaries. The study found that these conduits have funnelled collectively 47 per cent of corporate offshore investment from tax havens. The Netherlands is the largest conduit, channelling 23 per cent of offshore corporate investment. Ireland is the fifth largest, channelling 1 per cent of offshore corporate investment.

Other major OFCs such as the Cayman Islands, Hong Kong, Bermuda, and the British Virgin Islands operate more as sinks: they are recipients of funds, but do not act as major sources of FDI. I interpret the conduit/sink classification as representing different positions within corporate chains: conduits act as intermediaries, while sinks serve as the end points.

The categorization of jurisdictions into conduits and sinks – intermediaries and end-of-chain destinations – highlights a common confusion between tax planning and profit shifting. End-of-chain subsidiaries in low-tax jurisdictions can serve as useful, tax-efficient vehicles for financial functions, such as treasury operations, investment, hedging, or syndicated financing. But while a subsidiary in the Cayman Islands might avoid paying tax on profits, the Cayman Islands lack bilateral double tax treaties with other countries. Unless the corporate group is prepared to keep cash holdings in the Cayman Islands indefinitely, any attempt to repatriate those profits to other subsidiaries is likely to trigger taxation. Consequently, without additional structures controlling these subsidiaries, any profits repatriated to the parent company will ultimately be taxed (Forstater, 2018).

A study commissioned by Jersey Finance, an arm of the Jersey government, explains that Jersey, like other OFCs, creates an environment where international business can operate 'without fear of double taxation, or legislative and administrative bias in favour of a "home" counterparty' (Debono et al., 2016, 2). In other words, Jersey provides a 'neutral' space to conduct financial operations. But the real work of arbitraging occurs within the intermediary jurisdictions that manage and control these end-of-chain subsidiaries. From the discussion here, we can infer that the potential for arbitrage rises significantly among intermediary subsidiaries located in jurisdictions that specialize in providing regulatory advantages. The critical factor in regulatory arbitrage is not the location of the subsidiary in an OFC per se, but its specific position within the corporate chain (Forstater, 2018).

I suspect therefore that end-of-chain subsidiaries, or 'sinks' in OFCs, are more likely to house investment income, royalties, or financial assets rather than being the main operational hubs. They cannot, on their own, reduce the group's overall tax burden, because tax authorities in higher-tax jurisdictions can apply anti-avoidance rules, withholding taxes, or CFC provisions to prevent direct repatriation of untaxed income. Thus, while these subsidiaries may serve genuine functions – such as managing intra-group financing, treasury operations, or investment funds – their real power in tax structuring depends on their positioning within a larger network of intermediaries (Forstater, 2018).

The Elsewhere, Ideally Nowhere Strategy

A coveted form of arbitraging would be an activity or a transaction allowing a company to slip through the cracks of regulatory oversight altogether by making it appear an activity is taking place in another jurisdiction – or even across multiple jurisdictions (Nesvetailova and Palan, 2014). Such an activity would be intentionally structured to exist in a legal grey area, where no single jurisdiction has clear authority over it. More specifically, by setting up entities across multiple jurisdictions and transferring the appearance of the activity between them, corporate planners create enough ambiguity that no regulatory body can definitively claim responsibility. Each is led to believe the activity either takes place elsewhere or falls under the oversight of another entity. For instance, a transaction might be designed so that a jurisdiction believes it is conducted offshore, while the offshore location perceives it to be executed domestically.

The ultimate arbitrage is designed to make an activity or transaction appear, from the perspective of a regulatory authority, as if it takes place elsewhere, in a different regulatory environment, whereas in reality, it ends up in a regulatory vacuum. Since every regulatory authority believes the activity takes place elsewhere, it remains unregulated.

Intermediaries and Blockers and Stoppers

Many of the techniques of jurisdictional arbitrage that are practised internationally evolved first in the federated structure of the United States and were then exported by American companies and adopted by others as well. Although a history of the concept of the intermediary subsidiary company remains to be told, I believe its origins can probably be traced to tax avoidance techniques described in the parlance of US tax advisors as 'blockers' or 'stoppers'.

The term 'blocker' was applied by American lawyers to describe a technique that exploits US exemption rules granted to certain charitable entities (Silber and Wei, 2015; Taylor, 2010). US tax rules allow charities to engage in market transaction under the category of an unrelated business taxable income (UBTI). The purpose of the UBTI was to allow charities and other tax-exempt entities to engage in business transactions but not gain an unfair advantage. UBTI is used, then, to preserve the charitable status of the charitable entity. But although UBTI has been introduced to prevent such tax-exempt entities from having an unfair advantage, corporate groups often insert entities described colloquially as a 'blocker' between the tax-exempt charity (which could be the parent entity or operating subsidiaries) and other group subsidiaries. The blocker pays taxes on income it receives from UBTI, allowing it to shield the charity's tax status. After taxes, the blocker can pass income to the tax-exempt entity in a way that does not trigger UBTI, preserving the tax-exempt status.

It seems that the concept of the blocker was then extended to describe a particular type of entity used to help foreign investors avoid the United States' effectively connected income (ECI) tax and its associated US tax filing requirements. ECI regulations stipulate foreign investors engaged in a US trade or business are subject to federal net income tax. To avoid these taxes, a foreign investor sets up a US

Intermediaries and Blockers and Stoppers 105

company as a blocker. The blocker company shields the foreign investor from taxes, and the obligation to file a federal income tax return falls on the blocker, not the foreign investors (Mattingly, 2020). It did not take long for OFC entities to begin to serve this blocker function internationally as well. By setting up a blocker corporation in an OFC jurisdiction such as the Netherlands or Ireland, where favourable tax regimes are tailored to corporate needs, especially for US firms, companies can defer paying US taxes on foreign income until that income is repatriated to the United States.

The mechanics of the blocker corporation work as follows:

1. A US company sets up a subsidiary corporation in an OFC.
2. The blocker corporation is located on the corporate chain as an intermediary and invests in various assets or business activities, that is, in lower-level subsidiaries.
3. The blocker corporation, an intermediary in, say, the Netherlands or Ireland, earns income from its investments or activities in lower level subsidiary.
4. Instead of bringing profits directly back to the US parent (thus triggering US tax), the blocker structure allows downstream subsidiaries to pay dividends upstream to the intermediary without triggering immediate US tax.
5. The American parent may opt to 'park' funds within the OFC blocker to delay repatriation taxes, keeping profits in the OFC subsidiary.
6. When the US parent company wants to access the funds, it can receive them as dividends, which may be taxed more favourably than other forms of income.

The blockers are used, as Kim Clausing observes, to encourage American firms to shift profits to offshore tax havens, where they are subject to lower tax rates and might eventually benefit from favourable repatriation treatment (Clausing, 2019, 7), This practice contributes to the phenomenon of 'trapped' funds – profits held in low-tax jurisdictions rather than being returned to the United States. These trapped funds are estimated to be somewhere between US$1.9 and US$3.0 trillion in cash or near-cash instruments (Clausing, 2016; Dowd et al., 2017; Kaye, 2014; Keightley, 2013; Levin et al., 2013; Phillips et al., 2017; Tørsløv et al., 2018; Zucman, 2014, 2015). to the erosion of the US tax base (Fleming et al., 2014).

Paradoxically, international blockers can be used for the opposite purpose as well, to transfer losses and hence gain tax credit in the United States. To explain how blockers and stoppers take advantage of foreign losses, let me delve briefly into the history and philosophy of US taxation. Michael Graetz (2016) argues that in the United States, perhaps more than any other country, tax policy is shaped by doctrinal positions. One such doctrine, which influenced US tax policy for a long time, was the principle of capital export neutrality (CEN) (Graetz, 2016, 94).[8] CEN, which predates the League's tax agreement of 1928 (discussed in Chapter 2), holds that tax policy should not influence a resident's choice between domestic and foreign investments.

To support CEN neutrality and prevent double taxation of its residents, the United States introduced a system of tax credits and deferral. The tax credit offsets US tax liabilities by the amount of tax paid to foreign governments, while deferral allows residual tax on foreign-source income earned by US-owned foreign corporations to be postponed until that income is repatriated to US shareholders.

In a further erosion of CFC rules, Congress introduced the 'check-the-box' rules, granting companies flexibility in determining how their foreign subsidiaries are classified for US tax purposes. Under these rules, eligible foreign entities can elect to be classified as a corporation, a partnership, or a disregarded entity (if single-owned). If classified as a corporation, the subsidiary may be treated as a CFC if it meets ownership requirements, but if classified as a partnership or a disregarded entity, it generally escapes CFC treatment. In this way, the OFC subsidiary declares itself a conduit. This is particularly advantageous if the downstream subsidiaries can report losses.

The US tax system allows, then, affiliated groups of US corporations to file consolidated tax returns, but foreign subsidiaries (such as those in Luxembourg) are typically excluded from these consolidated filings. Previous analysis revealed Amazon uses its Luxembourg subsidiaries to 'fold' up losses to the US parent, where they are used to offset taxable income in the United States, reducing the parent company's federal tax obligations (Phillips et al., 2021). Losses reported in this manner can

---

[8] CEN has come to mean that if the source country imposes tax, the residence country should grant a credit for the foreign tax. In contrast, the principles of capital import neutrality require all investments in a given country to pay the same marginal rate of income taxation regardless of the residence of the investor (Graetz, 2016, 94). For a critique, see Avi-Yonah (2020).

be deferred for tax purposes; they either offset future taxable income or are carried forward to reduce tax liabilities in future years. This technique allows US companies to optimize tax obligations over time and manage cash flow more strategically. I suspect Amazon leverages these specific loopholes to reduce its taxable income in the United States, exploiting losses abroad in ways that minimize its US tax liability while benefiting from the flexibility of international tax regulations.

To sum up, the US system of tax credits and deferral incentivizes US-based CCMCEs to manipulate international earnings and use their foreign blockers to either block profit repatriation or report foreign losses.

Advent of Corporate Treasury Operations

The blocker strategy favoured by American CCMCEs evolved from a tactic for tax and liability insulation into a full-scale organizational structure within CCMCEs, primarily through the development of corporate treasury operations.

Corporate treasuries originally had a limited role in managing cash flow within corporate groups. They were focused on the financial tasks of organization such as cash management – ensuring liquidity, handling currency exchanges, and managing intra-group loans. But as the need for centralized control over finances grew, treasuries took on new roles, such as funding, risk management, and hedging for the entire group (Helliar and Dunne, 2004; Mazzi, 2013; Polak, 2010; Stewart, 2008). With the establishment of subsidiaries in different countries, large CCMCEs began to set up legal and accounting departments to oversee complex compliance issues. These legal and accounting departments have mushroomed, and have tended to merge in time with the corporate treasuries.

These departments that initially were designed to comply with local rules began to be used proactively not only to limit risks but also to take risks. Organizations began to set up subsidiaries in low-tax areas, often small island economies, and registered large portions of their operating profits as if they were sourced by these subsidiaries (Birkinshaw and Morrison, 1995; Dowd et al., 2017; Forte, 2016; Greggi, 2019; Grubert and Mutti, 1991; Polak et al., 2011; US Department of the Treasury, 2016). In this way the blocker function merged with corporate treasuries.

Companies began then to set such treasuries in preferred OFCs such as the Cayman Islands, but more often in the Netherlands, Irelands, Luxembourg, Switzerland or Singapore, and lately Dubai.[9] Treasury functions gravitate to OFCs to take advantage not only of low taxation but also of other facilitating rules involving liability, governance, and the like (Garcia-Bernardo et al., 2017; Gumpert et al., 2016; Hines, 1988; Hines and Rice, 1994; Polak and Roslan, 2009; Zucman, 2015).

Singapore is aggressively seeking to attract corporate treasury operations (Dizkırıcı, 2012; Polak and Roslan, 2009). Part of its attraction is a favourable tax regime, including a reduced corporate tax rate of 8 per cent on income from qualifying treasury services and activities. Singapore also offers withholding tax exemptions on certain interest payments and has an extensive network of tax treaties (eighty-three countries). Corporate treasuries are attracted by Singapore's well-developed capital markets, foreign exchange trading centre, a large banking sector, a lack of restrictions on capital flows in and out of the country, and support for investors. These factors combine to make Singapore an attractive location for companies to establish regional or global treasury centres, allowing corporations to centralize operations, manage risk effectively, and optimize their financial activities in the Asia-Pacific region.

Corporate treasuries are not solely focused on taxation. They tend to be located in jurisdictions that provide a comprehensive menu of rules and legislation tailored to appeal to parent companies wishing to operate as passive investors. By offering flexible legal structures, streamlined regulatory requirements, and advantageous financial frameworks, these jurisdictions allow corporate treasuries to manage and grow assets efficiently, minimize administrative burdens, and protect investments.

Unsurprisingly, the rise of corporate treasuries has been nothing short of spectacular. OFCs openly compete with one another by offering a range of incentives, including tax holidays, to attract MNCs to establish regional treasury centres. Singapore introduced its Finance

---

[9] Clark et al. note: 'Investors also use offshore jurisdictions for other forms of institutional arbitrage, such as ease of raising funds, speed and lower costs of company formation, and access to reliable legal jurisdictions' (Clark et al., 2015, 238).

and Treasury Centre incentive scheme in 1991 and later enhanced its provisions in response to a similar scheme offered by Hong Kong. This competition has given rise to a dynamic market for administrative and financial services, purportedly reducing the overall operational costs of large businesses and benefiting consumers and workers worldwide (Desai et al., 2006).

To sum up, treasury departments generally comprise in-house teams of lawyers and accountants, responsible for managing cash payments, compliance, currency transfers, insurance hedging, and financial investments for the entire corporate group. Over time, these departments have evolved into profit centres in their own right, tasked with developing innovative arbitrage strategies. Performance-based incentives, such as bonuses linked to successful arbitrage techniques, encourage teams to find creative methods to optimize financial outcomes, making corporate treasuries drivers of both operational efficiency and tax strategy within the CCMCE.

What the Literature Has to Say about Subsidiary Proliferation

The argument thus far suggests arbitraging encourages the proliferation of subsidiaries within corporate structures. And, in fact, this seems to be taking place.

Mary Zey and Brande Camp argue modern MNCs evolved from what Alfred Chandler described as the multi-divisional form to a multi-subsidiary form, commonly known as the multi-subsidiary firm or MSF (see Chandler, 2005; Cohen, 2007; Dörrenbächer and Geppert, 2011; Dunning, 1988; Dunning and Lundan, 2008; Zey and Camp, 1996). The drivers of the MSF firms and subsidiary proliferation, they suggest, were as diverge as the groups themselves, and they included a mixture of genuine operational reasons, such as joint ventures, brand development, and expansion into new markets, to risk hedging and tax mitigation, in other words arbitrage (Zey and Camp, 1996; Zey, 1999; Zey and Swenson, 1998).[10]

---

[10] To maximize post-tax profits of the group, a parent holding company may opt to own the majority of a subsidiary and extract value from it, while limiting its own financial risk exposure (Zey and Camp, 1996). Debt from the sale of bonds can be transferred between subsidiary and parent or between subsidiaries, and the parent can sell stock in the subsidiary (Zey, 1999). Firms

Organizational theorists argue high information processing requirements, coupled with growth in size (assets), complexity, environmental uncertainty, and interdependence of work flow, encourage the decentralization of organizational decision-making (Zey, 1999). In times of uncertainty, MNCs benefit from an ability to adjust their value-chain activities, including production and sales, among affiliated firms located in different countries. In other words, MNCs preserve upside potentials and curb downside risks with the help of flexible responses to favourable and unfavourable changes in the macro-economic conditions of their investment countries (Kogut and Kulatilaka 1994).[11]

As far as I can tell, only one study has directly addressed the question of corporate structure and subsidiary proliferation. Katrina Lewellen and Leslie Robinson (2013) from Dartmouth's Tuck School argue the default view assumes firms develop their structures under a 'pure historical accident' scenario. In this framework, 'the choice of ownership structures is irrelevant for the firm (as in Modigliani-Miller), and consequently, the structures may evolve randomly over time' (Lewellen and Robinson, 2013, 7). Lewellen and Robinson also acknowledge that in some cases, firms design their internal structures to circumvent tax and legal constraints imposed by host countries. They suggest understanding these deliberate structuring choices is crucial for evaluating which policies might be effective, but they consider such cases the exception rather than the rule, implying most corporate structures do not intentionally exploit regulatory frameworks but evolve organically over time.

I believe this is a misreading of the Modigliani-Miller theorem (Modigliani and Miller, 1958). The theorem assumes firms' value (i.e., market capitalization) is impervious to capital structure and financial arbitrage. The Modigliani-Miller theorem addresses the question of

---

may adopt complex equity structures, for example, to integrate or restructure their divisions and new acquisitions as direct subsidiaries in a non-taxable way (Zey and Swenson, 1998). Such arrangements may involve parents setting up a central treasury hub or a series of regional treasury centres, a decentralized or hybrid model that includes, global, regional, and decentralized treasury operations.

[11] Another theory suggests a great deal of intra-firm trade within the MNE's subsidiary network is driven by the requirements of operational flexibility. The argument is similar to the real options argument that MNCs can preserve upside potentials and curb downside risks with the help of flexible responses to favourable and unfavourable changes in macro-economic conditions in their investment countries (Kogut and Kulatilaka, 1994; Pantzalis et al., 2001).

financial arbitrage, not tax or regulatory arbitrage. However, while financial arbitrage and regulatory arbitrage may seem related, they yield, as I argued in Chapter 1, fundamentally different outcomes. An attentive reading of Modigliani and Miller reveals they understood the necessity of considering tax implications in financial decisions under real-world conditions. This insight suggests that instead of supporting the pure historical accident scenario, the Modigliani-Miller theorem might represent a missed opportunity to develop a broader theory of arbitrage in economics, one that could account for both financial and regulatory contexts.

It seems to me that arbitrage has consistently been ignored in economics because of a productionist bias. The dominant view emphasizes the firm as a production unit rather than a complex entity that also engages in strategic arbitrage. In this production-centric view, arbitrage is treated as a secondary activity, something that occurs between markets (e.g., in financial trading), not a core strategy shaping firm behaviour or market structures.

Conclusion

Although the CCMCE coordinates transactions among its subsidiaries, these transactions are legally conducted between companies that are formally independent. Transactions routed through intermediary subsidiaries, or a network of such intermediaries, carry inherent regulatory implications. By design, intermediary entities are often strategically located in jurisdictions with favourable tax, legal, or regulatory environments, and they bridge transactions between the parent company and end-of-chain subsidiaries.

We may conceptualize a CCMCE, therefore, as a three-dimensional (3D) fractal-like organization with three distinct types of entities:

1. Parent or holding company, the core entity that oversees the entire structure, setting the strategic direction and ensuring coordination across subsidiaries.
2. Intermediary subsidiaries, entities that facilitate transactions between the parent company and end-of-chain subsidiaries. These can often take the form of 'splitters', and both intermediaries and splitters can be involved in arbitrage owing to their placement in favourable regulatory environments.

3. End-of-chain subsidiaries, the final entities in the chain, interacting directly with external markets and subject to local regulatory and tax requirements.

While traditional studies of MNCs focus on the relationship between the parent company and end-of-chain subsidiaries, the true world of arbitrage lies in the in-betweeners – the intermediaries and splitters that connect different parts of the corporate chain. They play pivotal roles, enabling CCMCEs to channel profits, transfer risks, and manage regulatory burdens in ways that maximize efficiency across borders. Yet the CCMCE and the intermediary realm remain largely unexplored in MNC research. Traditional analyses overlook this critical layer, focusing instead on direct parent–subsidiary dynamics. A comprehensive study of the CCMCE necessarily involves examining the strategic functions of intermediaries – how they facilitate regulatory arbitrage, support intra-firm transactions, and enable the corporate group to navigate diverse jurisdictions. Understanding this intermediary layer is central to understanding the complexity and strategic manoeuvring that define modern MNCs in a globalized economy.

4 Corporate Tax Arbitrage

Introduction

Corporate taxation is a relatively new development. The first corporate income tax return in the United States was due on Monday, 4 March 1895, but the Supreme Court nullified the corporate income provisions (King, 2006, 26). Many trace the origins of corporate taxation in the United States therefore to 1909, when Congress enacted a special excise tax for doing business (Avi-Yonah, 2005).[1] In the United Kingdom, corporation tax was introduced as a distinct tax on company profits in 1965 (Ferran, 1999). Before that, companies were subject to income tax and profit tax. In Germany, the modern corporate tax system, known as Körperschaftsteuer, was formally introduced in 1920 (Landwehrmann, 1974), while Impôt sur les sociétés was introduced in France in 1948. This latter tax was designed to be an annual levy on the profits made by corporations and other entities operating in France (Morgan, 2016).

With the rise of corporate taxation, multinational corporations (MNCs) initially took advantage of their centrally coordinated multi-corporate enterprise (CCMCE) modality to shift activities and profits to countries with low or no tax, minimizing their tax burdens. Over time, the techniques of tax arbitrage became increasingly sophisticated. The global minimum tax proposal of 15 per cent, agreed upon in 2021, represented a significant step towards reforming the international tax system, but its impact on taxation and arbitrage remains uncertain, as implementation is still pending (Johannesen, 2022; Schjelderup and Stähler, 2024).[2] This chapter describes the technique

---

[1] During the nineteenth century, most advanced countries treated corporate taxation as 'pass-through' taxation, whereby the corporate group was seen as an extension of individuals; hence, individuals paid tax on the profits they gained from the corporate activity (Avi-Yonah, 2007).
[2] The recently agreed-upon two-pillar solution to the OECD/G20 Inclusive Framework on Base Erosion and Profit Shifting (the so-called Biden tax)

of tax jurisdictional arbitrage as it evolved within the framework of the international business taxation regime established by the League of Nations nearly a century ago.

League of Nations and International Business Taxation

The international business taxation regime formulated by the League of Nations in 1928 'has survived remarkably intact' (Graetz, 2016, 1023), despite the sweeping changes in the global economy. The League was concerned, however, with tax evasion and double taxation for individuals and companies, not with corporate tax avoidance as we understand it today. The League's regime was also designed with the concept of the traditional manufacturing company in mind, leaving aside the question of services (Jogarajan, 2018). Unsurprisingly, the League's notion of company and taxation was predicated on the concepts of tangible and financial assets, overlooking intangible assets such as intellectual property (IP) and trademarks. This historical context is significant, as the framework's original objectives left substantial gaps, not addressing the kind of sophisticated tax planning strategies employed by modern CCMCEs.[3]

Lorraine Eden argues that in the context of taxation, MNCs pose three interrelated questions for governments: where MNC activities fall under legal authority (jurisdiction), how income and expenses are distributed across borders (allocation), and how assets and transactions are valued for tax and regulatory purposes (valuation) (Eden, 2009, 596). The League was mostly concerned with jurisdiction, and the discussions of its experts show they were aware of the question of

---

(OECD, 2021) is arguably the biggest reform. The effects will take years to be felt and hence are not covered by the CORPLINK study.

[3] In preparation for a regime of international taxation, the League set up a commission of experts and solicited the views, among others, of the international chamber of commerce. It also drew on a wealth of experience gained in bilateral double taxation treaties dating as far back as 1899 (Vogel, 1988). But discussions took place long before the concept of the MNC was recognized as a distinct area of research, although some of the challenges posed by MNCs were alluded to in the testimonials of expert witnesses, and these helped shape the final agreements. Discussions focused on issues related to sourcing raw materials and production, with little or attention to services or the complexities introduced by intangible assets.

allocation but paid less attention to the question of valuation.[4] The difficulty with double taxation arose, the League's experts recognized, with the treatment of business with a head office in one country and business activities in another. Interestingly, the deliberations included contributions from some countries that were considered developing countries at the time (Jogarajan, 2018).

The main discussion among the League's expert centred on the potential conflict between corporations' host and home countries. Broadly speaking, capital-importing countries tended to favour taxation at the source, where profits were presumed to be generated, while capital-exporting countries preferred taxation based on residence; that is, where the investor or parent company was based.[5] To avoid double taxation, the tax regime agreed upon in 1928 allowed countries to tax income earned within their borders, regardless of the taxpayer's residence, known as source taxation. This approach typically applied to active business income, such as profits from a local branch or subsidiary (Cobham and Janský, 2018; Jogarajan, 2018; Sandler, 1998; Slemrod and Yitzhaki, 2002; Tiley et al., 2004; Vogel, 1988). Residence taxation allowed home countries of parent corporations to tax repatriated profits as they deemed appropriate. Over time, however, most countries moved away from taxing passive income on a residence basis; by the early twenty-first century, only the United States and the Netherlands maintained this approach (for a discussion, see Matheson et al., 2013). These principles were then clarified and reinforced by the Organisation for Economic Co-operation and Development's (OECD's) 1963 Model Income Tax Convention.

In retrospect, the 1920s tax regime established four core features that profoundly shaped international business taxation as well as tax avoidance strategies for the next century.

---

[4] Representatives from developing countries raised the question of the nature of profit. What about a foreign oil company that sources the raw material in that country, but sells the product in a third country? How can we compute the profits made from sourcing oil in one country and selling it in another? The assumption that the price the firm would charge its subsidiary selling in another country would correspond to the price it would have to pay on the spot market was an economist's perspective.

[5] Bilateral tax treaties aimed at resolving these conflicts by allocating taxing rights between countries and providing mechanisms for relief from double taxation (Avi-Yonah, 2005; Graetz, 2016; Kudrle, 2019).

First, the League resolved the jurisdiction question in a way that aligned well, whether intentionally or not, with the emerging CCMCE modality of MNCs. As independent companies, subsidiaries were supposed to pay taxes in their respective legal domiciles, that is, source taxation. The parent company or an intermediary parent company (see Chapter 3) also paid source taxation in its own country, but in this case, the source was revenues accrued from assets abroad (i.e., subsidiaries). Each country retained the sovereign right to define its own approach to source taxation. Naturally, this meant some nations chose to exempt revenue streams from foreign assets from taxation, creating opportunities for diverse fiscal policies and potential arbitrage strategies. Therefore, the League of Nations' approach to international tax incentivized tax strategies that functioned through transfers within the same corporate group, highlighting tax arbitrage as an intra-firm activity.

Second, the League's tax regime created incentives for governments to curtail tax abuse by companies (parents or subsidiaries) operating within their borders, as the revenue from enforcement directly benefited their public finances. However, governments had little motivation to prevent tax abuses by parents or subsidiaries of corporate entities that operated in their territories that impacted other countries, as they stood to gain nothing from such efforts. This dynamic even led some governments to view foreign tax payments by 'their' corporations – that is, corporate groups who had their parent or headquarters in their country – as a disadvantage, potentially weakening these companies' competitive standing internationally (Avi-Yonah, 2019; Graetz, 2016).

This meant that at least in theory, some governments might be tempted to 'help' companies they considered as 'theirs' to minimize tax payments abroad, fostering a paradoxical win–win logic: companies could enhance profitability and competitive position without necessarily facing an increased tax burden at home (I discuss this option in Chapter 8). Under such circumstances, the principle of *suum cuique* (to each his own) is likely to prevail over cooperation, making international tax collaboration and enforcement inherently challenging. Efforts by multilateral organizations such as the OECD and the United Nations to curb tax avoidance have historically faced significant challenges, leading to a fragmented and inconsistent regulatory framework.

Third, it appears the League's regime was founded on a simplified assumption associated with the world of 'things' – the assumption that market exchange involves transfer of goods or services or finances, that is, debt instruments, from one place to another, and the question of the transfer of property titles, let alone intangible assets, is residual. A related assumption seems to have been that a parent company would establish one subsidiary in each country and focus on repatriating profits. In this model, the primary conflict requiring resolution within the international tax regime is between the claims of the parent country and those of the host country.[6]

This traditional framework assumes international business expansion is driven solely by the profit motive and fails to account for the complexities of modern corporate groups. These groups are not merely extensions of the parent company; in some cases, the so-called parent might actually function as another form of subsidiary. Moreover, the group's strategy may prioritize, as we saw earlier, augmenting its overall market value; in other words, corporate goodwill rather than concentrating exclusively on the repatriation of profits.

Fourth, the international business taxation regime has incentivized countries with limited potential for substantial source taxation to develop alternative revenue streams. Instead of relying on corporate or capital gains taxes, these countries have focused on revenue sources such as licensing fees for corporations and residual income from legal, accounting, and financial services. This shift represents an unforeseen development within the framework of the international tax regime. These strategies were adopted primarily by smaller nations or territories that had limited prospects otherwise. Such licence-oriented income stream states have become known as tax havens (Palan, 2006). As far as I can tell, the idea that some nations would be uninterested in taxation was not contemplated by the League's experts.

That means that CCMCEs were given the option to establish subsidiaries in two distinct cost regimes: those driven by tax-based costs and those reliant on licence-based costs. This choice allows corporations to strategically align their operations with the most

---

[6] The international community began to address the question of multiple subsidiaries of the same companies located in some countries only few years ago under the BEPS country-by-country reporting, Action 13 of the OECD's Base Erosion and Profit Shifting (BEPS) Action Plan, specifically Action 13. (For discussion, see De Simone and Olbert, 2022; Tang and Schultz, 2017.)

advantageous financial environment. Over time, licence-based regimes have expanded their offerings to target other regulations and/or specialized as homes for corporate treasury operations. This makes sense because they are interested in licence fees and related professional services, and hence by expanding their offering they have expanded their licence fee business. In doing so, they create environments where various forms of arbitrage can be combined under one regulatory umbrella, allowing corporations to maximize not only tax efficiencies but also to arbitrage other rules (Eden, 2009, 599.)

The international tax regime introduced in the late 1920s, therefore, set dynamics in play that went on to shape corporate tax avoidance tactics for decades. The framework encouraged governments to focus on domestic tax enforcement, while limited incentives existed to prevent cross-border tax avoidance, leading to a fragmented international approach and the eventual rise of tax havens as low-tax jurisdictions tailored to attract foreign corporate structures.

Advent of the Offshore Corporation

Another issue with the League's framework was its alignment – or lack thereof – with pre-existing British tax principles. Long before the League reached an agreement in 1928, the United Kingdom was already on its way to establish certain tax principles that would prove highly effective in arbitraging the League's regime. The context for those developments was the particular legal structure of the British Empire. The British Empire's extensive reach meant British companies frequently operated across multiple colonies and territories, each with distinct governance, tax systems, and regulations. Colonial administrations applied different tax methods to individuals and businesses, and that led to conflict. It was left to the courts to resolve the conflict.

Since, as we saw in Chapter 2, corporations were increasingly treated towards the end of the nineteenth century as legal persons, British courts approached the question of corporate taxation by employing the metaphor of a human body to determine a corporation's location for tax purposes. In doing so, they reached the view that the corporate 'head' – representing central management and financial control – was crucial in defining a corporation's tax residence. Unlike today's common treatment of subsidiaries and affiliates as independent entities, British taxation viewed subsidiaries or branch offices as extensions of the main corporation, executing strategies and decisions set by the head office. They were symbolized as 'limbs'. This perspective placed central management and control as the factors defining tax residency, with subsidiaries functioning as instruments of the corporation rather than separate entities (Picciotto, 1992).

The British approach led to the understanding that the tax residence of a corporation was tied to its central management and control. In the *Egyptian Delta Land and Investment Company* case (1929), the court determined the Egyptian Delta company which was registered in London had its central management and control in Egypt, and hence should pay tax to the Egyptian authorities. This and similar cases created an option for a British company to be legally incorporated (and thus a resident) in one country while being considered a tax resident in another, because of where its central management and control were exercised. This scenario gave rise, argues Sol Picciotto, to the concept of the offshore corporation, where a company could be incorporated in one jurisdiction but be taxed in another with favourable legal and regulatory conditions (often referred to as a tax haven) where its management and control took place (Picciotto, 1992). The concept of the offshore corporation is a British imperial legacy that applies not only to the modern United Kingdom and its dependent territories, such as the Cayman Island or British Virgin Islands, but also to ex-imperial outposts such as Hong Kong or Ireland (Cogman and Koller, n.d.; Gross, 2004; Nougayrede, 2016; Vlcek, 2014; Wei and Palan, 2023).

The timing of the Egyptian Delta case is significant: it took place in 1929, just one year after the League's agreement. Soon the Egyptian Delta decision began to expose vulnerabilities in the League's framework. Critically, under the League's framework, the rules meant to clarify these differing interpretations – defining the nature of subsidiaries and their relationship to the parent – were left to individual countries to interpret. Each country retained the authority to resolve legal, tax, and regulatory questions as it saw fit. This flexibility led to inconsistent application of tax rules, opening avenues for jurisdictional arbitrage and challenging the coherence of the international tax framework established by the League.

Thus, while the League of Nations established foundational principles of international taxation, almost concomitantly, a group of countries that were once part of the British Empire unintentionally developed the tools for arbitraging those very principles. With careful structuring, a subsidiary could be incorporated in one country but considered tax resident in another. The arrangement was initially exploited by wealthy individuals and families who adapted corporate tax avoidance techniques to create chains of shell companies spread across various offshore financial centre (OFCs). This loophole opened up possibilities for tax avoidance, enabling these entities to operate in a regulatory grey area across multiple scenarios (Palan, 2010).

Act 1: Intangible Asset and Source Taxation

From the outset, MNCs exploited a crucial blind spot in the League's conceptual logic: the CCMCE modality and the limited understanding of the role intangible property can play in corporate planning. The exploitation represents a classic case of arbitraging a two-dimensional perspective (as if there are only two types of property, tangible and debt instruments) through a three-dimensional action in corporate tax planning (tangible, incorporeal or financial, and intangible assets) to take advantage of the distinctions (or gaps) between two main dimensions of tax policy (source and residence taxation) by introducing a third layer, such as intangible assets or intermediary jurisdictions.

While physical assets such as factories or machinery are fixed to specific locations, intangible assets are not bound by geography. A decentralized CCMCE can easily allocate intangible assets (as understood by Commons) such as IP, patents, or trademarks, to licence-fee state regimes rather than tax-regime countries. The subsidiaries with substantial intangible assets located in licence-based countries can charge subsidiaries in tax-based regimes a hefty price for the use of these assets. Since licence-fee-based regimes have no impact on profitability, the practice could be termed as profit shifting from high to low tax regimes. These subsidiaries are often 'exempted' companies in licence-based tax regimes (I return to the subject later).

Of course, this is not as simple as it sounds. Tax-based countries tried to protect themselves against the erosion of their tax bases, and countered with a variety of anti-abuse tactics. The first countermeasure was the introduction of the 'arm's length principle'.[7] This

---

[7] The concept of arm's length originated in the United States with the 1917 War Revenue Act, which authorized the commissioner to require related corporations to file consolidated returns. The principle was expanded in the 1926 Revenue Act, evolving into what is now known as the arm's length

Act 1: Intangible Asset and Source Taxation

mandates that transactions between related entities be conducted as if between independent, unrelated parties. The arm's length price is thus the price that two unrelated parties agree upon through negotiation in a competitive market. This principle aims to ensure intra-group transactions reflect market values, limiting, at least in theory, the ability of MNCs to shift profits across borders to reduce tax liabilities. The arm's length principle faces significant challenges, however, when applied to intangibles. Unlike physical goods, intangible assets such as patents or trademarks often lack comparable market prices, making it difficult to determine an arm's length price.

As I mentioned earlier, controlled foreign company (CFC) rules can be arbitraged using intermediaries. In response to potential arm's length manipulation, many countries have introduced general anti-avoidance rules to limit tax benefits from transactions deemed artificial or lacking economic substance. However, CCMCEs adapt by ensuring their subsidiaries in low-tax jurisdictions meet minimal economic substance requirements. They do this, for instance, by assigning these subsidiaries tasks under corporate treasury operations discussed in Chapter 3. Over time, rules have become harder, denying cross-border tax relief, establishing exit taxes, applying thin capitalization rules (discussed later), and implementing tougher CFC legislations.

The transfer of IP to subsidiaries located in low-tax jurisdictions is also subject to various rules. But as tax rules have tightened globally in response to aggressive tax planning, the basic challenges and complexities associated with intangible assets persist and are even more pronounced today, particularly with the rise of platform companies. These companies generate significant revenue, not from traditional goods or tangible assets but from processing information, data analytics, and digital services, all of which amplify the complexities of taxing intangible assets.

Digital platforms can generate substantial profits in multiple countries without having a physical presence or even personnel there. This decoupling of economic activity from physical operations challenges traditional tax rules, which historically relied on tangible indicators,

---

principle (Avi-Yonah, 1995). Arm's length proper was introduced in the United States in 1928, the League in 1933, and the OECD in 1963. As Eden notes, 'Under the arm's length standard, the associated enterprises are treated as separate entities for tax purposes, rather than as parts of an integrated multinational enterprise' (Eden, 2009, 600).

such as factories or offices, to determine tax obligations. Platform companies can create 'nowhere income', where profits seem to lack any specific 'origin'. By routing intangible-based revenues through multiple jurisdictions, often using stateless entities or IP boxes in low-tax countries, companies minimize their tax burden by keeping profits in jurisdictions with favourable (or absent) tax regimes (Keightley, 2013; Park, 2018).

Although anti-abuse measures, such as the OECD's Base Erosion and Profit Shifting (BEPS) initiative, have introduced guidelines to curb profit shifting, digital intangibles present unique enforcement challenges. Recognizing these challenges, countries and organizations are pushing for digital service taxes and global minimum tax agreements aimed at platform companies. These policies, such as the OECD's recent push for a global minimum corporate tax and digital taxation frameworks, seek to capture value from intangibles and platform-based income.

The crux of the problem is that the international tax regime is not well suited to the world of intangibles, nor does it take account of the two types of state business models: tax-based and licence-based, nor does it acknowledge companies are actually CCMCEs. Jurisdictional arbitrage techniques take advantage of this series of inherited blind spots in the international tax regime.

Act 2: Disarticulation of Registration

Intangibles are mobile, but what about immovable objects such as real estate?[8] Or apparently tangible assets such as container ships or oil rigs? In the commercial and residential real estate market, as well as the shipping and airline industry, a commonly used technique involves reallocation of apparent location based on the common confusion between the 'thing' and the title to the thing: things might be difficult to move, but property titles are far more mobile.

The idea is as follows. A building, a mine, a ship, or an oil rig can be incorporated as a company, and the company can be owned by another company, and so on. Soon enough, the transfer of the thing becomes a transfer of ownership over a corporation, and the chain

---

[8] This section describes techniques of arbitrage that were relayed to the author by Jean-Philippe Robé.

of corporations typically heads in the direction of licence-based jurisdictions and offshore corporations.

Consider an example. A wealthy foreigner wishes to purchase a house in London, England, worth, say, £10 million. If the purchase is the buyer's first residential property in the United Kingdom, the Stamp Duty rate on the purchase will be 12 per cent or £1.2 million. If the buyer wishes to buy the property through an offshore company, the Stamp Duty rises to 15 per cent or £1.5 million. Now, let's assume the seller made £8 million in capital gains tax (i.e., the seller bought the house ten years ago for £2 million). In this case, the seller (assuming they are a well to do individual) is likely to pay 28 per cent in capital gains tax, and £2.24 million is considered to be the seller's capital gains. Overall, the transaction should bring £3.44 million in taxation to the Inland Revenue.

Now consider a different scenario. The seller had a good tax lawyer at the time of the original property purchase. The seller bought the property through a company (company A). then established a company in an OFC, say Bermuda, called company B and ensures company A is owned by company B. The seller then set up another company in Bermuda (company C). Company C owns company B which owns company A, and hence, for all intent and purposes, owns the London property. In this scenario, the seller does not sell the house in London. Instead, company C, a Bermudan company, sells company B, a Bermudan company, to company D, a Caymanian company. Company D is now the owner of company B, which owns company A and hence the property in London. As the sale takes place in Bermuda, a tax-free jurisdiction, the UK Inland Revenue gets no tax at all from the sale. The technique allows the buyer, the person who owns or controls company D, to move into the house in London. The person who owns company D might even 'rent' the house as a business enterprise from company A (which ultimately this person owns), and get a tax deduction on business in the United Kingdom.

On the face of it, the ownership of the London property is organized through three separate companies, each owning the other, while companies B and C are doing nothing. Company B may appear as a shell (see Figure 4.1).

Practically all commercial vessels of any type, including many decent size yachts, are structured as special purpose vehicles (SPVs), that is, separate and independent companies. The same is true for commercial and private aircraft. These SPVs can be structured similarly through a chain of holding to avoid taxation.

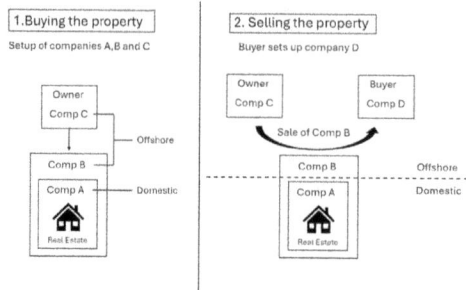

Figure 4.1 Real-estate tax arbitrage scheme.

In 2022, the United Kingdom introduced the Register of Overseas Entities as part of the Economic Crime (Transparency and Enforcement) Act (Vickery, 2023). The legislation requires offshore companies owning UK property to disclose their true beneficial owners publicly. It was discovered that over 87,000 properties in England and Wales are owned by anonymous companies registered in tax havens. The value of these properties is estimated to be at least £56 billion, potentially exceeding £100 billion. Whether the Act will be successful remains to be seen. It is a safe assumption that most companies employ the simple mechanism of disarticulation of the location described earlier for tax purposes.

One of the reasons for the proliferation of chains of CCMCE subsidiaries is their holding of real estate or assets such as ships or machinery. These apparently tangible assets are incorporated under separate SPVs and can be subject to arbitrage.

Act 3: Arbitraging Subsidiaries as Active or Passive Investors

As discussed in Chapter 3, one of the great advantages of the CCMCE model is the expanded option of financing of a subsidiary. MNCs as singular corporations with foreign branches face certain restrictions on financing those branches, limiting their flexibility in structuring their operations for tax efficiency. For instance, many countries have regulations restricting how branches can be financed, especially with respect to foreign debt. Some countries also limit interest deductibility to prevent MNCs from using excessive debt to shift profits out of high-tax jurisdictions (known as thin capitalization). Since a parent or intermediary parent company does not own a subsidiary but merely controls it through equity holding, the parent can decide whether to act as an active or a passive investor in the subsidiary.

In a CCMCE scenario, profits are typically repatriated in one of two forms. If the parent or intermediaries along the chain are positioned as passive investors, the subsidiary pays source taxation on profits in host countries and repatriates the rest as dividend up the chain. These payments are then subject to residency taxation rules in the parent's or intermediary subsidiary country (hence the intermediary will be located typically in zero or near zero tax jurisdiction). Dividends often qualify for more favourable tax treatment. Profits can also be repatriated in the form of interest payments on loans. The subsidiary's source taxation is reduced owing to interest payments, while the interest payments to the parent are classified as income for the parent and taxed based on the parent's residency location.

The optionality allows CCMCEs to develop various techniques of arbitraging these tax rules. An intermediary company occupies a dual role: as we saw earlier for the CFC rules, while it remains a subsidiary of the ultimate parent company, it is also considered the parent of its own subsidiaries for tax purposes in its country of residence. This structure creates a chain of resident taxation issues, wherein the transfer of funds up the chain is subject to each country's tax rules. Simultaneously, from the perspective of the ultimate parent company's home country, the intermediary is considered (typically, but not always) as if it pays source taxation in its own place of residence. In essence, the intermediary is viewed from one perspective as subject to resident taxation and from another as subject to source taxation. This duality presents opportunities to arbitrage the differences between resident and source taxation rules, enabling MNCs to optimize tax outcomes by strategically navigating the tax regulations of each jurisdiction in the chain.

A relevant technique that has evolved over time is known as thin capitalization (Blouin et al., 2014), the practice where a subsidiary takes on a high debt-to-equity ratio, borrowing extensively from the parent or corporate treasury. By structuring these loans with high interest, the subsidiary incurs substantial interest expenses. The corporate treasury in the low-tax jurisdiction receives the interest income from the high-tax one. Since the treasury is located in a low-tax jurisdiction, this income is taxed minimally or not at all, maximizing tax efficiency. In many countries, interest payments are tax deductible, allowing the subsidiary to reduce its taxable income in the high-tax jurisdiction. This lowers the local tax burden in the host country of the subsidiary.

Aware of these schemes, countries began to apply thin capitalization rules to deduct interest expenses for highly leveraged companies and prevent excessive debt financing (Blouin et al., 2014). Companies responded by developing ever more sophisticated measures such as back-to-back loans. In these loans, the low-tax corporate treasury subsidiary, considered legally as a separate and independent entity, 'decides' to lend money to an unrelated bank. The bank, in turn, 'lends' to the high-tax subsidiary of the same group. This financial arrangement is structured then as two unrelated transactions. This technique allows the CCMCE to circumvent some thin capitalization rules that only apply to related-party debt.

Hybrid Mismatch Entities

Another technique that has evolved to bypass thin capitalization rules involves the use of hybrid instruments – financial instruments treated as debt in a high-tax country but as equity in a low-tax one. This allows companies to claim interest deductions in the high-tax country without triggering corresponding taxable interest income in the low-tax country (Johannesen, 2014; Nessy and Rahayu, 2019; OECD, 2012).

As Omri Marian's (Marian, 2017) analysis of the Luxleak documents reveals, the technique involves manipulating the method of financing, either through equity or debt with the aid of a pull-jurisdiction (Christians, 2014). Following a thorough analysis of the Luxleaks, Marian says sarcastically, 'It would be great for the investor if he could devise a financing instrument that is treated as equity from country A's perspective, but as debt from country B's perspective' (Marian, 2017, 225. He demonstrates how Luxembourg positioned itself as an intermediary by creating mechanisms that 'switch' the classification of financial flows, making dividends appear as interest payments, or vice versa, depending on the tax advantages (Marian, 2017, 223–224).

Refining Global Value Chains

The techniques of incorporations, intangibles, and arbitrage can be refined in global value chain strategies. Companies spread production activities across countries not only to exploit cost efficiencies (such as labour) but also to strategically structure their operations to leverage regulatory, tax, and legal advantages. They do so by disarticulating the value chain, breaking it into finer, legally distinct components and re-articulating these pieces through connected subsidiaries.

To understand how they do it, consider a hypothetical soda company, a competitor to Coca-Cola or Pepsi. In a simplified version, the company will have to set up the following series of contractual relationships to proceed:

1. Contracts with suppliers for such raw materials as water, sugar, flavouring agents, and carbonization. Assume for the sake of argument that contracts for each item are assigned to a specialized subsidiary. This means one subsidiary (or a group of subsidiaries) handles the sugar contracts, while another handles the flavouring agents, and so on.
2. The company signs contracts with manufacturing plants, which could be owned by the company or outsourced to third-party manufacturers. These agreements will detail the production processes, quality control standards, and delivery schedules. Many of these contractual relationships could be assigned to one or more subsidiary.
3. The company secures contracts with logistics and distribution companies to handle the transportation of finished products from manufacturing facilities to various markets. This might include warehousing, freight services, and local distribution networks. Each task can be assigned to a different subsidiary.
4. The company engages advertising agencies and marketing firms to create and execute promotional campaigns. These contracts cover the development of advertising materials, media buying, and market research, and can be assigned to a specialized subsidiary or group of subsidiaries.
5. The company establishes agreements with retail chains, supermarkets, and convenience stores for shelf space and promotional activities. This might include pricing strategies, promotional discounts,

and merchandizing support. As before, these tasks are assigned to one or more subsidiary.
6. The company assigns trademarks, patents, and other IP rights to specialized subsidiaries, possibly in jurisdictions with favourable tax laws. These subsidiaries will then license the IP back to the main operating company and other affiliates.
7. The company sets up a specialized unit of lawyers and accountants that ensures compliance with local, national, and international regulations. This involves contracts with legal and regulatory experts to navigate food and beverage laws, health and safety standards, and environmental regulations. All can be assigned to specialized subsidiaries.
8. The company sets up customer service operations, including call centres or online support, to handle consumer inquiries, complaints, and feedback and assigns these tasks to a subsidiary.

The company, facing a choice in structuring its international operations, has several strategic options for organizing contractual relationships across entities. These options range from centralized control of all of these contracts under a single entity – this seems to be the view adopted by current firm theory, whereby a firm is considered a nexus of contracts (Alchian and Demsetz, 1973; Demsetz, 1974, 1988), to a fully disaggregated structure, with each contractual relationship assigned to a specialized subsidiary or SPV. The latter will yield a group of companies not dissimilar to the Equity Maps (EMs) 2–4 in the Introduction.

The decision to bundle or unbundle operations into so many subsidiaries and affiliates is taken in the context of a decision on where to locate the subsidiaries in terms of the country or the corporate chain (i.e., options one, two, and three or end-of-chain; see Chapter 3).

A bundled approach centralizes operations, simplifies management, and reduces transaction costs, while an unbundled approach enables the CCMCE to dissect and allocate various contractual relationships across multiple subsidiaries or affiliates. The unbundled approach is used in typical profit shifting through transfer pricing (Beer et al., 2020a; Eden, 2009; Eden et al., 2001; Grubert and Mutti, 1991; TAXUD, 2018; Taylor et al., 2015). Transfer pricing techniques rely on the disarticulation of a product or service into its constituent parts – each representing specific property rights or contractual arrangements that can be allocated across a network of subsidiaries in multiple jurisdictions. Subsidiaries with rights over intangible property such as patents and trademarks are located in low-tax jurisdictions. They charge other subsidiaries for the use of IP, and these charges transfer profits from high- to low-tax jurisdictions.

What this tells us is that a unbundled approach will inevitably contain an excess of subsidiaries and obviously higher transaction costs – some of which may be interpreted as 'shells' (see Chapter 3), allowing the corporate group greater freedom to decide on the best regulatory environment applicable to each stage in the production process.

Arbitraging Tax Residency Rules: The Case of Apple

These techniques of corporate tax avoidance are made far easier because MNCs are in reality CCMCEs; that is, the parent and the subsidiaries are considered separate and independent legal persons. A good example of the way CCMCEs arbitrage international taxes was revealed in a US Congressional investigation of the Apple corporation.

Until recently, Ireland adopted a variant of British incorporation rules with the option of the offshore corporation, that is, an Irish registered company that is not Irish tax resident (see Chapter 3 discussion of the offshore corporation). The United States, in contrast, defines the tax residence of corporations based on the place of incorporation. A corporation could incorporate in Ireland but locate its management in the United States, thereby creating an entity that is 'foreign' from the point of view of both Ireland and the United States. If such a tax arbitrage scheme is successful, no country asserts tax jurisdiction over the corporation (Marian, 2017, 207). That is exactly what Apple did. It employed a variant of the blocker strategy discussed in Chapter 3, but the blocker in Ireland was structured in such way that it fell between two conflicting rules of tax residency (known as nexus rules) (Gindis, 2009; Loar, 1982; O'Hara and Ribstein, 2009; Saittakari et al., 2023). This anomalous situation arose out of conflicting sets of tax residency rules as described by Marian (2017).

Figure I.3 is an equity map of the Apple group's subsidiary structure in about 2019; that is, it represents all entities held directly or indirectly at 50.01 per cent by Apple Inc., as reported in Palan et al., 2021). The subject of the dispute about Apple's tax planning is highlighted in the following box.

> **Apple's Tax Planning Structure**
>
> This option was noted by Apple's own submission to the European Commission. It says: 'The Apple Group includes companies incorporated in Ireland. Among the companies of the Apple Group incorporated in Ireland, a distinction can be made between companies headquartered in Ireland and are also tax resident in Ireland ... and companies that are incorporated in Ireland but are not tax resident in Ireland' (European Commission, 2016, 2.1.2, 45). AOI, an intermediary subsidiary, served as the 'gateway' or 'regional parent' for a group of more than thirty corporate entities in twelve countries (the entity at the top of the chain in the box), But AOI had no employees and insufficient physical presence in Ireland to meet Ireland's tax residency requirements. AOI was not a tax resident in the United States either. It was essentially a tax resident nowhere. AOI's location at the top of a chain of subsidiaries made it the de jure parent company of the subsidiaries on that chain, and hence was entitled to the profits generated by subsidiaries on that chain. AOI reported a net income of US$29.9 billion between 2009 and 2012, constituting nearly 30 per cent of Apple's total profit during those years. With 97 per cent equity in AOI, Apple Inc. chose not to repatriate those funds, thus avoiding potential US residency taxation.

Another Irish entity down the same chain, ASI played a more active role in Apple's affairs, serving in 2012 as a repository for Apple's non-US IP rights. According to the Levin Commission, in 2012, ASI was a subsidiary of Apple Operation Europe (AOE), another intermediary Irish SPV, which, in turn, was a subsidiary controlled by AOI. The line of ownership was changed sometime between 2012 and 2020 (for unknown reasons), and ASI is now directly controlled by AOI (Palan et al., 2021). Taking advantage of the fiction that ASI was a separate legal entity, ASI entered into a cost-sharing agreement with Apple Inc., the parent company, over the development of the iOS software. On that basis, as per an agreement with the parent company (under the fiction that these were two separate and independent companies signing a commercial agreement), ASI had rights over a considerable portion of income generated from Apple's sales of software outside the US market, whereas under the cost-sharing agreement, Apple Inc.

had rights over the remaining portion.[9] In addition, ASI bought many of Apple's finished products from manufacturers in China, some of which were Apple's subsidiaries as well, and resold them at substantial markup to other Apple affiliates. As a result, ASI accumulated substantial income, with net revenues of about US$74 billion between 2009 and 2012.

As subsidiaries controlled by AOI in Ireland, AOE and ASI were not subject to the United States' CFC rules, and as subsidiaries located in the same country (Ireland), they were not subject to Irish CFC rules either.[10] But like AOI, ASI did not meet the requirement for tax residency in Ireland. Indeed, it did not claim tax residency anywhere, though this changed in 2012.[11]

The Apple case is a vivid demonstration of the way the internal organization of subsidiary chains can be used by planners to arbitrage tax or other regulatory rules. It also shows the common focus on statuary corporate tax rate is often misplaced. Ireland's nominal corporate tax of 12.5 per cent –considered low when compared with other OECD countries but not particularly low when compared to many non-OECD jurisdictions – played a negligible role in the scheme. To all intents and purposes, Ireland could have had a nominal rate of corporate taxation closer to the OECD's average or perhaps higher. It would not have mattered, because the key to Apple's scheme was the arbitration of tax residency rules, not Ireland's rate of taxation. Ireland's willingness to accept the scheme at face value, rather than asking tough questions about the purpose of such non-tax resident entities located in its territory, combined with the location of those subsidiaries on corporate chains as intermediaries and equally, the sequence of control established between them, is what mattered in this case.

In the case of Apple, the entities without tax residency were used for the purpose of hoarding cash. Amazon took advantage of precisely the

---

[9] The Levin Congressional Committee considered the cost-sharing agreement between ASI and Apple Inc. a sham because there was no evidence of ASI performing significant or contracting out any research and development work (Levin et al., 2013); hence the accusation of artificiality.

[10] These Irish subsidiaries had their own CFCs in low tax jurisdictions, but as Apple did not try to divert funds from the Irish hubs to the lower subsidiaries, it did not fall foul of Irish CFC rules.

[11] Unlike AOI, ASI ended up paying a small tax on real-estate holdings in France in 2011, amounting to about 0.05 per cent of overall revenues.

same set of rules and principles, namely entity law, the internal affairs doctrine (see Chapter 1), and US CFC rules, not to hoard cash abroad, but to transfer losses from its international operations to benefit from generous US tax deferral rules, using three intermediary subsidiaries in Luxembourg (Phillips et al., 2021; The Fairtax Mark, 2019). Thin capitalization is permitted in Luxembourg.[12] As I explained earlier in the chapter, a company is considered thinly capitalized when its level of debt is much greater than its equity capital; such companies are characterized by a high gearing or leverage ratio, often expressed as a debt-to-equity ratio. Excessive debt can increase the risk of insolvency, but it can also be used to generate excessive interest deductions.

Estimating the Magnitude of Accounting Value Controlled by OFC Intermediaries: Evidence from the CORPLINK Study

The importance of intermediary subsidiaries is becoming clearer. In all the cases mentioned, an intermediary subsidiary located in an OFC played a crucial role in arbitraging national tax rules. The CORPLINK project sought to estimate how much of overall corporate revenues and profits are controlled by such subsidiaries. Problematically for this type of analysis, subsidiaries in many OFCs are not required to file annual reports. Financial information from such intermediary subsidiaries in OFCs is difficult to ascertain, but an EM can aggregate the revenue and profits accruing to subsidiaries that are controlled by such intermediary subsidiaries in low-tax countries.

The CORPLINK project created panel data of the top 100 non-financial firms in the world by revenue, excluding cases where the global ultimate owner (GUO) was a state (see Phillips et al., 2020). The largest 100 non-financial firms in the world possessed 70,291 subsidiaries in 2018. Forty firms in this group reported a parent (identified as the GUO in Orbis) in North America (all forty were in the United States), thirty-nine had a parent in the European Union, and sixteen had a parent in East Asia. Five firms were located outside these three

---

[12] Luxembourg had informal rules. Historically, tax authorities used an informal debt-to-equity ratio of 85:15 to address thinly capitalized companies, but this informal ratio is no longer the point of reference. As of 2020, the OECD guidance on financial transactions is the new reference for determining appropriate debt-to-equity.

regions. The distribution of subsidiaries corresponded broadly, therefore, to the regional location of the groups.

To identify subsidiaries located in OFCs, CORPLINK used a classification system based on two key sources from the Tax Justice Network (TJN):

1. Financial Secrecy Index (TJN, 2020): The index ranks jurisdictions according to the degree of financial secrecy they provide, which can shield corporate information from external scrutiny. Jurisdictions ranked high on this index tend to have low disclosure requirements, making them ideal locations for subsidiaries to maintain operational and financial opacity.
2. Corporate Tax Havens Index (TJN, 2019): The index identifies the top ten jurisdictions where corporate tax havens are prevalent, highlighting locations with favourable corporate tax regimes for tax avoidance and profit-shifting. Subsidiaries registered in these jurisdictions benefit from low tax rates and minimal financial disclosure obligations.

An additional filter was introduced to exclude OFC-based subsidiaries serving only local markets and not participating in OFC arbitrage. For instance, a Dutch holding company that only manages other Dutch subsidiaries is considered a non-OFC subsidiary.

The rest of the analysis centred on the structural position and location of those intermediaries located in OFCs. Of the largest 100 companies in the world, thirteen with a combined number of 4,597 subsidiaries had not established any intermediary subsidiary in any OFC. The remaining eighty-seven companies controlled 12,626 of their 68,060 subsidiaries, or 18.5 per cent, through an intermediate OFC subsidiary. Most of those OFC subsidiaries, 84 per cent, were end-of-chain subsidiaries. This is important. As discussed in Chapter 3, end-of-chain subsidiaries are likely to represent financial activities and are not necessarily involved in tax arbitrage.[13] Once those entities were excluded, the number of intermediary OFC subsidiaries held

---

[13] As Phillips et al. (2020) report, in nearly all observable cases, the pre-consolidated value of stand-alone OFCs was a small fraction (less than 10 per cent and typically less than 5 per cent) of the pre-consolidated value under the control of in-betweeners. The majority (75 per cent) of stand-alone firms registered a pre-consolidated index equal to only 1 per cent of the consolidated parent.

by the top 100 non-financial firms was 1,257, or 1.7 per cent of the subsidiaries of this group of companies.

These 1,257 subsidiaries controlled, in turn, 6,208 subsidiaries. In other words, nearly 8.4 per cent of the subsidiaries in the top 100 non-financial firms were controlled by OFC intermediaries. Yet the median scale of pre-consolidated index value for those subsidiaries was 66 per cent of operating revenues and 40 per cent of net income of the entire CCMCE group's overall operating revenues and net income! This does not mean, of course, that all these subsidiaries are used to arbitrage taxation, but it does mean that in planning terms, the top 100 non-financial firms have created what can be described as 'opportunity spaces', corporate structures that can be used for arbitraging purposes, and whereas those structures amount to only 1.7 per cent of subsidiaries, they account for a very substantial portion of revenues.

This is probably the strongest evidence for the widespread use of arbitraging schemes by corporate groups to date.

Conclusion

The techniques of jurisdictional arbitrage tend to route registrations to jurisdictions with low or no taxes. In some cases, firms seek to avoid tax obligations altogether by creating arrangements where no clear tax jurisdiction applies. This is accomplished by manipulating the allocation of profits governed by rules for intra-firm transfers and valuations shaped by the specific rules governing asset and transaction values within each jurisdiction. The aim of tax planning is to combine all three dimensions of taxation while manipulating the allocation of transactions through the group's internal economy – the realm of intra-firm transfers – while placing assets within diverging legal 'wrappers'.

5 | *How the European Union Became a Facilitator of Global Corporate Tax Avoidance*

Introduction

One of the most striking – and controversial – developments in recent years has been the emergence of European jurisdictions as hubs for global corporate tax avoidance strategies. The rise of some European middle size countries to prominence, especially during a period of intense scrutiny on tax avoidance, is paradoxical. The European Commission has placed itself at the forefront of the fight against corporate tax abuse (European Commission, 2015a; Monès et al., 2010; Panayi, 2015; Richard, 2018; Tsakalis, 2021), but as Rolf Eicke (2009) makes clear, European intermediaries are pivotal to US companies' corporate tax planning worldwide.

This chapter connects the narrative of the European rise with key insights into arbitrage. Arbitrage operates, as I argued previously, whenever there is a 'law market' and within the sphere of intra-firm trade, strategically positioned within corporate chains through intermediary subsidiaries. In this chapter, I explain how certain critical decisions about the structure of the European Union created a European law market – the rest, I contend, was inevitable.

European Conduit Companies and Jurisdictions

No regulatory authority seems more concerned with corporate tax avoidance than the European Commission. Since 2013, the EU Competition Department has launched multiple investigations into the tax affairs of several multinationals, including Apple Inc. (European Commission, 2016), Fiat and Starbucks in the Netherlands (European Commission, 2015b), Belgian tax schemes (European Commission, 2016), and Amazon (EU Commission, 2019). To the consternation of specialist corporate lawyers (Giraud and Petit, 2017; Lovdahl Gormsen, 2016; Richard, 2018; Traversa and Flamini, 2015) and the

US Department of the Treasury (2016), without exception, these investigations ended in detrimental rulings to the multinational enterprises under investigation.

Additionally, the European Commission has introduced two powerful measures. The Common Consolidated Corporate Tax Base Directive is widely recognized as one of the strongest measures available for dealing with abusive tax schemes (Dourado, 2016; Morgan, 2016; Seabrooke and Wigan, 2016; Spengel et al., 2018). As for the second, albeit away from the headlines, the European Commission's Taxation and Customs Union has launched a series of in-depth investigations into aggressive tax planning practices (TAXUD, 2018).

Interestingly, while the European Commission actively pursues corporate tax avoidance, there is growing evidence that many of the most effective conduits for corporate profit shifting are located within the European Union. Whereas in the 1990s, research on tax havens focused on small Caribbean jurisdictions and British dependencies, recent research in various social science disciplines highlights the global role of certain European countries, including the Netherlands, Ireland, Luxembourg, and Switzerland, as well as that of Singapore (Aalbers, 2018; Avdjiev et al., 2018; Buckley et al., 2015; Clark et al., 2015; European Parliament, 2019; Garcia-Bernardo et al., 2017b, 2019b; Haberly and Wójcik, 2015a, 2017; Hall, 2017; Zucman, 2015). A study conducted by Garcia-Bernardo and Janský (2021) using aggregate datasets and country-by-country reporting, reveals the Netherlands, Switzerland, Ireland, and Luxembourg rank among the largest destinations for shifted profits. These countries stand out, not only as some of the largest offshore financial centres (OFCs) globally but also as European states whose characteristics closely resemble those of traditional tax havens.

The central role of European countries in global financial flows is pointed out in a number of mapping and estimation studies. Using foreign direct investment (FDI) statistics, Haberly and Wójcik (2015) and Garcia-Bernardo et al. (2019) note the prominent positions of certain European countries in the global financial network. Kim Clausing (2016) shows that of the top nine locations of US multinational firms' affiliates gross profits in 2012, seven were tax havens with tax rates of less than 5 per cent: the Netherlands, Ireland, Luxembourg, Bermuda, Switzerland, Singapore, and the UK Caribbean Islands (including Cayman Islands). Echoing the findings of these economic geographers, economists Damgaard, Elkjaer, and Johannesen (2019b) estimate the global FDI network by disentangling real investment and phantom investment. Together, these studies show how FDI data can be analysed to expose the flow of capital through both legitimate investments and tax-driven structures.

Employing a different research strategy based on the Orbis database, Garcia-Bernardo et al. (2017) show the Netherlands, United Kingdom, Switzerland, Singapore, and Ireland are the largest conduit jurisdictions in the world. Another influential study of national accounts and other country-level data source reports Ireland is the biggest tax haven in terms of shifted profits, with Switzerland, the Netherlands, and Luxembourg the fourth, fifth, and sixth largest, respectively (Tørsløv, Wier, and Zucman, 2020). These European conduits also come out on top in studies of the location of regional headquarters of US groups (Clausing, 2020; Cobham and Janský, 2019; Guvenen et al., 2021; Zucman, 2014). Other research by economists on profit shifting has been recently reviewed by Beer et al. (2020) and Cobham and Janský (2020). Only a minority of the reviewed studies include estimates for specific tax havens, but those few point a finger at one set or another of European tax havens.

That some of the largest conduits and tax havens worldwide are in Europe has been confirmed by studies commissioned by EU institutions themselves (Loretz et al., 2017b). For example, in its Annual Report on Taxation published in May 2021, the European Commission uses more diplomatic language than most academic studies but confirms findings about the roles of the EU member states. It observes that within the European Union and relative to each country's gross domestic product, Luxembourg has extremely high FDI, Ireland and the Netherlands have the highest outgoing royalty flows (charges paid to rest of the world for the use of intellectual property), Cyprus, Luxembourg, and the Netherlands have the largest interest flows, and Malta, Luxembourg, and Cyprus have the highest outgoing dividends (Union, 2021).

As is often the case, the discussions focus on tax avoidance but overlook how these European conduits serve, in fact, as financial command centres for multinational firms, managing liquidity, debt issuance, and risk (Polak, 2010; Stewart, 2005, 2008). They are, in fact, as key hubs for corporate treasuries of large centrally coordinated multi-corporate enterprises (CCMCEs), discussed in Chapter 3.

These treasury functions are not just about tax efficiency but also about regulatory, accounting and financial arbitrage.

Rise of the European Law Market

The emergence of European conduit jurisdictions as key players in global tax avoidance strategies has not surprised legal scholars. Europe is likely to become, wrote Christina Panayi in 2006, 'a fiscal paradise for corporate aggressive tax planning' (Panayi, 2006a, 2006b, 142). Legal experts have been warning that several high-profile European Court of Justice decisions have resulted in firms being able to pick and choose their preferred gateway jurisdiction into the EU single market (Gelter, 2019; Gerner-Beuerle et al., 2017).

The evolution of European conduits closely mirrors the trajectory of the United States, as outlined in O'Hara and Ribstein's (2009) discussion of the 'law market' in Chapter 1. A law market emerges, as we saw, in the context of a fragmented yet integrating market, where local authorities, in this case European states, retain significant autonomy in crafting their laws of incorporation and taxation. This was precisely the case when the European Union adopted the principle of subsidiarity as defined in Article 5(3) of the Treaty on European Union.[1] The article states that the European Union shall act only if and insofar as the objectives of the proposed action cannot be sufficiently achieved by the member states. In other words, states have a presumed priority in setting up rules, including rules of incorporation and taxation.

The principle of subsidiarity remained somewhat vague and open to interpretation, and it was left, therefore, to the European Court of Justice to adjudicate on subsidiarity issues. From the outset, European member states were divided along two main theories regarding corporate mobility. Some states, for example, the United Kingdom and the Netherlands, adopt the incorporation theory. Accordingly, a company

---

[1] The principle states:

Under the principle of subsidiarity, in areas which do not fall within its exclusive competence, the Union shall act only if and insofar as the objectives of the proposed action cannot be sufficiently achieved by the Member States, either at central level or at regional and local level, but can rather, by reason of the scale or effects of the proposed action, be better achieved at Union level. (Lenaerts, 2003)

is governed by the laws of the country where it is incorporated, regardless of where it conducts business. Others adopted the Real Seat Theory, with a company being subject to the laws of the country where its central administration (or 'real seat') is located, rather than where it is legally incorporated. This approach was traditionally followed by Germany and France (Baelz and Baldwin, 2002).

In the context of the European Union, the real seat theory was seen as better adept at preventing companies from engaging in regulatory arbitrage. Its main purpose was to ensure companies were governed by the laws of the country where they operated and were not able to choose a more favourable legal regime elsewhere.[2] But in a number of seminal cases including the Daily Mail (1988), Cadbury Schweppes (2006), Centros (1999), Überseering (2002), and Inspire Art (2003), while obviously aware of the possibility of abusive practices, the European Court prioritized the principle of fundamental freedoms. It emphasized that the mere fact that a resident company established a secondary establishment (i.e., a subsidiary) in another member state did not justify a general presumption of tax evasion. A national measure restricting freedom of establishment could only be justified when it specifically related to wholly artificial arrangements aimed at circumventing the application of the legislation of the member state concerned (Panayi, 2013, 344–345).

These rulings created opportunities for what is known as the gateway issue. Multinational corporations (MNCs) could now use any country as a gateway into the entire EU market and set up subsidiaries in other EU jurisdictions controlled by the gateway jurisdiction. Unsurprisingly, most foreign MNCs, and in fact, as we will see, European as well, used gateway jurisdictions that offered tax and regulatory advantages. The decisions of the European Court of Justice are believed to have triggered a 'Delaware effect' in corporate governance rules or a race to the bottom among European states. Gelter (2009, 2019), Meussen (2007), and others warn about the possibility that firms might use intermediating holding companies in those EU countries whose tax regimes they find preferential as gateways into European markets.

---

[2] This debate has implications beyond the narrow question of taxation. Real seat theory, argues Cristina Panayi, did not offer a great deal of protection to creditors (or shareholders); rather, it protected a country's authority to determine the law of business entities operating within its territory (Panayi, 2015).

Evidence from the CORPLINK study

As mentioned in Chapter 4, the CORPLINK study found thirteen companies among the top 100 firms in the world that maintained no subsidiaries in OFC jurisdictions. Of the 87 companies who did have these subsidiaries, 12,626 or about 18% of the subsidiaries were controlled by an OFC intermediary, and nearly half of these (6,167, or about 49 per cent) were in the European Union. This shows that US firms generally refrain from employing such structures within North American markets. The study reveals that American companies have controlled, on average, 45 per cent of their EU subsidiaries in the European Union via European gateway jurisdictions. Their East Asian counterparts controlled about 30 per cent of their EU subsidiaries in the European Union through intermediary subsidiaries located in those European gateways.

Even more remarkably, European-based firms also leverage these gateways extensively, controlling 3,150, or 51.07 per cent, of their own subsidiaries through European intermediary jurisdictions. The CORPLINK data reinforce the idea, discussed in previous chapters, that conduit jurisdictions serve as hubs for intermediary subsidiaries within corporate chains. These jurisdictions are central to the structural design of MNCs, facilitating the flow of capital and the strategic positioning of assets within complex global networks.

European Intermediaries and Developing Countries

Beyond their use as investment vehicles in European markets, there are strong signals that European gateways are used for investment purposes in other markets as well, particularly in East Asia and the rest of the world. A United Nations Conference on Trade and Development (UNCTAD) study using CORPLINK data found nearly all FDI directed into developing countries is channelled through intermediary jurisdictions, mostly European. Between 65 per cent and 80 per cent of subsidiaries in the Global North were held indirectly; the figure rises to between 70 per cent and 95 per cent in the Global South. Less than 9 per cent of US FDI is aimed at directly controlled subsidiaries in the Global South (or what was described as 'simple structure' in Chapter 3). The figures rise slightly for Germany, France, Japan, the Republic of Korea, and the United Kingdom; on average, their

CCMCEs have 19 per cent of their investments controlled directly in the Global South (UNCTAD, 2023).

UNCTAD suspects this routing means the bulk of economic value creation related to investments in the South, including high-value services and profit generation, such as legal services, accounting, finance, and corporate treasury functions, is carried out in and through those intermediary jurisdictions, rather than in the developing countries where raw materials or basic manufacturing occurs. As a result, developing countries receive limited benefits beyond raw material extraction or basic manufacturing, even though they are the nominal destinations of FDI.

The UNCTAD study found another disturbing trend in its analysis of FDI into developing countries, specifically in the relationships between intermediary and end-of-chain subsidiaries. In the majority of direct equity investments in end-of-chain subsidiaries in the Global North, UNCTAD says, the value of income statement reporting is typically greater than balance sheet reporting. In contrast, both directly and indirectly structured equity investments into the Global South exhibit a nearly equivalent distribution of income and balance sheet dominated entities. As we will see in Chapter 7, balance sheet entities provide far less information on their activities and may reflect some form of dormant activities.

The UNCTAD study raises concerns that the intermediary use of FDI might distort the true economic impact of foreign investments in developing countries. By routing value-adding functions and profit-generating activities through intermediary jurisdictions, multinationals deprive developing economies of the full benefits of FDI, which could otherwise support local development and economic diversification. This phenomenon calls into question the developmental role of FDI in these regions and highlights the need for policies that ensure value creation stays within the host countries where resources are sourced (UNCTAD, 2023).

Conclusion

The emergence of Europe as a global hub for corporate tax avoidance underscores the powerful dynamics of the law market, as described by O'Hara and Ribstein (2009). Regardless of efforts by the European Commission and individual member states to curb tax avoidance, the EU's political structure inherently fosters a dynamic and competitive legal landscape. Indeed, paradoxically, Europe's strong reputation for combating tax abuse may actually enhance the role of key gateway jurisdictions, allowing them to function as conduits not only for investment into Europe but also for capital flows beyond its borders.

The resulting concentration of corporate tax avoidance mechanisms in Europe reflects structural features – fragmented sovereignty, overlapping legal regimes, and competitive tax policies – not intentional efforts to attract these activities.

6 A World of Fuses and Splitters

Introduction

So far, the focus of the discussion has been on taxation, but what about liability arbitrage? Legal systems throughout the world recognize corporate liability as a necessary counterpart of the legal privileges of corporate personhood (Curzi, 2020, 279). If corporations have legal rights as persons, they should also bear legal responsibilities. Just as individuals are liable for their actions, corporations should be accountable for theirs.

According to economic theory, liability concerns are central to the successful expansion of foreign direct investment (FDI). Exposure at personal and corporate levels adds a layer of risk, making it essential for companies to ensure their foreign operations are in full compliance with local laws and international standards (Bratton and McCahery, 1997; Dodge, 2011; Petrin and Choudhury, 2018). The risks associated with FDI are heightened by the potential discovery of hidden or unknown liabilities, such as environmental hazards (e.g., asbestos exposure), which can have substantial legal and financial repercussions (Kellard et al., 2022). If such liabilities are revealed, they could not only threaten the viability of the foreign subsidiary but also infect the parent company and its investors, causing significant financial losses and damaging shareholder value. This risk of contagion underscores the importance of rigorous due diligence, compliance, and risk management processes before and during foreign investments.

Companies face, as a result, multifaceted sets of risk. Directors, officers, and managers of a foreign corporation face personal liability for violations of laws or regulations in the host country where the corporation operates. Personal liability can arise from breaching duties of care or fiduciary duties or failing to exercise proper oversight and implement compliance measures to prevent corporate misconduct. Multinational corporations (MNCs) may face the risk of rogue behaviour by local managers, lower standards owing to the quality of local management personnel, or exposure to volatile political conditions (Arlen and Weiss, 1995; Ribstein, 1991; Weissman and Weissman, 2007). In addition, MNCs can be held criminally liable for illegal actions or violations of laws committed abroad by their subsidiaries or affiliates. Some countries have laws extending their jurisdiction beyond national borders, allowing them to prosecute companies for overseas offences, such as bribery, corruption, environmental crimes, and human rights violations (Arlen and Weiss, 1995).

It is well known, therefore, that companies spend considerable resources on corporate planning and risk mitigation (Baskin Jr, 1999; Harrigan, 1986; Mathis and Tor, 2021). MNCs rely on a web of bilateral investment treaties to provide legal protections and recourse in the event of expropriation or unfair treatment. Many acquire insurance to cover potential losses, including political risks, such as expropriation, nationalization, and political violence. They engage in local partnerships, forming joint ventures or strategic alliances with local firms to reduce the visibility of foreign ownership and provide local insights and influence, potentially reducing political risk. They use flexible contracts with flexible terms that can be adjusted in response to changing political environments. They may seek to implement robust corporate social responsibility programmes to build goodwill with local communities and governments.

But the literature on risk mitigation tends to be written from the perspective of singular MNCs planning for risks and corporate liabilities and ignoring techniques of risk liability perpetrated by centrally coordinated multi-corporate enterprises (CCMCEs). As Jane Dine explains, 'There are numerous cases of parent companies exporting dirty and dangerous business to poor countries where regulations are minimal or unenforced; or of paying exploitatively low wages; and/ or ignoring the environmental effects of corporate operations' (Dine, 2012, 47). Dine has little doubt about the underlying cause of the failure to prosecute these corporate offenders: jurisdictional arbitrage.

This chapter outlines how liability-defeating schemes operate through techniques of jurisdictional arbitrage, showing how they rely on a combination of legal fragmentation and selective jurisdictional choices to shift responsibility, avoid compliance costs, and minimize exposure to financial or legal obligations. The chapter explains these mechanisms, illustrating how jurisdictional arbitrage becomes a powerful tool for crafting liability-resistant corporate structures.

Dissolving Subsidiaries and the Texas Two-Step

One of the best known techniques used by CCMCEs to avoid liability involves setting up subsidiaries and dissolving them in the face of potential liability (Cheng, 2010; Hespe, 2013; Strasser, 2004). This includes establishing subsidiaries in jurisdictions with favourable corporate laws and providing benefits such as limited disclosure requirements or enhanced protections for corporate shareholders. Once a subsidiary faces significant liabilities, it may be liquidated, restructured, or moved, thereby limiting the legal exposure of the parent company.

A famous case in this context was *Adams v Cape Industries*. Cape Industries, a British company involved in asbestos mining, was sued by workers and residents exposed to asbestos in South Africa. Although Cape Industries operated primarily in the United Kingdom and South Africa, the plaintiffs brought the case in Texas because the state's legal frameworks were more favourable to asbestos-related personal injury claims. The claimants won their case, but Cape Industries had no assets in Texas, so they could not get monetary compensation there. The claimants sought to enforce the claims in England, where Cape Industries has its head office and considerable assets, but the English Court of Appeal held the award could not be enforced in England.

Meanwhile, Cape Industries restructured its subsidiaries after the Texas litigation as a strategic move to limit liability and shield itself from future claims related to asbestos exposure. The US subsidiary was liquidated and ceased to exist, and two new companies were formed: a company in Liechtenstein whose shares were held by a subsidiary of Cape Industries and an Illinois company. The two companies were also put in charge of US marketing. The purpose of restructuring, argues Janet Dine (2012), was blatant. These moves were clearly intended to avoid liability for the outstanding claims for asbestosis injury which Cape Industries knew were in the pipeline.

Some countries have rules that can be used, wittingly or unwittingly, for liability protection purposes. Among the best known is a strategy developed in Texas known as the Texas two-step (associated with a country music dance) (Daniels and Martin, 2005). In the Texas two-step, a corporation facing serious litigations undergoes a 'divisive merger', a move allowed under Texas law. The corporation splits into two separate entities – one retaining the core business operations and assets and the other assuming the liabilities such as mass tort claims. The scheme involves the original parent company entering into a 'funding agreement' to provide payments and/or indemnification to the bankrupt subsidiary to theoretically pay creditors in full over time. The newly created subsidiary company containing the liabilities then files for bankruptcy, often in a plaintiff-friendly jurisdiction such as North Carolina. The bankrupt subsidiary seeks an extension of the automatic bankruptcy stay or a preliminary injunction to halt litigation against the parent company related to the assigned liabilities. The goal is for the bankrupt subsidiary to establish a trust through the bankruptcy plan to compensate claimants using the funding from the parent, while also securing releases discharging the parent from any further liability related to the assigned claims (Daniels and Martin, 2005).

The Texas two-step was attempted by Johnson & Johnson, but in this case, the tactic failed. When Johnson & Johnson was sued by consumers alleging some of its talcum-based baby powder products contained asbestos and ordered in 2021 by a Missouri appeals court to pay US$2.1 billion to the claimants, it responded by setting up a new subsidiary and transferring its talcum-related liabilities to that subsidiary, along with a US$2 billion trust to fund any potential future claims.[1]

While the Texas two-step specifically refers to the divisive merger statute in Texas, a few other US states, including Delaware, Pennsylvania, and Arizona, have enacted similar laws allowing companies to split into two entities – one retaining assets and the other assuming liabilities. Instead of a divisive merger, other companies may explore more traditional corporate spin-offs or split-offs to separate liabilities into a new entity before putting that entity into bankruptcy.[2]

---

[1] Recent court rulings, such as the LTL Management and 3M Aearo cases, have rejected the Texas two-step strategy, signalling increased judicial scrutiny of such bankruptcy manoeuvres by large, profitable corporations, although a recent report suggests Johnson & Johnson succeeded with a modified form of the Texas two-step (Indap, 2024).

[2] Some companies may attempt to establish trusts through the bankruptcy process and secure 'channelling injunctions' to halt litigation against non-bankrupt affiliates related to the assigned liabilities, but courts are increasingly scrutinizing such arrangements (Rock and Wachter, 2001).

These tactics are easier to enact internationally, as courts of licence-fee jurisdictions may be inclined to be more pliable. Problematically, if there is a violation, for instance, of environmental rules, the subsidiary company will generally not be sued, either because the venture is in a state that is politically unstable and/or lacking in effective environmental regulation or enforcement practices, or because the subsidiary can be starved of finance by the parent and placed in danger of insolvency. When subsidiaries are treated as independent legal entities, the separation can shield the parent company from liabilities incurred by its subsidiaries – this is called the corporate veil (Dine, 2014). Meanwhile, suing the parent company is problematic because each company in the CCMCE scenario is constructed as a completely separate entity (Petrin and Choudhury, 2018).[3]

Leveraging Passive Investor Play to Avoid Corporate Liabilities

The technique of adding or eliminating subsidiaries is reactive and typically employed in response to legal action taken against a company. However, most corporate planning focuses, as I argued in Chapter 3, are anticipatory. These proactive strategies are usually structured around the legal distinction between ownership – the common perception that an MNC fully owns its subsidiaries – and control. In reality, the parent company often holds only a controlling share in a subsidiary, thus allowing it to exert influence without full ownership. This distinction plays a pivotal role in corporate risk management and liability shielding.

As an equity holder in a subsidiary, the parent can opt to emulate, as I explained in Chapter 3, the role of an active or passive investor. Passive investors generally have a reduced degree of liability compared with active investors. The more the parent-shareholder successfully

---

[3] The issue of the 'corporate shield' is increasingly scrutinized, with calls for more stringent regulations or reforms, such as piercing the corporate veil in cases of fraud, abuse, or where the subsidiary acts as a façade for the parent company's operations. In contrast, in a branch structure, there is no legal separation, and the parent company bears full responsibility for the actions and liabilities of its branches. The choice between a subsidiary and a branch can therefore have significant implications for legal liability and corporate accountability (Blumberg, 1985; Cheng, 2010; Petrin and Choudhury, 2018; Strasser, 2004).

emulates passive investor behaviour, the better the parent's protection from financial liability to victims (Skinner, 2015).

If subsidiaries are organized as intermediaries on a corporate chain, the parent company can play the game of passive or active investor along the chain. The parent's emulation of the role of passive investor in a subsidiary is often supplemented, as we saw in Chapter 3, by the disarticulation of the physical location of the entity's business activities from the location of its legal registration. In this way, CCMCEs can benefit from lower taxation and register activities in jurisdictions with less stringent liability rules or more favourable corporate governance rules, while still maintaining operational activities where there is access to specialized labour, suppliers, or other strategic advantages. This separation allows companies to optimize their legal and financial positioning without sacrificing their operational needs – but it raises concerns about regulatory avoidance and the potential for evading responsibility for legal and tortious misconduct.

A sophisticated corporate entity may opt to obscure some of its liability mitigation practices by strategically relocating its financial investments. This involves hedging corporate treasury operations not just to jurisdictions with tax benefits but also to those offering a blend of political and legal stability, favourable financial conditions, and, crucially, robust investor protection. For example, the United Kingdom traditionally had strong protections for institutional shareholders.[4] Similarly, over the last two decades, Luxembourg has developed as a jurisdiction of choice for private equity and venture capital investors/funds. It offers flexibility in structuring companies and allows various shareholder rights to be included in articles of association or shareholders' agreements. These are some of the factors that have made these two countries among the favourite conduit jurisdictions.

In Search of Plaintiff-Friendly Jurisdictions

Some jurisdictions offer legal frameworks favourable to corporations, including more favourable procedural rules, leading to a type

---

[4] The interests of institutional shareholders dominate the institutions of lawmaking and enforcement, such as the Financial Conduct Authority, Financial Reporting Council, and Takeover Panel. Large institutional investors in the United Kingdom typically oppose any form of suspected favouritism toward corporate controllers (Davies, 2015).

of 'forum shopping', whereby CCMCEs shop for jurisdictions offering 'favorable court access and choice-of-law decisions' (Whytock, 2010, 490) and helping them avoid plaintiff-unfriendly jurisdictions (Juenger, 1988).

Such dynamics evolve in any dissected market economy, whether a federated legal system or the international economy. For instance, much of the recent discussion about Delaware as a tax haven may be misleading. Experts agree that perhaps the most important dimension of Delaware's attractiveness is a series of enabling statutes providing flexibility for corporations to structure their governance as they see fit (Cary, 1974). What makes Delaware particularly successful is its judiciary, which strongly upholds the 'business judgment rule', thus protecting directors from liability. Delaware business judgment rule has a presumption that in making a business decision, the directors of a corporation act on an informed basis, in good faith, and in the honest belief that the action taken is in the best interests of the company. Delaware law, for instance, allows corporations to include provisions in their charters limiting or eliminating director liability for duty of care violations (Arsht, 1976; Dyreng et al., 2013; Manesh, 2011; Seligman, 1976).

Delaware's corporate-friendly legal framework, known for its emphasis on protecting business judgements and management discretion, often makes it challenging for plaintiffs to pursue claims against corporations. In contrast, California's laws provide broader protections for plaintiffs, with stricter regulations on corporate behaviour and a legal environment that tends to scrutinize corporate practices more closely. This disparity illustrates how jurisdictional differences can shape the outcomes of corporate litigation, influencing where plaintiffs choose to file and the strategies they employ (Alva, 1990; Manesh, 2011).

Delaware also has an extensive body of corporate case law built up over decades, providing clear guidance on management's rights and responsibilities. The long history of judgement gives management significant protection against second-guessing by courts. In addition, Delaware law allows various anti-takeover defences that protect incumbent management and provides broad rights for corporations to indemnify directors and officers against legal claims. In this way, Delaware is attractive far beyond taxation.

The Cayman Islands are actively seeking to emulate Delaware's rules and regulations (Fichtner, 2016; Greguras et al., 2008; Wei and Palan, 2023). It adopted a creditor-friendly regime. The Cayman Islands do not have the equivalent to the US Chapter 11 bankruptcy that might impede the enforcement of security arrangements.[5] In addition, the Cayman Islands' exempted company structure provides significant flexibility – appealing for syndicated lending arrangements. Cayman also allows various types of security interests to be created over different asset classes – useful for structuring syndicated loans with diverse collateral. Finally, there is no statutory prohibition on Cayman companies providing financial assistance for the acquisition of their own shares – useful in certain syndicated loan structures. All these have made Cayman an important location to end-of-chain subsidiaries.

Cayman is thus an attractive jurisdiction for companies seeking to protect their management from personal liability and to benefit from a business-friendly regulatory framework. One of the reasons for the prevalence of sink investments in the Caymans is that these investments gain from enhanced liability protection and/or flexible corporate structure. Tax is a bonus.

The British Virgin Islands (BVI) have developed a reputation for having a robust and sophisticated court system – a significant attraction for international businesses and investors. BVI is home to one of two commercial divisions of the Eastern Caribbean Supreme Court High Court of Justice. The combination of a specialized commercial court, a strong legal framework based on English Common Law, efficient arbitration capabilities, and a robust appellate structure makes the BVI court system very attractive to international businesses and investors. This judicial infrastructure supports BVI's position as a leading offshore financial centre (OFC) (Maurer, 2000, 1995).

Singapore has contemplated adopting a statutory codification of the business judgment rule, similar to Delaware's. The United Kingdom has also emerged as a significant competitor to Delaware for corporate law and incorporation.[6]

---

[5] Although the introduction of a new restructuring officer regime in 2022 brings the Cayman Islands closer to having a Chapter 11-like process, Cayman still maintains distinct features suited to the jurisdiction's legal framework and business environment.

[6] Some aspects of Delaware corporate law have been adopted in Israel (Baum and Solomon, 2022), and Panama has enacted corporate law statutes modelled after Delaware (Moon, 2021).

The Cayman Islands play both roles, offering strong protection to both management and shareholders through several key features of its legal and regulatory framework. Cayman law allows companies to indemnify directors and officers against certain liabilities incurred in their official capacities. There are minimal requirements for directors, shareholders, and record-keeping locations. The courts generally defer to directors' business decisions as if they are made in good faith and with due care. Directors' personal information is not publicly available, offering privacy protection. Finally, the Caymans Islands offer a high degree of investor protection and confidentiality, beneficial for complex syndicated loan structures.

Today, an OFC is much more than just a low-tax jurisdiction. The era of the pure tax haven is a thing of the past; contemporary OFCs compete by providing sophisticated liability protection or favourable incorporation laws and court systems. Consequently, the distribution of subsidiaries to these types of jurisdictions may not be driven wholly, or even primarily, by tax considerations.

Advent of the Fuse Corporate Structure

A common, if less discussed, technique used by CCMCEs to avoid liabilities can be described as a fuse structure, emulating an electric circuit breaker or electric fuse that trips to prevent current surges from damaging electronics (Palan et al., 2021). Like electric fuses, a corporate fuse is inserted along corporate chain of subsidiaries to protect the parent from damage.

The technique plays on the distinction between the concepts of general and limited partners that originated as early as the Middle Ages in European commercial law, particularly in Italy and France. This structure has evolved based on the principle of the partnership, not the corporation, allowing passive investors known as limited partners (LPs) to invest capital without taking on unlimited liability. A separate set of investors, known as general partners (GPs), manage the business and assume full liability (Weber, 2003).

In the United States, the concept of LP was gradually adopted by various states early in the nineteenth century. In 1822, both New York and Connecticut legislatures allowed companies to form an LP entity. The partnership consisted of two types of partners: GPs, who ran the company and hence were subject to legal proceedings, and special partners, who had no managerial authority, and whose liabilities were limited to their investment (Lamoreaux, 2004). The GPs had decision-making authority, managed day-to-day operations, and were liable for the partnership's debts and obligations and as such could be sued on behalf of the partnership (Ribstein, 2000). The special partners invested capital into the business but had no managerial authority or control over daily operations. They were not held personally responsible for the partnership's debts beyond their investment; as passive investors, they were shielded from potential liabilities and court cases (Hayes, 1997).

This structure was an important innovation in business law, as it permitted a combination of active management and passive investment within a single business entity. It encouraged investment by allowing individuals to contribute capital without risking their entire personal wealth while maintaining a clear management structure. Such structures are pervasive today in financial investment vehicles, such as hedge funds (Gross, 2004).

Similar structures seem to have migrated to the corporate world. What is often described as a hedge fund is generally a group of independent companies. The hedge fund is usually structured so that investors are organized into series of LPs. There can be many LPs in one fund. The fund manager acts as the GP. The GP controls the fund's investment strategy, manages day-to-day operations, collects fees and pays bills, and assumes unlimited liability for the fund's debts. The GP is typically structured as a limited liability company (LLC) or an LP to limit the personal liability of individual fund managers. Many LPs are passive investors and have no say in fund operations. As such, they have limited liability and can only lose their investment amount.

The LP/GP is often a 'split' two-tiered structure (Figure 6.1). One subsidiary or chain of subsidiaries emulates the role of a GP, the active investor, and another subsidiary or chain of subsidiaries emulates the LP, the passive investor. The subsidiary emulating the GP role owns a small stake in a lower-layer subsidiary (typically holding 1 per cent or less in the subsidiary company). The GP is then fully liable for the investment losses – the GP is after all considered an active investor. But the GP's liabilities amount to the GP's investment, which is 1 per cent or less. The subsidiary emulating the LP role typically holds 99 per cent majority of the lower-layer subsidiary. This controlling subsidiary (or chain of subsidiaries) remains, at least formally and in the eye of the law, a passive investor in the lower-layer subsidiary.

Advent of the Fuse Corporate Structure

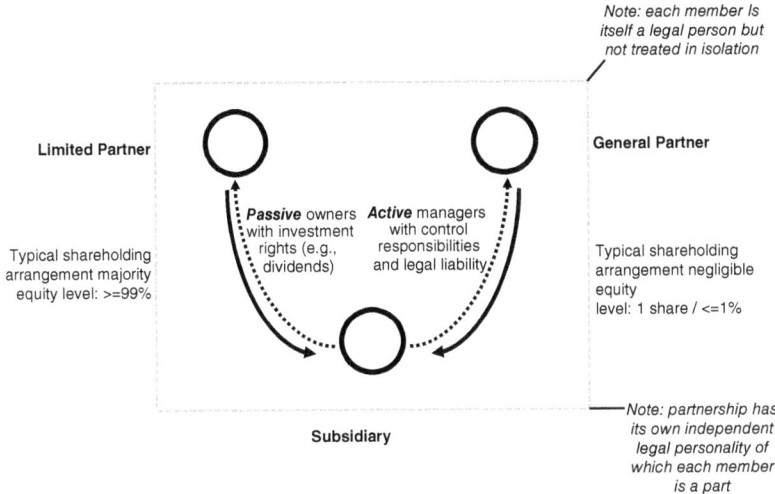

Figure 6.1 Corporate fuse.
Source: Reprinted from Palan et al. (2021) (original work published 2023)

The organization can thus ensure the GP maintains control of lower-level subsidiaries. The simulated GP is subject to legal proceedings in case of misdemeanour. In the event of trouble, the simulated LP will go bankrupt. But with little financial stake in the entity (1 per cent or so), the liability attached to the simulated GP is limited.

The simulated LP is formally a passive investor and cannot be held liable for the failing of the investment. It may lose a considerable portion of its investment, but the parent or regional parent is protected from litigations. Both the simulated GP and the simulated LP are controlled by the same parent, and the whole structure may be considered a sham. But rarely, if ever, are courts prepared to challenge such schemes (Blumberg, 1993). That is the essence and the beauty of the corporate veil.

The strategy of the liability fuse ultimately relies on a court accepting the fiction of the partnership and refusing to lift the corporate veil. But there is always a risk that courts may decide in a particular case to do so. Therefore, many CCMCEs introduce another layer of fuses located in different jurisdictions to insure against the risk that courts in one country will find against such an arrangement. For this reason, a double fuse structure frequently traverses a number of jurisdictions. The double fuse involves additional jurisdictions; accordingly, litigants could potentially face more courts located in different countries, raising the costs while reducing the chance of success. Many subsidiaries involved in such schemes may appear to be shells or phantom investment, suspected of tax avoidance, but they have an important role to play.

Some jurisdictions, including Germany and Scotland, as well as OFCs such as the Netherlands or Luxembourg, have legal regimes that are particularly amenable to the creation of such fuses. Germany, for instance, allows a unique hybrid combining a limited liability company as GP with an LP corporate form (GmbH & Co. KG). Here, some LPs can hold assets and enter contracts, whereas others have a limited liability option through the Kommanditgesellschaft (KG) structure (Laundry, 1967). The KG is a type of limited partnership in Germany that combines elements of both general and limited partnerships (for discussion see Wirth et al., 2024).

In contrast to UK partnerships, Scottish partnerships have a separate legal personality, and partners can limit their liability through LPs. The Scottish LPs offer additional privacy protections (Hardman, 2021). The implication of such a structure is that a number of important legal distinctions, such as who bears the liability risk, the level of risk, and even the location of tax residency for the transactions involved, are not givens dictated by law, but decisions based on the contracts set up between the parties involved in the hybrid entity. Whenever a splitter structure is located in one of these jurisdictions, I suspect it is intended to serve as a liability fuse.

In terms of the corporate equity map (EM), a fuse often displays as a split ownership, typically as 1–99 per cent (but not always) equity holding of the downward subsidiary. The CORPLINK study's investigation of the branch of Apple branch described in the box in Chapter 4 revealed several such holding structures can be inferred from the prevalence of 99.9 per cent holding arrangements among several entities. However, there is no way to determine whether these structures were set up intentionally as fuses.

Interestingly, an analysis of the European Commission case against Amazon, combined with an EM of Amazon, reveals a somewhat different split ownership arrangement located at the gateway of Amazon's international investment through Luxembourg that could potentially be a fuse. This fuse-like arrangement is not discussed in the European Commission case. Moreover, for reasons not made public, the fuse-like arrangement was removed following the investigation (Phillips et al., 2021).

Trump: The King of Fuses

The prevalence of splitters in a corporate EM implies a group that is concerned with liability issues. Such fuse structures appear in the Trump Organization. This is not a corporate group in the technical sense. It operates like a loose collection of businesses under Trump's ownership and control (Warren and Eisen, 2024). After being sued, the Trump Organization appears to create new LLCs, such as Trump Organization II, in an attempt to restructure and avoid liabilities associated with the named defendants. For example, Trump Organization II LLC was registered in Delaware on 21 September 2022 – the day prosecutor James announced her US$250 million fraud lawsuit against Trump and his company (Warren and Eisen, 2024).

Figure 6.2 is an EM of the Trump Organization produced by the CORPLINK project. The EM highlights (in red) the split ownership

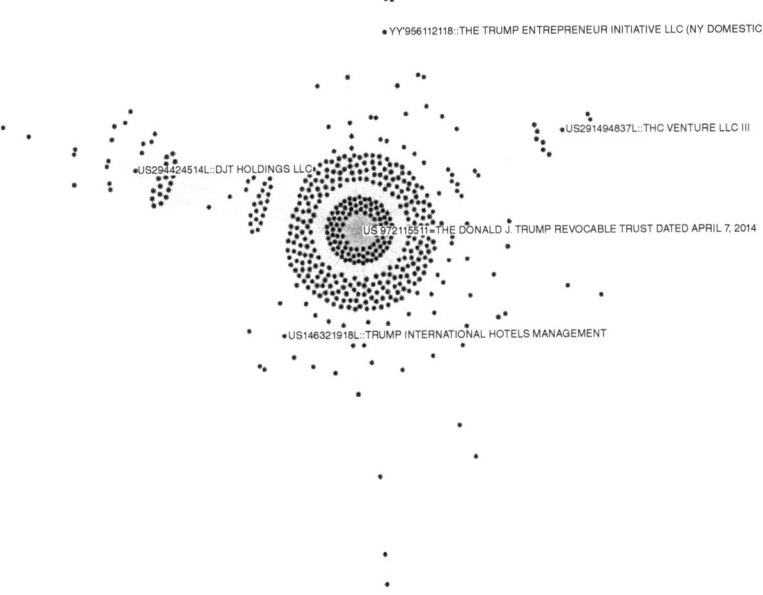

Figure 6.2 Trump Organization equity map, *c.* 2021.

structure that approximates the 1–99 per cent arrangement in that organization. The purple dots reproduce the GP versus LP arrangement. It seems the Trump Organization is one large set of fuses upon fuses.

Conclusion

The techniques of liability arbitrage are similar to those of tax planning arbitrage, and the former are often confused for the latter. The emulation of the parent and regional parents of the CCMCE can certainly be used for tax purposes – because active and passive investments are subject to different rules of taxation – but they can be used for liability and risk mitigation purposes as well. Often the two sets of purposes merge into one, and jurisdictional arbitraging schemes become multitasking ones. Such legal outcomes, Dine concludes, are commonplace: 'This means that companies can export potentially liability-attracting activities from the rich world to poverty-stricken areas where any sort of employment, including scavenging from rubbish tips, is welcome and there are fewer, or no, inconvenient checks on health and safety, environmental or labour standards [and] regulatory controls are frequently bargained away' (Dine, 2012, 48).

These realities mean MNCs can play regulatory or jurisdictional arbitrage, seeking out the jurisdiction with the fewest protections in order to maximize profit. This is the well-known race to the bottom, encouraged and protected by commercial law, just as the slave trade was in earlier times.

7 How Not to Tell by Telling
Reporting and Disclosure Arbitrage

Introduction

One often overlooked aspect of jurisdictional arbitrage is its impact on corporate reporting. The period under discussion in this book, from the late nineteenth century onwards, coincided with the emergence of numerous business regulations, including mandatory reporting requirements. Regulatory bodies worldwide began requiring companies to disclose performance metrics, such as financial statements which must be filed with securities regulators, as well as environmental compliance data submitted to environmental agencies and workplace safety statistics provided to labour departments.

In addition to these mandatory disclosures, many companies today engage in voluntary reporting, offering sustainability reports, corporate social responsibility initiatives, investor presentations, and earnings calls. These voluntary disclosures aim to enhance transparency and align with stakeholder expectations, but they also highlight the uneven global landscape of reporting standards and the resulting opportunities for companies to exploit jurisdictional inconsistencies.

Most of what is known about corporate performance stems from private and publicly mandated reporting requirements. Multinational corporations (MNCs) have a vested interest in controlling the information they disclose to stakeholders, however, as this information shapes perceptions of financial performance, tax contributions, and strategic positioning vis-à-vis competitors.

There is a vast literature on corporate disclosure and opacity. But the literature is predominantly focused on MNCs as a unified entity. While there is substantial research on arbitrage through tax havens (Brown et al., 2019; Taylor et al., 2015; van 't Riet and Lejour, 2018), techniques of opacity and disclosure arbitrage at the subsidiary level remain comparatively under-explored. Thus, the literature overlooks a critical dimension of how MNCs manage and manipulate information disclosure across their global operations.

In this chapter, I discuss the nuanced strategies of jurisdictional and reporting arbitrage at the pre-consolidated, or subsidiary, level, exposing how dispersed subsidiaries located in diverse jurisdictions are used to arbitrage corporate disclosure rules.

Two Problems with Consolidated Accounts

Historically, cost accounting emerged during the Industrial Revolution when businesses needed better ways to measure and control production costs in large-scale operations. Today, it plays a crucial role in pricing strategies, budgeting, and decision-making across various industries, not just in production but also in services and project management.[1] Financial accounting originally developed as a way to record and report business transactions, but by the late nineteenth century, as businesses grew and external financing became more common, creditors and shareholders needed reliable financial information to assess whether managers were using corporate resources responsibly. Financial statements – such as the balance sheet, income statement, and cash flow statement were developed to help creditors evaluate a company's financial health, liquidity, and ability to repay debts (King, 2006, 55).[2]

Investors, particularly in large corporate groups, were generally less concerned with the performance of individual subsidiaries and more interested in the overall financial health and profitability of the parent company. As a result, the system of financial reporting evolved to focus on consolidated financial statements, which aggregate the financial information of all subsidiaries under the parent company. The argument was that stand-alone subsidiary accounts may include intra-group transactions that distort financial analysis. Consolidation eliminates these to present a more accurate financial position. Hence, consolidated

---

[1] Cost accounting is not required to adhere to external accounting standards such as Generally Accepted Accounting Principles or International Financial Reporting Standards, allowing more customized and frequent reporting. Application of management accounting varies as a result, based on circumstances, and includes both financial and non-financial information (Holland, 2005).

[2] Some of the earliest examples of financial reporting in the United States came from the railroad companies, which often had complex corporate structures with multiple subsidiaries (Commons, 1919).

accounts provide a clearer picture of a corporation's total assets, liabilities, revenue, and profits, rather than fragmented reports from individual subsidiaries.[3] The equity ownership, however, fundamentally changed the role of financial accounting. Investors began using financial statements not just to assess a company's financial health but also to value shares in capital markets. This introduced a tension in accounting, as financial reports were now linked to remuneration and bonuses.[4]

By the early twentieth century, governments began using financial accounting to assess corporate profits and determine tax liabilities. However, whereas financial accounting seeks to represent economic reality, tax accounting is often based on legal and regulatory frameworks, focusing on taxable income rather than economic performance. The result was that systems of accounting and information disclosure designed for management purposes evolved to serve one set of constituencies, investors, whose interests are not the same as those of the managers, and then further evolved to serve another set, governments, whose interests are aligned with neither management nor investors (King, 2006, 27). Consequently, corporate accounting and reporting must maintain a delicate balance between different sets of interests: managers, investors, and governments.

That means that consolidated accounts aim to satisfy diverse constituencies; external stakeholders demand transparency and accuracy, while internal management prioritize flexibility and discretion. At the same time, different jurisdictions and regulatory regimes impose varied requirements on subsidiaries, creating discrepancies in accounting standards, tax obligations, and reporting rules. One solution to this conundrum is that MNCs often maintain multiple sets of accounting books, each serving different purposes and complying with distinct

---

[3] British companies began adopting these reporting methods around the late nineteenth century as well, influenced by American practices and their own evolving corporate structures. For a discussion of consolidated reporting, see Walker (2006).

[4] 'It is not clear that financial accounting', writes Thomas King 'was ever designed to aid investors in the forecasting of future earnings and cash flows' (King, 2006, 55). Following the financial crisis of 1929, the Securities and Exchange Commission (SEC) was given powers to prescribe financial accounting principles and specify the form and content of financial statements filed with the SEC. A 1934 Act required public firms to issue periodic financial statements audited by independent accountants, but the SEC required auditors to verify the accounts. Auditors are paid by the corporate group, not the investor, contributing to a second known area of conflict of interest.

regulatory requirements. The inherent flexibility in consolidation practices – such as transfer pricing, allocation of intercompany transactions, and treatment of liabilities – creates incentives to arbitrage rules where possible, with companies looking for grey areas between compliance and strategic manipulation to maximize their benefits within legal boundaries.

That is true at the aggregate, consolidated level. But there is another problem that affects accounting and disclosure. Edith Penrose, in *The Theory of the Growth of the Firm* (Penrose, 2009), highlighted the problem of defining the boundary of the firm. As we saw, MNCs operate through a complex corporate structures that I prefer to describe as centrally coordinated multi-corporate enterprises, including subsidiaries, joint ventures, franchises, and partnerships. As a result, the distinction between what is 'inside' the firm and what is external is not always clear. But if the boundary of the firm is uncertain, then consolidated financial statements may not fully capture the economic reality of the business. Companies may exclude certain entities from consolidation, creating 'off-balance-sheet' (OBS) structures.

For all these reasons it may be worth returning to the question of reporting and disclosure at subsidiary level,

Boundary Arbitrage of Disclosure Rules

Although not a great deal had been written about reporting arbitrage at the subsidiary level, some techniques of boundary arbitrage have been identified in recent studies, shedding light on how firms exploit these gaps to manage transparency and accountability strategically.

One famous case was the Enron Corporation, a major US energy and commodities company. A key part of Enron's fraudulent financial practices was the use of off-balance sheet (OBS) entities to conceal debt and inflate profits. Under the Generally Accepted Accounting Principles (GAAP) rules at the time, a company could exclude a special purpose entity (SPE) from its balance sheet if an independent investor held at least 3 per cent equity in the entity. Enron manipulated this rule by using SPEs that lacked genuine third-party investors and were still controlled by Enron executives (e.g., Andrew Fastow personally managed LJM while being Enron's chief financial officer) (McLean and Elkind, 2013).

Another technique of boundary arbitrage that has been attracting attention lately is the strange case of disappearing subsidiaries in the

K-10 reports of Google and Oracle (Gramlich and Whiteaker-Poe, 2013).[5] Jeffery Gramlich and Janie Whiteaker-Poe note that Google's 2009 K-10 report mentions 117 subsidiaries, including twenty-five in tax haven countries, but in 2010, Google K-10 lists only two significant subsidiaries, both in Ireland. In a simple online search, the two authors discovered thirty-eight of the missing subsidiaries, and they suspect many more remain active. The majority of these disappearing subsidiaries 'just happened' to be in tax havens. Similarly, Oracle's Securities and Exchange Commission (SEC) Form 10-K filed in July 2010 discloses 428 subsidiaries, 100 of which are in fourteen foreign tax haven jurisdictions. Oracle's Form 10-K for the fiscal year ending 31 May 2011 reports only six!

Gramlich and Whiteaker-Poe's (2013) analysis of disappearing subsidiaries shows the subsidiaries themselves are not the issue. Rather, the SEC's definition of the concept of 'significant subsidiary' was open to arbitrage. The SEC's rules on significant subsidiaries are so complex, they argue, that Google and Oracle were able to arbitrage these rules.

Similarly, the CORPLINK analysis discovered that following the EU case against Apple (see Chapter 4), as reported in the Orbis dataset, one of Apple's subsidiaries in Singapore displayed extraordinary growth, from about US$3 billion in revenues in 2012 to nearly US$60 billion in 2016. One possible explanation was that the subsidiary grew in response to Ireland's announcement of the closing down of the Double Irish, Dutch Sandwich tax scheme, but there was no way of knowing precisely how the Singaporean entity is being used for tax purposes. Although it reached US$60 billion in revenues per annum, there is no mention of it on Apple's K-10 form in 2016! Other studies suggest most American firms comply with the US disclosure requirements (Hoopes et al., 2018).

Another recently discovered technique is that of 'floating' subsidiaries. I referred to the Trump Organization in Chapter 6, describing it as a loosely set of corporate entities with little or no equity relationship among them, controlled by Trump. It seems the Trump Organization is set up intentionally to avoid scrutiny or centralized auditing. Similar techniques are found elsewhere. Nesvetailova et al. (2020) report that some energy trading companies in Africa adopted a disparate 'franchise-like'

---

[5] Form 10-K is a comprehensive annual report required by SEC for publicly traded companies.

corporate organization.[6] The Sahara Energy Trading Company presents itself as one unit to the market in its brochures. Yet the group does not exist as a familiar corporate group in the sense that there was no common holding of equity. Such an organization is not subject to the corporate governance auditing and reporting requirements described earlier. This could be a concern, because it is not clear who bears responsibility for the group's actions (Nesvetailova et al., 2020).

In another study, Xinyi Wei and I discovered Chinese state-owned banks tend to establish strings of floating subsidiaries in Hong Kong and beyond, often in offshore financial centres (OFCs), with no known equity ties to the parent or to the Hong Kong holding companies (Wei and Palan, 2023). For instance, the China Construction Bank (CCB) had 132 floating subsidiaries in 2022, approximately 31 per cent of its subsidiaries. Some of these subsidiaries are listed in CCB's consolidated accounts (in 2020) or mentioned in operational and financial actives, and some are even consolidated into the group's financial statements. But these subsidiaries have no known equity ties to the parent or to any of the three Hong Kong holding companies of CCB. These subsidiaries present little information about their history or development, including their association with the group. Wei and Palan found the case of Bank of China (BOC) was similar. Some of these floating entities are disclosed in the IPO prospectus of BOC Aviation in 2016, where they are deemed subsidiary companies of BOC Aviation, even though they have no visible equity link to the company.

Gravitating towards Low-Disclosure Jurisdictions

Another technique of disclosure arbitrage emulates the tax and liability arbitrage techniques discussed earlier. Corporations operate across reporting jurisdictions, giving them opportunities to select the amount, quality, and frequency of information communicated to external stakeholders.

A favoured technique involves simply setting up subsidiaries in low-disclosure jurisdictions. For example, although the Cayman Islands comply with the latest international rules of disclosure and transparency

---

[6] These organizations, for example, the Sahara group, a Nigerian energy trading company, are more akin to the United Kingdom's notion of a quasi-partnership. A quasi-partnership is a concept in business law that describes a business relationship resembling a partnership, even though it is not formally recognized as such under partnership law (for a discussion, see Lewellen and Robinson, 2013).

and require companies to file an annual filing of corporate accounts,[7] it has a system of *exempted* companies, and those companies are not required to undertake an annual audit and follow the rules. Exempted companies conduct their business primarily outside the Cayman Islands and do not hold a licence to operate within the jurisdiction.[8] They are offshore companies as far as the Cayman Islands are concerned. Yet, as Bransens (2021) notes, exempted companies 'are the most common form of offshore company in the Cayman Islands and are incorporated or registered under the Companies Act (2021 Revision)'.[9]

The concept of the exempted company is popular in other OFCs as well. In the British Virgin Islands, international business companies are not required to file annual financial statements with the government. They must keep financial records that reflect the company's financial position, but these records are not submitted to any authority. In Bermuda, Guernsey, and the Isle of Man, exempted companies are not required to file annual financial statements with the government. In Jersey, certain types of companies, such as Jersey Private Funds, are exempt from filing annual financial statements. Together, these exempted companies create a global informational black hole.

In the United States, the disclosure requirements for private companies are governed by state laws in the state where the company is incorporated. These laws vary significantly, but they generally impose minimal requirements for ongoing disclosures beyond the initial formation documents, such as articles of incorporation. Public companies provide disclosures, available on the SEC EDGAR database (SEC EDGAR, n.d.), but the disclosure typically has little financial

---

[7] Under pressure from the Organisation for Economic Co-operation and Development (OECD), companies regulated by the Cayman Islands Monetary Authority are required to prepare and file annual financial statements. Unfortunately, those filings are not made public.

[8] Companies must now file an annual return confirming compliance with the Companies Act, but this does not include detailed financial statements unless they are specifically regulated. In other words, offshore companies are exempt from filing.

[9] Exempted companies are frequently used to facilitate offshore financial and trust business. They have several advantages over companies incorporated in other jurisdictions. These include minimal annual reporting requirements, no requirement for Cayman resident directors or shareholders, the ability to close the register of shareholders from public inspection, no requirement to hold an annual meeting of its shareholders, the ability to issue shares with or without nominal or par value, and the ability to deregister from the Cayman Islands and be reregistered in another jurisdiction (Bransens, 2021).

information; the company will inform who its owners are and who it owns, leaving aside the issue of the missing subsidiaries.

The result of the widespread use of subsidiaries in OFCs is that consolidated reports produced by MNCs may or may not be subject to third-party verification. To address this, the CORPLINK project developed the *visibility index* comparing insights gained from public subsidiary data to those from the more opaque parent-level reporting (Phillips et al., 2020).

With the help of the visibility index, the CORPLINK project discovered that for the top 100 firms in the world, aggregating the information provided by subsidiaries accounts for an average of 66 per cent of the operating revenues of these groups. In other words, on average, only two-thirds of these companies' operating revenues were reported in jurisdictions whose subsidiaries provide information that is available to third-party or public scrutiny. However, when it comes to net income – an accounting value that plays a more significant role in taxation – only 32 per cent of net income reported by subsidiaries appears in the consolidated accounts. In other words, it appears that many MNCs ensured that a far greater portion of their net income will be registered in opaque jurisdictions.

Granular Analysis of Poor Reporting Practices

The visibility index raises the question of whether the location of subsidiaries in OFCs genuinely influence data quality and transparency.[10] Here again, the CORPLINK project was ground-breaking, developing a comparative study of data quality in two types of companies, independent trading companies such as Glencore and Trafigura, and integrated energy companies, such as Shell or BP. The CORPLINK project began by evaluating the quality of data produced from the two groups of non-OFC subsidiaries (see Chapter 3 for OFC subsidiary classification). Table 7.1 is a sample of companies used as data sources for analysis in this chapter.

Figure 7.1 compares the quality of information disclosed by subsidiaries from the two group of companies that are located in

---

[10] This section draws on a comprehensive and detailed but unpublished comparative study of reporting quality. The analysis and data were provided by Richard Phillips, with conceptual and technical support from Professor Yuval Millo, Warwick Business School. I am deeply grateful for their permission to include this valuable information.

Table 7.1 *Independent and integrated trading companies (CORPLINK/OECD study)*

Independent Energy Traders	Integrated Energy Traders
Macquarie Bank	ENI
Trafigura Group	Exxon
Glencore	Sinopec (trading arm UNIPEC)
Vitol	CNPC/Petrochina
Mercuria	Shell
Gunvor	BP
–	Litasco
–	Total

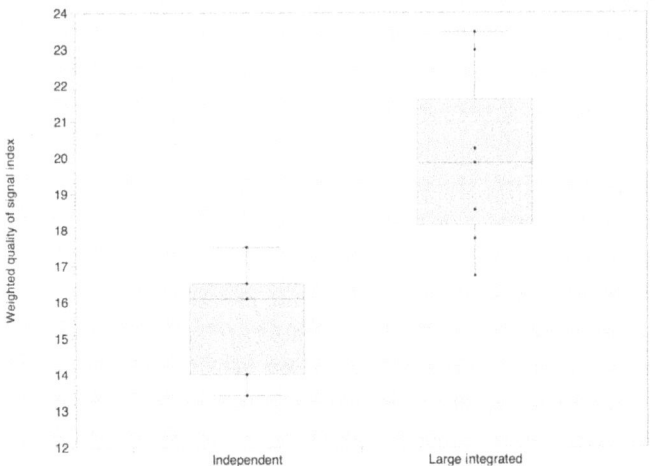

Figure 7.1 Weighted quality of signal received from OFC subsidiaries.

OFCs. It shows that subsidiaries of OFCs are rather opaque, providing little financial information. But there is an interesting divergence in the quality of financial data disclosed by independent energy companies and integrated energy companies. This discrepancy suggests independent firms are exploiting jurisdictional reporting arbitrage in OFCs to a far greater extent. The question, then, is how independent trading companies use OFCs to achieve a greater degree of reporting opacity?

A common contributor to low disclosure quality at the subsidiary level is the prevalence of dormant subsidiaries. Dormant companies typically report only a balance sheet, whereas active companies report both a balance sheet and an income statement. While definitions of the concept of the dormant company vary by jurisdiction, a dormant subsidiary generally refers to an entity with no active operations. Fossil companies described in Chapter 3 are likely to be dormant companies. They are a common occurrence among energy companies,

Dormant subsidiaries fall into two main categories:

1. Ceased Operations: These subsidiaries were once operational but have halted business activities. They might remain on the books for administrative reasons or as part of tax and financial planning, yet they contribute little to the overall financial transparency of the corporate group.
2. Future Operations: Some subsidiaries are established pre-emptively, with the intention of using them for future business activities. These entities remain dormant until they are activated to meet business needs in a particular jurisdiction.

Owing to their inactive status, dormant companies inherently provide limited financial disclosure, as they lack substantial financial transactions, revenue, or profit to report.

Although entirely legitimate, the effect of dormant subsidiaries in a group that provides only a balance sheet will be to lessen the appearance of the quality of information made available by the group as a whole. The CORPLINK project examined the prevalence of dormant companies among two groups – large integrated energy firms and independent energy trading companies – to assess whether the observed divergence in disclosure quality between the two could, in part, be explained by the greater reliance on dormant subsidiaries within the independent segment. The integrated sector possesses, on average, many more dormant companies than the independent sector. That makes sense – energy companies are often involved in exploration that is not successful, leaving them with dormant or fossil companies.

As Figure 7.2 shows, the lower quality of the information footprint produced by the independent energy sector cannot be attributed to the prevalence of dormant entities. Another possible explanation for the information gap between the two groups is not the sheer number of dormant subsidiaries, or fossils, but the proportion of subsidiaries that behave like dormant companies – subsidiaries that report very little information, typically only balance sheet information without accompanying income statements or cash flow data. Figure 7.3

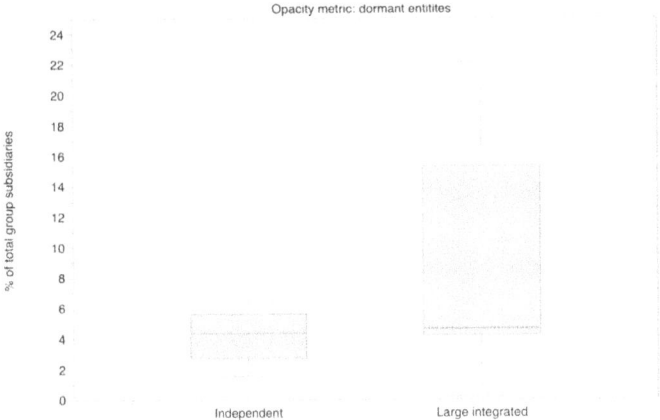

Figure 7.2 Prevalence of dormant companies among independent and integrated energy trading companies.

Figure 7.3 Dormant-like behaviour of corporate subsidiaries.

supports this hypothesis, showing the independent sector has a significantly higher portion of subsidiaries providing only minimal disclosures, akin to dormant entities, than the integrated sector. It appears the independent energy sector is leveraging the less rigorous regulatory enforcement typically found in OFCs to create entities that mimic dormant companies.

This practice sheds light on the overall lack of transparency. More subsidiaries in the independent group, particularly those located in

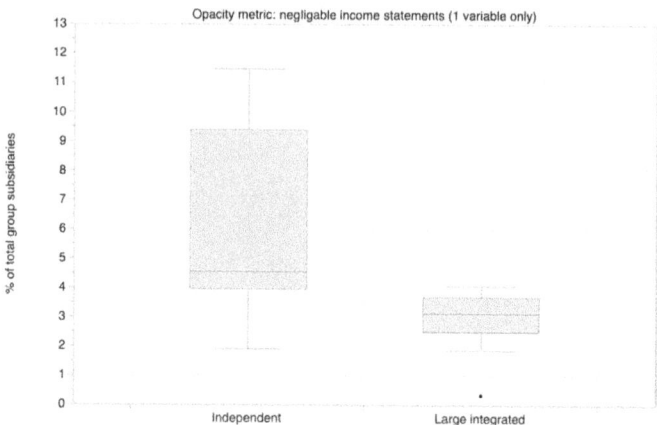

Figure 7.4 Income statement quality of OFC-based subsidiaries of independent and integrated oil trading companies.

OFCs, are providing basic, balance-sheet-only reports, limiting external visibility into their financial activities.

Figure 7.4 compares the income statement quality of the OFC subsidiaries of the two groups, focusing on the proportion of subsidiaries that report only a single income statement variable. This metric provides insight into the depth – or lack thereof – of income statement disclosures within each group's subsidiaries. The findings align with previous observations: subsidiaries of independent companies tend to provide significantly lower-quality information than those of integrated companies. Specifically, a higher proportion of independent-sector subsidiaries report only one variable in their income statements, such as revenue or net income, without accompanying details on expenses, operating costs, or other financial metrics. This limited reporting reduces the utility of the income statement and precludes a full understanding of the subsidiary's financial performance.

The implications are that existing transparency regulations, with their inherent gaps, are insufficient on their own. These regulatory gaps create opportunities for jurisdictional arbitrage that companies, particularly those in the independent sector, can exploit. As countries face pressure to amend or remove legislation aimed at increasing transparency, these gaps persist, particularly within OFCs, where there is little to compel companies to provide high-quality financial disclosures. This underscores the need for stronger international regulatory standards that not only require financial disclosures but also establish clear quality criteria for those disclosures, especially within OFCs, to prevent strategic under-reporting and improve overall corporate transparency.

Conclusion

The CORPLINK study offers compelling new evidence that complex corporate structures and OFCs enable companies to strategically withhold information when desired, creating an information blackout at the subsidiary level. This lack of subsidiary-level disclosures significantly reduces transparency and hampers the ability to verify the financial integrity of consolidated accounts, raising concerns about accountability and oversight.

This chapter highlights that reporting and disclosure arbitrage represents a critical, yet often overlooked, aspect of jurisdictional arbitrage. It underscores the pressing need for stronger international standards to ensure consistent disclosure quality across jurisdictions, particularly for subsidiaries operating in OFCs. Addressing the issue of strategic non-reporting is essential to safeguard the credibility of consolidated accounts. Only through comprehensive, quality-focused regulatory reform can the information opacity exploited through jurisdictional arbitrage be mitigated.

8 Geopolitics and Jurisdictional Arbitrage
Does the United States Arbitrage the World?

Introduction

The discussion so far has been predicated on the common assumption that centrally coordinated multi-corporate enterprises (CCMCEs) are well designed to arbitrage national regulations. Certain countries have long been suspected of tailoring their legislation to facilitate regulatory and tax arbitrage, becoming tax havens catering to non-resident business needs. But could countries – particularly those with well-developed legal systems, such as the United States – also be leveraging arbitrage as a tool for geopolitical strategy? If true, this would not be unprecedented. As Kai Raustiala argues, the United States has a history of seeking strategic control over other countries by 'unilaterally manipulating legal differences to better serve its interests' (Raustiala, 2011, 7).

In Chapter 3, I discussed the possibility that some governments may view foreign tax payments by 'their' corporations as disadvantageous, likely to weaken these companies' competitive standing internationally. If this is indeed the case, these governments may actively or tacitly support their corporations in arbitraging the tax rules of other states to gain a strategic edge. This chapter builds on that idea, drawing on the CORPLINK project's analysis of the world's 100 largest non-financial firms to present evidence suggesting US companies may be encouraged by the government to exploit foreign tax systems.

The evidence I present in this chapter is admittedly circumstantial but nonetheless revealing. It demonstrates that large US-based CCMCEs exhibit a distinctly bifurcated structure: they are organized in one manner domestically and adopt a markedly different configuration internationally. This duality reflects the kind of structural patterns commonly associated with arbitrage, suggesting a deliberate strategic design to exploit regulatory and tax disparities across jurisdictions.

Jurisdictional Arbitrage and Geopolitical Calculations

The economic rationale for governments to harness corporate arbitraging techniques to advance their geopolitical goals is straightforward: lower corporate tax rates are often associated with increased economic growth (see Gemmell et al., 2011; Lee and Gordon, 2005). If corporations from one country face lower effective tax rates on their global earnings – whether owing to intentional policy choices or to a lack of strict anti-abuse enforcement – those corporations enjoy a competitive edge in the global market.

An overzealous tax authority that aggressively enforces anti-abuse rules on domestic corporations' foreign earnings risks, therefore, placing those corporations at a disadvantage relative to competitors from countries with more lenient policies. In contrast, by strategically allowing or even encouraging certain tax-minimizing structures and practices, governments can boost the global standing of their corporations. This approach transforms corporate tax policy into a geopolitical tool, with governments selectively tolerating or promoting practices that enhance domestic firms' competitiveness abroad, sometimes at the expense of tax revenue.

Whether the US government or Treasury explicitly encourages corporations to avoid foreign taxes is an open question (Avi-Yonah, 2005; Clausing, 2019; Kudrle, 2019). While it has not been US policy to endorse tax avoidance abroad, some observers suggest there may be tacit or indirect support for such practices. Critics frequently argue the United States takes a lenient stance on international anti-tax avoidance. For example, the country has historically been less than enthusiastic about multilateral anti-tax abuse initiatives, such as those promoted by the Organisation for Economic Co-operation and Development (OECD), and has been particularly resistant to reciprocal information-sharing agreements on corporate taxation. For instance, Einfeld and Blomkamp (2022) argue behind-the-scenes 'nudging' may subtly steer US corporations towards minimizing foreign tax liabilities, despite official statements to the contrary. Meyer notes that the United States often enacts 'laws that proscribe or regulate conduct but that remain silent about whether [they] apply to acts that occur outside of the United States' (Meyer, 2010, 114). Such 'geo-ambiguous' extra-territoriality policies, he says, inadvertently encourage firms to use offshore jurisdictions. David Miller (2011) catalogues over thirty provisions of US federal and state law that encourage American taxpayers to operate through foreign tax havens (see also Hines and Rice, 1994; Tax Justice Network, 2015).

A notable case of regulatory arbitrage appeared when the United States introduced mandatory controls on direct investment abroad in 1968, limiting US-registered companies' ability to raise funds domestically for foreign operations. Following this policy shift, the US Bureau of Statistics identified a suspicious increase in US bank affiliates registered in the Netherlands Antilles (NA), a recognized tax haven at the time (Ellicott, 1969). Papke argues the Treasury adopted a permissive attitude towards this form of roundtripping through the NA because of its perception that US competitors gained advantages by operating through London's Euromarket (Papke, 2000; see also Boise and Morriss, 2009; Rosenzweig, 2012). The United States signed a treaty with the Netherlands that allowed US affiliates to raise capital on Euromarkets, just like their competitors, and like their competitors, they could avoid withholding tax on interest payments on borrowing channelled through NA affiliates. This was an early case of what Avi-Yonah (2005) calls the US policy of competitiveness.[1]

Similar arguments have been advanced to explain the US application of controlled foreign company (CFC) rules (see discussion in Chapter 3). In the beginning, CFC regulations gave the Internal Revenue Service the power to prevent American companies from abusing foreign taxes. But Congress soon began to erode the effectiveness of the original rules. After the adoption of Statement of Financial Accounting Standards 131, released in 1998 by the US Financial Accounting Standards Board, firms no longer had to disclose geographic earnings as was required by Subpart F in the original regulations (Hope et al., 2013). Meanwhile, Congress had introduced the so-called tick the box rules in 1996, whereby a parent could select the nature of a foreign subsidiary irrespective of its status in its home country. Tick the box rules were introduced to ensure consistency, or

---

[1] Once withholding tax was repealed in the United States in 1984, the situation rapidly reversed itself. By the end of 1993, the net outstanding debt of US companies vis-à-vis NA affiliates had been reduced to US$8.7 billion, and the negative direct investment was negligible (OECD 1998, 43). The repeal of US withholding rules explains, in no small part, the subsequent decline in the significance of NA as an offshore financial centre (OFC) (Papke, 2000; Weyzig, 2013).

so it was argued, for US companies at home and abroad.[2] Yet critics argue these rules 'allowed multinationals to create entities that were treated one way in a foreign jurisdiction and another by the United States' (Scott, 2014). In a further erosion of the original CFC rules, US courts declined to apply Securities and Exchange Commission Rule 10b-5 to foreign securities transactions, even though they were considered fraudulent in the United States (Meyer, 2010; also see Rosenzweig, 2012).

The tick the box rules saw an unprecedented rise in the number of European-based intermediaries of American companies. The US Treasury acknowledged that 'formalistic rules' allowed taxpayers to 'achieve partnership [i.e., conduit] tax classification for a nonpublicly traded organization that, in all meaningful respects, [was] virtually indistinguishable from a [state-law] corporation' (Scott, 2014).[3]

Given the persistent claims of ambiguity in US policy on tax havens, the CORPLINK project set out to investigate whether there was any concrete evidence at the subsidiary level that could support or refute this perception. Specifically, the project aimed to determine if US multinational corporations (MNCs) were systematically structuring their subsidiary networks to take advantage of regulatory gaps and tax benefits in offshore jurisdictions – actions that might indirectly reflect a permissive stance by the US Treasury on foreign tax avoidance.

Analysis of the Forty Largest US Companies by Revenue

The CORPLINK project investigated US-based companies, looking for a distinct pattern in how they structured their subsidiaries for American versus foreign markets. The analysis focused on the number of intermediary subsidiaries, the splitter arrangements, and the overall scope of subsidiary control within each corporation. The underlying assumption was that intermediary and splitter subsidiaries are

---

[2] These rules were supposed to emulate domestic rules, allowing firms to differentiate between two types of corporate entities under their control, corporations and conduits, with each treated differently for taxation purposes (Speck, 2015, 2583).

[3] A European Union case against Amazon found Amazon's Luxembourg entities elected for 'partnership' arrangements in the United States, thus transferring considerable international losses to be used in tax credit schemes.

typically employed, as I explained in Chapter 3, to facilitate various forms of arbitrage.

Of the original sample of the 100 largest MNCs (see Chapter 4), forty had their parent company in the United States. Of those, seven held no intermediary subsidiaries in OFCs (Phillips et al., 2020). The discussion that follows from now on is focused on the remaining thirty-three companies. The pattern of holding of companies in this sample was especially interesting. Of these thirty-three companies, eighteen firms, or 54 per cent, held none of their domestic subsidiaries through intermediary structures. Only four held more than 2 per cent of their American subsidiaries through such intermediaries, and Pfizer was the only company to exceed 5 per cent, holding 8.71 per cent of its domestic subsidiaries through OFC intermediaries.

The conclusion is obvious: large American-based CCMCEs are not using US-based intermediaries in jurisdictions such as Delaware to manage either US or international subsidiaries. This aligns with insights into Delaware's role as a corporate haven. As we saw in Chapter 4, Delaware primarily attracts parent companies, global ultimate owners, or specific direct subsidiaries without requiring intermediary structures. This arrangement contrasts with typical OFC intermediaries; instead, Delaware's legal and tax environment allows companies to operate with direct holdings that avoid additional intermediary layers.

It appears, therefore, that arbitrage within the United States, or regulatory arbitrage as defined in Chapter 1, has a different nature. Instead of using intermediaries to obscure ownership or manage tax obligations, companies leverage Delaware's favourable regulatory framework to gain tax efficiencies and confidentiality directly. This streamlined approach reflects a unique form of domestic regulatory arbitrage, whereby Delaware's specialized corporate laws facilitate tax and legal benefits without the need for complex intermediary arrangements commonly seen in OFCs.

The approach of American firms seems to shift significantly when it comes to foreign subsidiaries. Among the firms in the CORPLINK sample, eight (24 per cent) held more than 50 per cent of their foreign subsidiaries under intermediary structures, while seven held between 30 per cent and 50 per cent in this way. An additional eight firms held over 20 per cent of their foreign subsidiaries through such intermediary arrangements. This stark contrast is revelatory of a clear difference in how American firms structure their domestic and foreign operations.

A similar trend emerged in the use of the splitter structure among the thirty-three companies. Three companies, Kroger, CVS, and Express Scripts, had no splitter. Among the remaining firms, twenty-six had no splitter arrangements for controlling US domestic subsidiaries, and nine used splitter arrangements for fewer than 2 per cent of their domestic subsidiaries. However, this approach shifted dramatically for foreign subsidiaries. Two firms opted to control over 50 per cent of their foreign subsidiaries through a splitter arrangement, and an additional sixteen firms used splitters for over 10 per cent of their foreign subsidiaries.

The circumstantial evidence derived from the data suggests that American firms are highly bifurcated: they barely use intermediary subsidiaries or splitters domestically, but are avid users of these structures internationally. This strategy suggests a pattern of prioritizing global efficiency while maintaining compliance with US regulations at home.

Conclusion

The CORPLINK analysis suggests a complex interplay between geopolitics and corporate arbitrage. American multinational firms appear to adopt a dual strategy, leveraging domestic regulatory stability while actively pursuing jurisdictional arbitrage abroad. By structuring foreign operations through intermediaries, splitters, and offshore arrangements, they navigate international tax and regulatory environments in ways that minimize costs and enhance competitiveness, often capitalizing on discrepancies in global standards.

This approach underscores the geopolitical dimension of corporate arbitrage. Firms are not merely optimizing for tax or regulatory benefits; at times, they align with national interests by bolstering their global competitiveness. In this sense, the selective application of arbitrage techniques – concentrated in foreign markets – can be seen as part of a broader economic strategy that indirectly aligns with US geopolitical aims. By allowing corporations flexibility in structuring their foreign operations, the United States benefits from a powerful private-sector presence abroad, even as this approach creates challenges for global regulatory and tax cooperation.

Thus, while corporate arbitrage is often viewed as purely profit-driven, it operates within a geopolitical framework where national interests, regulatory gaps, and global competitiveness intersect. Addressing the complexities of corporate arbitrage in a geopolitical context will likely require greater international coordination to harmonize regulatory standards and close loopholes that enable selective transparency and cross-border tax avoidance.

9 The Hidden Empire
How MNCs Redefine Power through Arbitrage

Introduction

I have emphasized throughout this book that the techniques of jurisdictional arbitrage extend far beyond taxation. However, they are not solely about avoidance or evasion. Multinational corporations (MNCs) use these strategies to stabilize their operating environment, constructing intricate legal and financial frameworks to exert control over both their regulatory and tax landscapes.

Tax arbitrage techniques, as we have seen, are anticipatory, designed not only to mitigate current tax liabilities but also to shield against potential future taxation. In contrast, liability arbitrage and control over financial reporting serve to minimize exposure to the unpredictable and fragmented nature of the international system – where each state operates under its own distinct set of rules and political dynamics. These techniques allow corporations to navigate, exploit, and even shape regulatory inconsistencies across jurisdictions, reinforcing their strategic position in a world of inherently arbitrary and uneven governance structures.

Anyone who can exert control over their environment and selectively determine the institutional rules that apply to them wields a formidable source of power. The ability to shape one's regulatory, legal, and financial conditions is not just a strategic advantage – it is, in essence, a mechanism of autonomy, insulating actors from external constraints and granting them leverage over others. This raises a fundamental question: does jurisdictional arbitrage constitute a previously unrecognized form of power? If so, what mechanisms enable this power to operate, and who are its primary beneficiaries?

Throughout this book, the power of MNCs has remained in the background. Now, it is essential to bring it to the forefront. If arbitrage is indeed a hitherto unrecognized form of power, understanding its implications is critical to assessing the true nature of corporate sovereignty in the modern world.

Corporate Dominance: Theories of MNC Power and Global Influence

MNCs are widely recognized as powerful actors, exerting substantial influence over the global economy and international politics. Theoretical understandings of their power have been shaped by two seminal contributions: Robert Dahl's (1957) relational definition of power and Albert Hirschman's (1978) concept of 'voice or exit' dynamics.[1]

Dahl conceptualized power as an inherently relational dynamic, emphasizing the ability of one actor to influence another's actions. As he famously stated: 'A has power over B to the extent that he can get B to do something that B would not otherwise do' (Dahl, 1957, 203).

This formulation highlights the coercive or persuasive capacities of power: the greater the power one party wields, the more effectively it can compel another to act against its original preferences. In the context of MNCs, this framework suggests that power is measured by the ability to shape the decisions of states, regulatory bodies, and even consumers in ways that serve their strategic interests.

In one of the earliest analyses of the relationship between MNCs and states, John Fayerweather (1972) identified three primary areas of political conflict between MNCs and host governments, each rooted in the inherent tension between the global ambitions of MNCs and the nation-focused priorities of states. MNCs, driven by global optimization, he argued, concentrate manufacturing in a few strategically chosen locations based on internal economic criteria, such as cost efficiencies, supply chain integration, and access to key markets. In contrast, host governments seek to attract and retain manufacturing operations within their borders to stimulate domestic employment, foster industrial growth, and drive economic development. Similarly, MNCs seek to determine the location of research and development

---

[1] Originally formulated to address inefficiencies in organizations, Hirschman's framework has become a cornerstone for understanding the interplay between states and corporations. Voice represents the ability of corporations to influence regulatory and institutional environments through lobbying, negotiation, or advocacy, reshaping the rules to suit their interests. Exit is the capacity of MNCs to withdraw from a state's jurisdiction, relocating their resources or operations to more favourable environments. States hold the formal authority to impose regulations, but MNCs leverage their mobility and influence to challenge, evade, or reshape these constraints, redefining the boundaries of power in the globalized economy.

(R&D) facilities in regions that align with their strategic needs – areas with access to top talent, robust intellectual property protections, favourable tax incentives, and well-developed infrastructure. In contrast, governments view R&D facilities as vital to their own economic and technological aspirations.

At the core of Fayerweather's analysis – and echoing the insights of scholars such as Douglass North (North, 1990) and Stephen Hymer (Hymer, 1982) – lies a fundamental conflict over control. For MNCs, retaining control over their foreign subsidiaries and operations is essential. But for host states, control is the *sine qua non* for governing elites to achieve their national objectives (Fayerweather, 1972). This struggle for control places states and MNCs in direct competition, leading to a negotiation process often framed as a 'bargaining situation' (Bennett and Sharpe, 1979; Eden et al., 2005; Fagre and Wells, 1982; Grosse, 1996).[2]

The concept of bargaining between states and individual MNCs serves as a highly suitable and effective analytical framework in political science, particularly in the study of international political economy and global governance (Dörrenbächer and Geppert, 2011). Some MNCs, particularly those with vast global reach (e.g., Big Tech, financial giants, or energy firms), can exert more economic power than many states. Conversely, some strong regulatory states (e.g., the United States, European Union, or China) have the leverage to impose restrictions on MNCs, shaping corporate behaviour through laws, taxation, and sanctions. The bargaining model helps explain why some governments impose strict regulations on MNCs, while others offer favourable policies to attract investment. It accounts for policy variations across countries, shaped by factors such as MNC dependency, industry type, and domestic political pressures. Scholars such as Raymond Vernon with his 'Obsolescing Bargain Model' highlight how power can shift from MNCs to states over time, particularly in industries such as oil and natural resources (Vernon, 2013).

Considering the assumed power play between companies and states, political scientists and international political economists have

---

[2] Vernon (1971) argued multinationals face an 'obsolescing bargain' in their dealings with host-country governments. Before entry, the bargaining relationship favours the firm, but deteriorates once a physical investment in plant and equipment in the country is made, because such investments are 'held hostage' by government policies.

gathered evidence that MNCs leverage their considerable financial and political power to influence government authorities through lobbying, campaign contributions, and other expenditures in both home and host states (Hill et al., 2013; Kelleher et al., 2009). They use, in other words, 'voice' to try to influence states, engaging with regulators over extended periods, setting and influencing policy agendas at both national and multilateral levels (Irogbe, 2013).

When faced with intransigence from certain governments, MNCs have a powerful fall-back strategy in their arsenal: the threat to exit (Dörrenbächer and Geppert, 2011; Hill et al., 2013; Kelleher et al., 2009; Kim and Milner, 2019; Nye, 1974).[3] John Stopford and Susan Strange highlight the shifting dynamics between states and firms in *Rival States, Rival Firms* (1991). They acknowledge the growing trend of corporations to leverage their mobility as a bargaining chip. Threatening to leave – or actually leaving – a country that fails to provide a favourable regulatory environment is now a common tactic for MNCs. This mobility, coupled with their substantial financial and technological resources, allows MNCs to shape the policy frameworks of host states, compelling them to align with corporate priorities and to rethink their economic and regulatory policies. John Williamson (1993), for instance, urged Latin American countries to adopt what he called the Washington Consensus, a set of neoliberal economic policies designed to make countries more attractive to global capital and stave off the damaging effects of capital flight.

Over time, the concept of power evolved to include non-behavioural dimensions, and our understanding of the power wielded by MNCs similarly expanded. Peter Bacharach and Morton S. Baratz (Bachrach and Baratz, 1963), in what Lukes (2021) calls their theory of the

---

[3] The underlying conceptual framework is that of special interest group theory within competitive political systems. Mancur Olson's (2009) argument that concentrated interest groups can benefit at the expense of more dispersed groups, even when the latter have more at stake collectively, applies to MNCs. The MNC is a form of concentrated interest, highly focused on a goal. As Kim and Milner (2019) argue, 'MNCs' economic dominance reduces the relative cost of engaging in political activities, while their large-scale transnational operations increase the marginal benefits of influencing policy-making individually.' This perspective suggests MNCs, by virtue of their concentrated resources and global reach, are uniquely positioned to shape policy outcomes to their advantage, often at the expense of broader but less organized societal interests.

'second dimension of power', suggest power is not only about direct decision-making. Their argument goes as follows: 'A participates in the making of decisions that affect B; power is also exercised when A devotes his energies to creating and reinforcing social and political values and institutional practices that limit the scope of the political process to public consideration of only those issues' (cited in Lukes, 2021, 7). The second dimension includes institutional power and the power to set agendas (Graz, 2019). Rather than merely influencing outcomes within a predefined decision-making process, power in this sense involves shaping the very framework of decision-making – determining which issues are brought to the table and which are not.

Power as Autonomy

The relationship between states and MNCs is typically seen, therefore, through the lens of power relationship between two parties, whereby the stronger party achieves its aim by forcing the weaker party to change course. But there is another way of looking at the question of power. Warren J. Samuels (Samuels, 1972) argues that legal rules dictate the terms of access and participation in the economy for potential economic actors. In Samuels' view, economic actors may not necessarily seek power as traditionally understood; rather, they may want to find a means of expanding the range of options available to them within those rules. In this view, power is not merely about the ability to compel others to act against their will. It is also about achieving autonomy and optionality – it is about an actor's capacity to navigate within a rule-bound system in ways that maximize their freedom and flexibility. This interpretation of power shifts the focus from overt conflict to strategic adaptation and exploitation of institutional structures.

In a similar vein, Neil Fligstein (1993) argues that whatever the ultimate goal of a business enterprise, whether profit maximization, higher return on investment, or augmented market value, managers and entrepreneurs seek to achieve a degree of control over the internal and external environment.[4] Power is about autonomy or control over the environment.

---

[4] Fligstein's theory has many moving parts, some of which I would dispute, and others which are not particularly relevant to this book.

We can, therefore, conceptualize arbitrage as a form of power rooted in autonomy and control. Rather than lobbying for wholesale regulatory change, MNCs can use an alternative source of power, working within the system, identifying and utilizing weaknesses in the system of rules in order to expand their autonomy and choice. The techniques they use involved not only voice or exit but also finding legal and institutional pathways that grant them greater flexibility and control over the political and economic environment. As I have argued throughout the book, the centrally coordinated multi-corporate enterprise (CCMCE) modality that evolved from the late nineteenth century is perfectly designed to expand the range of available options and enhance the resilience of MNCs through the use of arbitraging techniques. This approach, arbitrage, minimizes conflict with regulatory bodies while maximizing strategic advantages.

Predator/Prey Dynamics

My understanding of the dynamics of power between MNCs and states as centred on achieving autonomy from institutional and regulatory constraints may seem novel from a political science perspective, but it is a common power relationship in the natural world: predator–prey dynamics. Extending this to the state–MNC relationship, states can be seen in this model as 'predators': states use their coercive power to impose taxes, regulations, and other constraints that can limit a corporation's freedom of action and profitability. Corporate groups are the prey, seeking ways to avoid capture or exploitation while striving to survive and thrive. In the predator–prey analogy, just as prey in nature seek to camouflage themselves or exploit the physical limitations of their predators, so too MNCs have developed four main strategies to escape detection and exploit states' limitations. They have adopted the CCMCE modularity to outsmart their predators.

In nature, predators are bound by their hunting grounds; their ability to pursue prey is limited by geography, environmental conditions, and their own physical capacities. Similarly, the corporate world has identified that although powerful, states are territorially constrained and can only enforce laws within their borders. The concept of territorial sovereignty restricts their reach and prevents them from acting effectively against corporations beyond their borders. Like prey that evade predators by fleeing to areas outside the predator's range,

MNCs leverage their CCMCE modality to relocate operations to regions where the state cannot reach or where conditions are more favourable.

Equally, in nature, certain terrains provide structural advantages to prey, where they take advantage of the predators' sensory limitations to camouflage or shelter. Similarly, the law of states unwittingly provides the corporate world with certain limitation corporations with a formal identity, and this is akin to the sensory limitations of states as predators. As Sebastian Orts argues: '[The law] plays an essential role in the social recognition, conceptual definition, and historical evolution of business enterprises, also known as firms ... Without the social technology and 'forms' provided by law, business firms would be indistinguishable from informal organized social groups, clubs, or gathering of people pursuing similar interests' (Orts, 2013, 1).

Just as prey exploit natural features to avoid detection or capture, the corporate world use the legal forms provided by states to structure their operations in ways that minimize regulatory exposure and maximize protection. These forms allow corporations to shield owners from liability (via fuses, playing the role of the passive investor, and the like as discussed in Chapter 6), accumulate capital, and operate globally under a single legal identity.

Predators are also known to use their environment to track and capture prey. States, through the law, gain the ability to regulate and oversee corporate behaviour. The law serves as a tool for states to impose taxes, enforce compliance, and extract value from corporations. However, the legal framework that empowers corporations can also obscure their full scope of actions and impacts.[5] They leverage their CCMCE modality to blend in or mask their presence. By setting up complex legal structures, corporations can minimize their visibility, obscure accountability, and deflect attention from their harmful practices. In this way, just as prey in nature seek to identify the physical limitations of predators to survive, so the corporate world exploits the limitations of states – the fact that they often lack the financial,

---

[5] Arbitrage is not to be confused with non-compliance. Compliance is not simply about adhering to regulations; it can be strategically manipulated to achieve desired outcomes. Non-compliance can go unpunished, particularly if the non-compliant party has a degree of power. A system of rules characterized by non-compliance is considered a demonstration of the controlling party's lack of power.

technological, or human resources to fully monitor and enforce regulations. The rapid pace of corporate innovation often outstrips the state's ability to regulate. Corporations can leverage this lag to deploy new technologies or business models before governments catch up (e.g., ride-sharing apps operating in legal grey areas).

The practice of jurisdictional arbitrage mirrors, then, the predator–prey dynamics observed in nature. However, as discussed in Chapter 1, such techniques can have significant costs. Establishing alternative pathways or overwhelming the monitoring capacity of states often requires the creation of numerous 'excess' subsidiaries across the globe and the employment of costly professional advisors to manage complex legal and financial structures.

In essence, jurisdictional arbitrage is a resource-intensive strategy of power. Its high costs make it available only to the most powerful and well-resourced organizations, further entrenching the advantages of those at the top of the global economic hierarchy.

From Profit Maximization to Augmenting Market Value

What, then, is the ultimate aim of a corporate group seeking autonomy by deploying arbitrage? Economists often argue corporate taxes are inherently nonsensical, merely costs passed on to consumers. In this view, the corporation – often conflated with the broader concept of the firm – functions as a tax collector for the state, serving as an intermediary without bearing the tax burden itself.

This perspective aligns with the productionist perspective of the firm, whereby firms are supposed to produce 'things' at lower costs, and any distortions produced by governments, such as taxes or regulations, simply increase the costs of those things. Corporate tax, when viewed through this lens, is just another cost of doing business, on a par with the costs of labour, raw materials, or logistics. Reducing tax liabilities becomes essential for lowering overall production costs, thereby enhancing profitability and allowing firms to offer competitive prices or reinvest savings into growth and innovation.

However, this perspective is one-sided, not considering the broader implications of corporate taxation and regulatory arbitrage on the market capitalization of corporate groups or the underlying logic of the investor. As I have repeatedly stressed, a core corporate strategy revolves around augmenting the market value of the firm. Investors evaluate the group's consolidated financial statements, which aggregate the results of the parent and its subsidiaries. An 'investment' in a subsidiary is typically recorded on the parent company's financial statements as a long-term asset called 'investment in subsidiary' or something similar. In the consolidated statements, however, this investment asset is eliminated and replaced with the actual assets and liabilities of the subsidiary. Goodwill, for instance, may be recognized on the consolidated balance sheet if the parent paid more than the fair value of the subsidiary's net assets at acquisition. In this way, the consolidated statements will show the total assets, liabilities, revenues, and expenses of the entire group as if it were a single economic entity.

This logic helps explain why corporate groups pursue autonomy so relentlessly. The ability of subsidiaries to operate with autonomy from regulatory constraints directly enhances their value as assets within the corporate group. When a subsidiary pays less tax either because of favourable local regulations or the use of jurisdictional arbitrage, its net income is likely to rise. This higher profitability enhances the subsidiary's valuation as an individual entity and contributes to the overall financial health of the corporate group. However, higher profitability in one subsidiary does not necessarily mean the group as a whole will pay more tax, because other subsidiaries within the group often absorb the tax burden, strategically offsetting the group's overall tax liability. Those subsidiaries may not add to the group's overall profitability as logged on the consolidated accounts, but they do not detract from the value of the group either (besides the cost of running them). Consequently, tax avoided at the group level will translate to higher market valuation of the group as a whole.[6]

Similarly, tort arbitrage refers to strategies companies use to reduce their liability exposure and costs related to potential lawsuits or legal claims (Chapter 7). Just like tax arbitrage, tort arbitrage can increase cash flows and profits by reducing liability burdens and thus lead to higher firm value, as investors often view effective liability management positively. Successful tort arbitrage offers competitive advantage

---

[6] Several economic and financial frameworks are used in management decision-making to account for taxation when evaluating investments. These frameworks integrate taxation into the assessment of project profitability, cash flows, and overall strategic value. For instance, the formula for net present value with tax adjustments evaluates the profitability of an investment after considering the time value of money and taxation.

over rivals less adept at managing legal risks and more efficient resource allocation based on economic rather than purely regulatory factors. Management is protected from potential liability and can take greater risks with the corporate organization.

Similarly, autonomous subsidiaries operating in jurisdictions with looser financial regulations or better credit conditions can borrow on more favourable terms. The access to cheaper capital allows growth and investment, further increasing the subsidiary's valuation. Equally, less transparent reporting can facilitate more aggressive tax avoidance strategies, and these, in turn, can reduce a company's tax burden and increase its after-tax profits. Opacity can create information asymmetries that may benefit insiders or sophisticated investors who are better able to interpret limited disclosures. This can lead to higher valuations in some cases. Less disclosure of sensitive business information can protect competitive advantages and prevent rivals from gaining insights into a company's strategies or operations. Opacity gives companies more leeway in how they report and present financial results, potentially allowing them to smooth earnings or meet market expectations more consistently

Autonomy grants subsidiaries the ability to adapt to local conditions, optimizing their operations and market strategies. Of course, this is not a one-way street. Excessive avoidance can sometimes reduce firm value owing to reputational risks, agency costs, and potential legal/regulatory backlash. Excessive tax avoidance may increase costs and have the opposite effect on corporate valuation (Duhoon and Singh, 2023).

An Economy of Unrealized Wealth

Who, then, gains from the higher valuation of the parent company yielded by arbitrage? Jurisdictional arbitrage exploits the fiction that each corporation or a subsidiary is a separate and independent legal person. The main beneficiaries of the rising value of corporate groups are management, large individual shareholders, and institutional investors. They reap significant financial rewards as shareholder value increases, driven by strategies that maximize profitability and optimize tax liabilities within the group.

Many companies tie executive compensation packages to metrics such as shareholder value, stock price performance, or return on equity. This incentivizes management to prioritize strategies that boost market capitalization, such as tax optimization, efficient operations, and jurisdictional arbitrage.

Large institutional investors – such as pension funds, mutual funds, and investment firms – typically hold significant stakes in publicly traded companies. Dividends, share buybacks, and stock price appreciation all contribute to their portfolio growth. Large institutional investors primarily distribute returns to their shareholders or beneficiaries, but they also allocate a considerable portion of the financial gains to their own management teams.

The most spectacular beneficiaries are large individual shareholders who own substantial stakes in highly successful corporate groups. These include individuals such as Elon Musk, Jeff Bezos, and other founders or early investors in major corporations. For these individuals, the rapid growth in the market value of their holdings often results in wealth accumulation far exceeding what management or institutional investors achieve, especially when tied to globally dominant firms.

What do these individuals do with their money? The ultra-wealthy, such as Elon Musk, Bill Gates, and Warren Buffett, possess immense wealth, much of which is tied to unrealized wealth – assets whose value exist mostly on paper and is not immediately subject to taxation. As I write this in 2024, the combined net worth of the world's 2,781 billionaires is an estimated US$14.2 trillion, much of which is unrealized wealth. Unrealized wealth is not taxed until it is sold or generates income (e.g., through dividends). This allows individuals to defer taxes indefinitely, keeping their wealth compounding within the asset.

The ultra-wealthy use several strategies to manage their unrealized wealth and minimize exposure to taxes, such as income tax, capital gains tax, or inheritance tax. For instance, instead of selling shares and realizing taxable gains, wealthy individuals often borrow against their assets to generate liquidity. Loans secured by shares, bonds, or real estate allow them to access cash without triggering a taxable event. By holding onto assets instead of selling them, they can defer capital gains taxes indefinitely. Upon death, many jurisdictions allow a step-up in basis, resetting the tax value of assets to their market value at the time of inheritance, thus avoiding taxation on accumulated gains. This strategy is known in the United States as 'Buy, Borrow, Die' (Heath, 2024).

Many ultra-wealthy individuals use trusts to shield their assets from inheritance tax and maintain control over their wealth for future generations. Wealth is often diversified into real estate, art, and other collectibles, which may have lower tax rates or specific exemptions.

There are therefore many techniques of arbitrage. But make no mistake. These are secondary forms of arbitrage, tools and tactics designed to amplify and secure the benefits of the primary form of arbitrage: jurisdictional arbitrage.

Rise of the Rule-Based Transgressor Elite

The distinction between primary and secondary arbitrage is crucial to understand the root causes of global wealth inequality, particularly in the context of tax havens. Much of the discourse around wealth concentration and tax justice focuses on secondary arbitrage tactics, such as offshore accounts or complex tax planning structures. While these strategies are visible and draw public attention, they obscure the deeper, structural dynamics of primary arbitrage, which fundamentally shapes the global financial system.

One of the key drivers of extreme wealth accumulation is jurisdictional arbitrage, where corporations and individuals (organized as corporations) exploit systemic disparities in tax regimes and regulatory frameworks. The techniques of jurisdictional arbitrage are widely regarded as legal, yet they embody a distinctive form of power that artfully combines compliance with transgression. Practitioners of jurisdictional arbitrage meticulously adhere to the formal rules of the jurisdictions in which they operate, ensuring legal compliance, but they often circumvent the broader regulatory intent, exploiting ambiguities and inconsistencies in legal and regulatory frameworks. Operating in a grey area where different jurisdictions intersect, these practitioners push the boundaries of what is permissible, walking a fine line between innovation and exploitation. In essence, jurisdictional arbitrage is a highly sophisticated strategy for manoeuvring through the complexities of international legal and regulatory landscapes, leveraging their disparities to achieve strategic advantages.

This dynamic extends to beneficiaries as well. These beneficiaries are transnationally organized and form what can be described as rule-based transgressor elites – a class of individuals and organizations highly skilled at complying with rules in order to transgress them.

This elite group excels in arbitraging rules, using legal and regulatory frameworks to maximize wealth and power while minimizing constraints. The managers of large MNCs and so-called born-global companies, such as Tesla and eBay, form the core of this group. They are joined by large investment houses such as BlackRock, Blackstone, and Vanguard, as well as leading international investment banks and elite legal, consultancy, and accounting firms that facilitate these practices. These entities constitute the backbone of the rule-based transgressor elite, leveraging their global reach and expertise to manipulate tax codes, liability regulations, and other rules to their advantage.

In addition to this core group, several ancillary groups contribute to the dynamics of wealth and power concentration. Among the most significant are mid-size corporate groups, many of which are privately held. These entities, numbering in the hundreds of thousands – possibly millions – employ strategies honed by larger corporations to arbitrage rules, minimizing exposure to corporate taxes, personal or group liabilities, and shareholder protection regulations.

Ricardo de Soares (2021) identifies another critical group: elites from developing countries who latch onto existing institutional and professional networks serving transnational elites. Once these individuals manage to transfer capital out of their own countries, they actively participate in global processes of wealth and power concentration. In short, rule-based transgression underpins the strategies of today's wealthiest and most powerful actors, creating a global system that perpetuates inequality and concentrates influence.

The problem is that the costs associated with rules and regulations designed to address these issues – such as infrastructure expenses or liabilities – do not simply disappear. The liabilities remain, as do the financial regulations intended to ensure the stability of corporate entities and the broader system. Similarly, reporting requirements, which enable a degree of oversight and activity monitoring, continue to serve their purpose, even if circumvented or minimized by certain actors. These costs and responsibilities are not eliminated but redistributed, often falling disproportionately on less powerful entities or the public at large.

Simply put, arbitraging is a technique for socializing costs, shifting them onto less powerful groups within society or across international borders. The existence of rules and regulations does not imply that the problems they were designed to address – such as liabilities, infrastructure costs, or financial stability – have been resolved. Instead, it means certain types of corporations are able to evade these costs, offloading them onto others while maintaining their own profitability.

Conclusion

Jurisdictional arbitrage is a rational, often identifiable decision-making process that seeks, in the words of Warren J. Samuels (1972), to expand options. As a form of power, jurisdictional arbitrage has remained largely invisible to political scientists and international political economists. But by employing the techniques of arbitrage, modern companies have developed a third dimension of power and are no longer restricted to a binary set of options. They can seek to change the rules, regulations, or taxation of their home or host states, and if all else fails, they may exit and shift operations to other countries. But they have another option: they can rearrange their subsidiaries in such a way that rules are arbitraged. In so doing, they can create a path of least resistance, forging their own preferred regulatory environment.

The power corporations derive from jurisdictional arbitrage is not adequately captured by traditional theories. These theories tend to attribute corporate power to omnipotent lobbyists, corrupt politicians, globalization, or neoliberalism. They often propose solutions such as restricting lobbying or improving transparency in the political process, but these measures do little to address the underlying power dynamics facilitated by arbitrage. The concept of jurisdictional arbitrage provides a compelling explanation for the increased power of corporate groups in recent decades, arguably more so than traditional notions of power.

To better understand and address the power of corporate groups, it is essential for international relations and international political economy to focus more on the legal structures of these corporations and the phenomenon of arbitrage as a source of power. Scholars and policymakers will recognize the sophisticated legal and strategic manoeuvres that underpin corporate power in the modern world and develop more effective strategies to regulate and balance the influence of MNCs in the global economy.

Conclusions

The book began as an empirical study of the tactics and strategies employed by multinational corporations (MNCs) to avoid or evade taxation and other regulations. When I first encountered the phenomenon of jurisdictional arbitrage, my perspective was largely aligned with conventional narratives, which often focus on their role in tax optimization and regulatory loopholes perpetrated by MNCs. It was tempting to frame these tactics, or what I thought were mere tactics, as a tale of avoidance and evasion, marked by the exploitation of rules and the creation of artificial constructs. It also made sense that these tactics remain largely under-explored in academic literature. They are complex, highly technical in nature, blending law, accounting, and economics in ways that is highly challenging for someone with little training in each of these disciplines. Moreover, these tactics often do not conform to established theoretical models. They are neither purely economic phenomena nor solely legal constructs; they are highly political in their impact, operating in a realm of power that does not fit into common theories of power.

Over time, I began to question, therefore, the prevailing view, sensing that there might be a different story behind jurisdictional arbitrage. Certain anomalies, which at first appeared unrelated, began to reveal underlying connections, pointing to a broader and more intricate dynamic at play.

While jurisdictional arbitrage is commonly framed through the lens of corporate taxation, I came to see taxation as merely a subfield of the larger phenomenon of regulatory arbitrage. This realization raises important theoretical questions: Does taxation serve as the paradigmatic form of arbitrage, with other forms – such as liability arbitrage or financial disclosure arbitrage – simply replicating its logic of avoidance, evasion, and artificial constructions? Or does the focus on taxation, as a widely acknowledged problem, obscure a much larger and more fundamental story about how firms strategically shape and navigate regulatory environments? If taxation is only one manifestation of a broader arbitrage strategy, then the implications extend well beyond fiscal policy and corporate tax planning. Instead, they point to a deeper structural transformation in the relationship between firms, regulatory institutions, and global governance, one that demands a rethinking of how we conceptualize corporate power and legal boundaries in a fragmented international system.

Then there is this odd anomaly – one that is often overlooked: MNCs are, in fact, centrally coordinated multinational corporate enterprises (CCMCEs). What makes this insight striking is that the CCMCE structure is inherently well suited for arbitrage. If one were given a blank slate and tasked with designing a corporate structure optimized for navigating and exploiting regulatory differences, the logical outcome would be a CCMCE – a networked, multi-jurisdictional entity with centralized strategic control but operational and legal fragmentation. Why, then, has this structural feature been largely ignored in discussions of MNCs? Why is arbitrage typically treated as a set of isolated financial or legal manoeuvres rather than as a systemic outcome of corporate design?

Then there is the question of the inexorable rise of intangibles in corporate valuations. As the global economy shifts towards intellectual property, brand equity, algorithms, and financial instruments, intangibles have become the dominant driver of corporate value. This shift is not just an economic trend – it has profound structural and strategic implications for arbitrage. Yet it so happens that transferring intangible assets among subsidiaries in different jurisdictions is far easier than transferring physical manufacturing assets, particularly in the context of the CCMCEs. Unlike factories or supply chains, intangibles can be relocated on paper, often with minimal regulatory friction. This gives firms unprecedented flexibility in shifting profits, liabilities, and risks across borders, reinforcing the effectiveness of arbitrage strategies.

The alignment between CCMCE structures, intangible assets, and jurisdictional arbitrage suggests that these anomalies may not be anomalies after all – they might be part of a larger entirely rational story. And then there is the question of power. Scholars have long recognized that the rise of MNCs presents deep challenges to states and societies, raising fundamental questions about sovereignty, governance, and accountability. However, discussions of corporate power have typically remained within traditional frameworks – focusing on market dominance, lobbying influence, or financial control.

Arbitrage is clearly a distinct form of power, one that operates in ways fundamentally different from conventional corporate influence. Rather than exercising power through direct confrontation – as in the case of lobbying or regulatory capture – arbitrage mimics predator–prey dynamics, where corporations navigate, adapt to, and exploit weaknesses within fragmented legal and regulatory ecosystems. It is a power of evasion, adaptation, and strategic positioning.

And yet, in line with the other anomalies, this form of power is largely ignored in mainstream analyses. It does not fit neatly into existing political economy frameworks, nor does it align with traditional theories of corporate control. Instead, it represents a more elusive, fluid form of structural power – one that allows firms to shape their operating environment without directly confronting it.

The four anomalies combined challenge the traditional framing of arbitrage as a technical or peripheral issue and instead position it as a central dynamic in global capitalism, one that blurs the lines between legal engineering, corporate strategy, and political economy. The aim of this book has been, therefore, to set the story of the proliferation of corporate subsidiaries and jurisdictional arbitrage schemes within a broader narrative of the development of the modern corporate form and the rise of the rule-based transgressor elite.

I have argued that to fully grasp the narrative of arbitrage, it is essential to embed it within a broader critique of capitalist interpretations, particularly concerning the misunderstood nature of intangibles during the twentieth and twenty-first centuries. A critical distinction must be made between incorporeal or financial instruments and intangible assets. The former primarily include debt instruments, which have contributed to the development of intricate, global wholesale markets for debt. The latter, however, are characterized by their estimated future earning capacities. Understanding these distinctions is key to comprehending the specific dynamics that these types of assets introduce into the global economy, influencing both market behaviour and economic theory.

In the modern economic narrative, the MNC is epitomized by a pivotal relationship: the centralized and coordinated management efforts operating through the corporate structure. MNCs are significant participants in financial markets, with many subsidiaries and affiliates strategically placed in offshore financial centres. According to Garcia-Bernardo et al. (2017), these entities often serve as 'end-of-chain' or 'sink' locations, primarily utilized for tax arbitrage purposes.

However, the role of MNCs extends beyond such financial manoeuvres. They are deeply involved with intangibles, where the augmentation of value involves a comprehensive set of strategies including arbitrage – favouring complex structures over simpler ones, despite the higher transaction costs associated. This complexity is often justified through cost advantages, which are readily apparent in tax contexts but less so in areas such as tort, liability arbitrage, or information asymmetries. Thus, the true cost advantage for MNCs does not lie in production or manufacturing costs but in the value generated – or, as some argue, the value extracted – through enhanced market capitalization of the corporate entity. This perspective shifts the focus from traditional views of cost to a broader understanding of value creation and extraction in global markets.

The conflation of finance and intangibles has led to a series of erroneous assumptions and interpretations, notably when these concepts are merged under the umbrella term 'financialization'. This conflation can obscure the unique roles and impacts of each sector. Finance, traditionally associated with the management of money and financial instruments, and intangibles, which refers to assets such as intellectual property, brand value, and technological patents, each influence the economy differently. When blended into the broad concept of financialization, the distinct economic functions and consequences of finance and intangibles are often misrepresented. This misrepresentation can lead to policy and strategic decisions that fail to address the nuanced ways these sectors operate and interact within the broader economy. A more precise delineation between finance and intangibles is crucial for accurate analysis and informed decision-making in economic policy and corporate strategy.

Jurisdictional arbitrage schemes give corporate groups the ability to sidestep a wide range of state-imposed restrictions and regulations. Importantly, these schemes are not simply the result of corporate ingenuity. Instead, they depend on a critical cadre of professionals who design and implement them – including legal, accounting, and financial experts. The growing influence of these professions, reflected in the proliferation of accounting firms, law firms, and consultancy agencies, is a tangible manifestation not only of the world of arbitrage but also clearly of the world of intangibles.

Conclusions

An intangible economy created then its own rule-based transgressor elite, which had significant consequences for global inequality and governance. By skilfully navigating and exploiting the complexities of legal and regulatory systems, it consolidates wealth and power, deepening existing disparities and undermining the ability of states to regulate effectively.

What to do? If something is to be learned from this study, it is the importance of avoiding simplistic conclusions that attribute outcomes solely to deliberate intent. While the benefits of jurisdictional arbitrage have overwhelmingly accrued to a select group of companies and their shareholders, these corporations, however powerful, did not create the underlying conditions they exploit. Rather, these conditions can be attributed to broader systemic forces – to long-term and transformative processes shaping the global economy; in short, to the evolution of economic and legal institutional conditions.

From the doctrine of incorporation and corporate personhood to the rise of corporate groups, the proliferation of intangible assets such as intellectual property and goodwill, and ultimately the nature of a market dissected among sovereign authorities – none of these institutional conditions can be easily dealt with. Business entities should be expected to systematically leverage these legal and economic transformations to their advantage.

Jurisdictional arbitrage is a product of, and one attempted solution, to structural contradictions deeply rooted in the historical emergence of modern capitalism and the state system. The fragmented regulatory landscape of nation-states, shaped by historical contingencies and political priorities, contrasts sharply with the global ambitions of MNCs. This dissonance creates fertile ground for arbitrage, as corporations navigate – and reshape – the boundaries of state sovereignty to their advantage. But it is difficult to see how these systemic features, sovereignty, market, technology, legal personality, and CCMCEs, are going to change, or be changed.

The systemic nature of jurisdictional arbitrage demands a re-evaluation of the frameworks used to understand corporate power and global economic governance. The traditional dichotomies of market and state, firm and market, or production and value creation fail to capture the complexities of modern MNCs. As my analysis of jurisdictional arbitrage suggests, the intricate interplay of legal, economic, and political forces is shaping the global economy.

A frequently proposed yet limited solution to arbitrage is a robust and coordinated international effort to close the loopholes and gaps enabling these practices. Without such measures, the foundational principles of fairness, accountability, and equity in the global economic system will continue to erode, leaving states and citizens to bear the costs of corporate transgressions. It is hard to argue against this solution – but precisely how can it be achieved? As I discussed in Chapter 3, there are inherent contradictions in the ambitions of states, and these often impede collective action. While most states broadly agree on the necessity of regulation, their agreement falters when addressing aspects of arbitrage that appear to serve their own narrow interests. This inconsistency highlights the challenges involved in forging truly unified global efforts to combat the systemic issues of jurisdictional arbitrage.

And then there is the question of what regulation can realistically achieve. Should we dispense with the doctrine of incorporation and entity law that lies at the core of jurisdictional arbitraging schemes? Many legal scholars have argued for this. As early as 1993, Philip Blumberg called for a shift from entity law to enterprise law, advocating for the treatment of corporate groups as a single legal entity (Blumberg, 1993). More recently, in the United States, the Biden administration's proposals for a global unitary tax on corporations marked a significant step in this direction. However, with the subsequent shift in administration, these initiatives have lost political momentum and no longer reflect the current US position. Such measures suggest a growing recognition of the need to address the structural foundations that enable arbitrage, but we do not know whether these initiatives can gain the necessary international consensus to be effective. Put differently, would these measures stop arbitrage or merely change its form?

Should we, or can we, dispense with a host of strategies that are deeply embedded in a world dominated by intangibles – a world where companies are not merely organizations designed to produce goods or services for profit but are themselves assets to be invested in? In such a context, management's role extends to augmenting the market value of intangible assets.

The strategy of enhancing future value – or shaping market perceptions of future value – incorporates arbitrage as a key strategic tool. No longer a tool of avoidance, arbitrage performs a subsidy-like function with the objective of maximizing institutional and environmental support while minimizing the associated costs. Firms who achieve this balance inherently increase their market value, making arbitrage not just an option but an integral component of their corporate strategy. Eliminating intangibles would strip away much of the rationale for arbitraging rules. But is this feasible? And if it is, would it be desirable?

I have more unanswered questions, perhaps best left for future research. Consider the inexorable rise of intangibles. Would the Ocean Como chart in the Preface look different if MNCs were truly singular entities rather than CCMCEs? I believe it would. I am not suggesting arbitrage is the sole mechanism driving contemporary wealth creation, but I do contend it is a critical dimension of today's economic landscape, often overlooked, perhaps wistfully. But if our modern billionaires are rule-based transgressors, benefiting enormously from corporate groups specialized in arbitrage, what does this imply about the relationship between the corporate economy and the state economy? How does the world of intangible property, with MNCs organized as CCMCEs, interact with the inequalities across and within states? These questions touch upon issues of development and demand further exploration.

Unfortunately, I have no clear answers to any of these questions. I hope this book inspires others to take up the challenge and empirically investigate these dynamics, shedding more light on how the structure and operation of modern corporations shape the economic landscape. The evidence presented in this book represents a starting point – and also hopefully a foundation for deeper inquiry into the intricate relationship between corporate organization, regulatory fragmentation, and the evolving global market system.

References

Aalbers, M. B., 2018. Financial Geography I: Geographies of Tax. *Progress Hum. Geogr.* 6, 916–927.

Adams, P., n.d. Jurisdictional Arbitrage: A Comparative Analysis of the Treatment of Income Arising from Patents in Australia-Irish and U.S.-Irish Jurisdictions [WWW Document]. Bond Univ. Res. Portal. https://research.bond.edu.au/files/36233105/Phillip_Adams_Thesis.pdf (Accessed 14 August 2025).

Aigner, D., Lovell, C. A. K., Schmidt, P., 1977. Formulation and Estimation of Stochastic Frontier Production Function Models. *J. Econom.* 6, 21–37.

Aigner, D. J., Chu, S. F., 1968. On Estimating the Industry Production Function. *Am. Econ. Rev.* 58, 826–839.

Alchian, A. A., Demsetz, H., 1973. The Property Right Paradigm. *J. Econ. Hist.* 33, 16–27.

Alef, D., 2009. *J. P. Morgan: America's Greatest Banker.* Titans of Fortune Publishing.

Allan, C. E., 1889. *The Law Relating to Goodwill.* Stevens and Sons.

Allen, D., 2005. Transaction Costs, in: Clark, D. (Ed.), *Encyclopedia of Law and Society: American and Global Perspectives.* SAGE Publications, London, pp. 893–916.

Allen, R. C., 1979. International Competition in Iron and Steel, 1850–1913. *J. Econ. Hist.* 39, 911–937.

Allen, L., Pantzalis, C., 1996. Valuation of the Operating Flexibility of Multinational Corporations. *J. Int. Bus. Stud.* 27(4), 633–653.

Alstadsæter, A., Johannesen, N., Le Guern Herry, S., Zucman, G., 2022. Tax Evasion and Tax Avoidance. *J. Public Econ.* 206, 104587.

Alstadsæter, A., Johannesen, N., Zucman, G., 2018. Who Owns the Wealth in Tax Havens? Macro Evidence and Implications for Global Inequality. *J. Public Econ.* In Honor of Sir Tony Atkinson (1944–2017) 162, 89–100.

Alva, C., 1990. Delaware and the Market for Corporate Charters: History and Agency. *Deleware J. Corp. Law.* 15, 885.

Andrews, D. S., Fainshmidt, S., Fitza, M., Kundu, S., 2023. Disentangling the Corporate Effect on Subsidiary Performance. *Strateg. Manag. J.* 44, 2986–3011.

Andrews, D. S., Nell, P. C., Schotter, A. P. J., Laamanen, T., 2023. And the Subsidiary Lives On: Harnessing Complex Realities in the Contemporary MNE. *J. Int. Bus. Stud.* 54, 538–549.
Ardeni, P. G., 1989. Does the Law of One Price Really Hold for Commodity Prices? *Am. J. Agric. Econ.* 71, 661–669.
Arlen, J., Weiss, D. M., 1995. A Political Theory of Corporate Taxation. *Yale Law J.* 105, 325–391.
Arsht, S. S., 1976. A History of Delaware Corporation Law. *Del. J. Corp. Law.* 1, 1.
Atkinson, G., 2009. Going Concerns, Futurity and Reasonable Value. *J. Econ. Issues.* 43, 433–440.
Avdjiev, S., Everett, M., Lane, P. R., Shin, H. S., 2018. Tracking the international footprints of global firms. *BIS Quarterly Review*, March, 47–66.
Avi-Yonah, R. S., 2020. Do Lawyers Need Economists? Review of Katja Langenbucher, Economic Transplants: On Lawmaking for Corporations and Capital Markets (Cambridge University Press, 2017). *AEL: A Convivium* 10(2), 1–4.
Avi-Yonah, R. S., 2019. *Advanced Introduction to International Tax Law: Second Edition*. Edward Elgar Publishing, Cheltenham; Northampton, MA.
Avi-Yonah, R. S., 2017. International Tax Avoidance – Introduction. *AEL: A Convivium* 7(2), 167–172.
Avi-Yonah, R. S., 2007. Why Was the U.S. Corporate Tax Enacted in 1909? in: Tiley, J. (Ed.), *Studies in the History of Tax Law*. Hart Publishing, Portland, OR, pp. 23–45.
Avi-Yonah, R. S., 2005. All of a Piece Throughout: The Four Ages of U.S. International Taxation. *SSRN Electron. J.* 58(3), 313–337.
Avi-Yonah, R. S., 2000. Globalization, Tax Competition, and the Fiscal Crisis of the Welfare State. *Harv. Law Rev.* 113, 1573–1676.
Avi-Yonah, R. S., 1995. The Rise and Fall of Arm's Length: A Study in the Evolution of U.S. International Taxation. *Va. Tax Rev.* 15, 89.
Avi-Yonah, R. S., Panayi, C. H., 2010. Rethinking Treaty-Shopping: Lessons for the European Union. Public Law and Legal Theory Working Paper 32.
Avraham, D., Selvaggi, P., Vickery, J. I., 2012. *A Structural View of U.S. Bank Holding Companies* (SSRN Scholarly Paper No. ID 2118036). Social Science Research Network, Rochester, NY.
Baars, G., Spicer, A. (Eds.), 2017. *The Corporation: A Critical, Multi-Disciplinary Handbook*. Cambridge University Press, Cambridge.
Bachrach, P., Baratz, M. S., 1963. Decisions and Nondecisions: An Analytical Framework. *Am. Polit. Sci. Rev.* 57, 632–642.

Baelz, K., Baldwin, T., 2002. The End of the Real Seat Theory (*Sitztheorie*): The European Court of Justice Decision in *Ueberseering* of 5 November 2002 and Its Impact on German and European Company Law. *Ger. Law J.* 3, E8.

Bankman, J., 2004. The Tax Shelter Battle, in: Aaaron, H., Slemrod, J. (Eds.), *The Crisis in Tax Administration*. Brookings Institution Press, pp. 279–316.

Bartlett, C. A., Ghoshal, S., 2002. *Managing across Borders: The Transnational Solution*. Harvard Business Press.

Barzel, Y., 2003. Property Rights in The Firm, in: Anderson, T. L., McChesney, F. S. (Eds.), *Property Rights, Cooperation, Conflict, and Law*. Princeton University Press, pp. 43–58.

Barzuza, M., 2011. *Market Segmentation: The Rise of Nevada as a Liability-Free Jurisdiction* (SSRN Scholarly Paper No. ID 1920538). Social Science Research Network, Rochester, NY.

Baskin, J. B., & Miranti, P. J., Jr., 1999. *A History of Corporate Finance*. Cambridge University Press.

Baum, I., Solomon, D., 2022. Delaware's Copycat: Can Delaware Corporate Law be Emulated? *Theor. Inq. Law.* 23, 1–36.

Beebeejaun, A., 2020. *The Double Irish and Dutch Sandwich Strategies and Tax Avoidance in Mauritius. J. Money Laund.* Control ahead-of-print.

Beer, S., de Mooij, R., Liu, L., 2020. International Corporate Tax Avoidance: A Review of the Channels, Magnitudes, and Blind Spots. *J. Econ. Surv.* 34, 660–688.

Bennett, D. C., Sharpe, K. E., 1979. Agenda Setting and Bargaining Power: The Mexican State versus Transnational Automobile Corporations. *World Pol.* 32(1), 57–89. https://doi.org/10.2307/2010082.

Benton, T. G., Solan, M., Travis, J. M. J., Sait, S. M., 2007. Microcosm Experiments Can Inform Global Ecological Problems. *Trends Ecol. Evol.* 22, 516–521.

Berk, G., 2004. Whose Hubris? Brandeis, Scientific Management, adn the Railroads, in: Lipartito, K., Sicilia, D. B. (Eds.), *Constructing Corporate America: History, Politics, Culture*. Oxford University Press, pp. 120–146.

Berle, A. A., 1950. *Corporations and the Modern State*. Future Democr. Capital.

Berle, A. A., 1947. The Theory of Enterprise Entity. *Columbia Law Rev.* 47, 343–358.

Berle, A. A., Means, G. C., 1948. *The Modern Corporation and Private Property*. Macmillan.

Biggs, M., 1999. Putting the State on the Map: Cartography, Territory, and European State Formation. *Comp. Stud. Soc. Hist.* 41, 374–405.

Biondi, Y., 2017. The Firm as an Enterprise Entity and the Tax Avoidance Conundrum: Perspectives from Accounting Theory and Policy. *AEL Conviv.* 7(2), 135–166.

Birkinshaw, J. M., Morrison, A. J., 1995. Configurations of Strategy and Structure in Subsidiaries of Multinational Corporations. *J. Int. Bus. Stud.* 26, 729–753.

Blair, M. M., 2002. Corporate Law and the Accumulation of Organizational Assets: Lessons from the 19th Century. *SSRN Electronic Journal*, 1–35.

Blouin, J., Huizinga, H., Laeven, M. L., Nicodeme, G., 2014. *Thin Capitalization Rules and Multinational Firm Capital Structure.* International Monetary Fund.

Blumberg, P. I., 1993. *The Multinational Challenge to Corporation Law: The Search for a New Corporate Personality.* Oxford University Press.

Blumberg, P. I., 1985. Limited Liability and Corporate Groups. *J. Corp. Law* 11, 573.

Boadway, R., Tremblay, J.-F., 2012. Reassessment of the Tiebout Model. *J. Public Econ., Fiscal Federalism* 96, 1063–1078.

Boise, C. M., Morriss, A. P., 2009. Change, Dependency, and Regime Plasticity in Offshore Financial Intermediation: The Saga of the Netherlands Antilles. *Tex. Int. Law J.* 45, 377.

Borga, M., Zeile, W. J., n.d. *International Fragmentation of Production and the Intrafirm Trade of U.S.* Multinational Companies.

Bostock, F., Jones, G., 1994. Foreign Multinationals in British Manufacturing, 1850–1962. *Bus. Hist.* 36, 89–126.

Botero, G., 1956. *The Reason of State.* Routledge & Kegan Paul.

BrandFinance, 2024. *Value of Global Intangible Assets Reaches All-Time $79.4 Trillion High*, Press Release, Brand Finance.

Bratton, W. W., McCahery, J. A., 1997. An Inquiry into the Efficiency of the Limited Liability Company: Of Theory of the Firm and Regulatory Competition. *Wash. Lee Law Rev.* 54, 629.

Broe, L. D., 2008. *International Tax Planning and Prevention of Abuse: A Study under Domestic Tax Law, Tax Treaties, and EC Law in Relation to Conduit and Base Companies.* IBFD.

Brossart, R. T., 2010. Tax Due Diligence, in: Rosenbloom, A.H. (Ed.), *Due Diligence for Global Deal Making: The Definitive Guide to Cross-Border Mergers and Acquisitions, Joint Ventures, Financings, and Strategic Alliances.* John Wiley & Sons, pp. 209–251.

Brown, R. J., Jorgensen, B. N., Pope, P. F., 2019. The Interplay between Mandatory Country-by-Country Reporting, Geographic Segment Reporting, and Tax Havens: Evidence from the European Union. *J. Account. Pub. Pol.* 38(2), 106–129. https://doi.org/10.1016/j.jaccpubpol.2019.02.001.

Buchanan, J. M., 1978. *Cost and Choice: An Inquiry in Economic Theory*. University of Chicago Press.

Buchanan, J. M., Tollison, R. D., 1984. *The Theory of Public Choice – II*. University of Michigan Press.

Buckley, P. J., Sutherland, D., Voss, H., El-Gohari, A., 2015. The Economic Geography of Offshore Incorporation in Tax Havens and Offshore Financial Centres: The Case of Chinese MNEs. *J. Econ. Geogr.* 15, 103–128.

Burke, K. C., 2012. Passthrough Entities: The Missing Element in Business Tax Reform. *Pepperdine Law Rev.* 40, 1329.

Burke-Kennedy, E., 2020. Explainer: Google and its double Irish tax scheme [WWW Document]. *The Irish Times*. www.irishtimes.com/business/economy/explainer-google-and-its-double-irish-tax-scheme-1.4190807 (Accessed 14 August 2025).

Byers, J. H., 1940. The Selden Case. *J. Pat. Off. Soc.* 22, 719.

Carmassi, J., Herring, R., 2016. The Corporate Complexity of Global Systemically Important Banks. *J. Financ. Serv. Res.* 49, 175–201.

Cary, W. L., 1974. Federalism and Corporate Law: Reflections upon Delaware. *Yale Law J.* 83, 663–705.

CFA, F. J. F., 1998. *The Use of Derivatives in Tax Planning*. John Wiley & Sons.

Chandler, A. D., 2005. *Leviathans: Multinational Corporations and the New Global History*. Cambridge University Press.

Chandler, A. D., 1993. *The Visible Hand: The Managerial Revolution in American Business*. Harvard University Press.

Chandler, A. D., Hikino, T., 2009. *Scale and Scope: The Dynamics of Industrial Capitalism*. Harvard University Press.

Cheffins, B. R., 2015. Delaware and the Transformation of Corporate Governance. *Del. J. Corp. Law* 40, 1–76.

Chen, H., Zeng, S., Lin, H., Ma, H., 2017. Munificence, Dynamism, and Complexity: How Industry Context Drives Corporate Sustainability. *Bus. Strategy Environ.* 26, 125–141.

Cheng, T. K., 2010. Form and Substance of the Doctrine of Piercing the Corporate Veil. *Miss. Law J.* 80, 497.

Christians, A., 2014. Lux Leaks: Revealing the Law, One Plain Brown Envelope at a Time.

Clark, G. L., Lai, K. P. Y., Wójcik, D., 2015. Editorial Introduction to the Special Section: Deconstructing Offshore Finance. *Econ. Geogr.* 91, 237–249.

Clausing, K. A., 2020. Profit Shifting before and after the Tax Cuts and Jobs Act. *Natl. Tax J.* 73(4): 1233–1266.

Clausing, K. A., 2019. *Profit Shifting Before and After the Tax Cuts and Jobs Act* (SSRN Scholarly Paper No. ID 3274827). Social Science Research Network, Rochester, NY.

Clausing, K. A., 2016. *The Effect of Profit Shifting on the Corporate Tax Base in the United States and Beyond* (SSRN Scholarly Paper No. ID 2685442). Social Science Research Network, Rochester, NY.

Coase, R. H., 1937. The Nature of the Firm. *Economica* 4, 386–405.

Cobham, A., Janský, P., 2020. *Estimating Illicit Financial Flows: A Critical Guide to the Data, Methodologies, and Findings*. Oxford University Press.

Cobham, A., Janský, P., 2019. Measuring Misalignment: The Location of US Multinationals' Economic Activity Versus the Location of Their Profits. *Dev. Policy Rev.* 37, 91–110.

Cobham, A., Janský, P., 2018. Global Distribution of Revenue Loss from Corporate Tax Avoidance: Re-estimation and Country Results. *J. Int. Dev.* 30, 206–232.

Cobham, A., Janský, P., Meinzer, M., 2015. The Financial Secrecy Index: Shedding New Light on the Geography of Secrecy. *Econ. Geogr.* 91, 281–303.

Coendet, T., 2021. The Concept of Regulatory Arbitrage, in: Mathis, K., Tor, A. (Eds.), *Law and Economics of Regulation*. Springer International Publishing, Cham, pp. 159–181.

Cogman, D., Koller, T., n.d. The Real Story behind US Companies' Offshore Cash Reserves | McKinsey & Company [WWW Document]. www.mckinsey.com/business-functions/strategy-and-corporate-finance/our-insights/the-real-story-behind-us-companies-offshore-cash-reserves (Accessed 14 August 2025).

Cohen, F. S., 1935. Transcendental Nonsense and the Functional Approach. *Columbia Law Rev.* 35, 809.

Cohen, S. D., 2007. *Multinational Corporations and Foreign Direct Investment: Avoiding Simplicity, Embracing Complexity*. Oxford University Press.

Collins, W. D., 2012. Trusts and the Origins of Antitrust legislation. *Fordham Law Rev.* 81, 2279.

Commons, J. R., 1934. *Institutional Economics: Its Place in Political Economy*. Transaction Publishers.

Commons, J. R., 1924. *Legal Foundations of Capitalism*. Transaction Publishers.

Commons, J. R., 1919. *Industrial Goodwill*. McGraw-Hill.

Cooley, A. A., Heathershaw, J., 2017. *Dictators without Borders: Power and Money in Central Asia, Dictators without Borders*. Yale University Press.

Cooper, J., 2007. Debating Accounting Principles and Policies: The Case of Goodwill, 1880–1921. *Account. Bus. Financ. Hist.* 17, 241–264.

Corey, L., 1930. *The House of Morgan; a Social Biography of the Masters of Money*. New York.

Cox, H., Cox, P., 2000. *The Global Cigarette: Origins and Evolution of British American Tobacco, 1880–1945*. Oxford University Press.

Coyle, D., 2017. Multinationals turn from 'Double Irish' to 'Single Malt' to avoid tax in Ireland [WWW Document]. *The Irish Times*. www.irishtimes.com/business/economy/multinationals-turn-from-double-irish-to-single-malt-to-avoid-tax-in-ireland-1.3292418 (Accessed 14 August 2025).

Crivelli, E., Mooij, R. A. de, Keen, M. M., 2015. *Base Erosion, Profit Shifting and Developing Countries*. International Monetary Fund.

Crouzet, N., Eberly, J. C., Eisfeldt, A. L., Papanikolaou, D., 2022. The Economics of Intangible Capital. *J. Econ. Perspect.* 36, 29–52.

Curzi, L. C., 2020. *Part IV A General Principle on Corporate Liability in International Law*. Brill.

Dahl, R. A., 1957. The Concept of Power. *Behavioral Sci.* 2(3), 201–215. https://doi.org/10.1002/bs.3830020303

Damgaard, J., Elkjaer, T., Johannesen, N., 2019a. Empty Corporate Shells in Tax Havens Undermine Tax Collection in Advanced, Emerging Market, and Developing Economies. *Fin. & Dev.* 56(3), 52–53.

Damgaard, J., Elkjaer, T., Johannesen, N., 2019b. What Is Real and What Is Not in the Global FDI Network? IMF Work. Pap. 2019, 1–51.

Daniels, S., Martin, J., 2005. The Texas Two-Step: Evidence on the Link between Damage Caps and Access to the Civil Justice System. *DePaul Law Rev.* 55, 635.

Darby, J. B., Lemaster, K., 2007. Double Irish More than Double the Tax Savings: Hybrid Structure Reduces Irish, U.S. and Worldwide Taxation. *Pract. USInternational Tax Strateg.* 11, 11–16.

Davies, P. L., 2015. Institutional Investors as Corporate Monitors in the UK, in: Hopt, K.J., Wymeersch, E. (Eds.), *Comparative Corporate Governance: Essays and Materials*. De Gruyter, pp. 47–66.

Davies, R. B., 1969. 'Peacefully Working to Conquer the World:' The Singer Manufacturing Company in Foreign Markets, 1854–1889. *Bus. Hist. Rev.* 43, 299–325.

Davies, W., 2016. *The Limits of Neoliberalism: Authority, Sovereignty and the Logic of Competition*. SAGE Publications.

Davoudi, L., McKenna, C., Olegario, R., 2018. The Historical Role of the Corporation in Society. *J. Br. Acad.* 6(s1), 17–47.

Debono, M. et al. (2016) *Jersey's Value to Europe: Investigating the Linkages between Jersey and Investment and Prosperity in the European Union*. Jersey Finance, St Helier.

De Simone, L., Olbert, M., 2022. Real Effects of Private Country-by-Country Disclosure. *Account. Rev.* 97(6), 201–232.

Demsetz, H., 1997. *The Economics of the Business Firm: Seven Critical Commentaries*. Cambridge University Press.

Demsetz, H., 1983. The Structure of Ownership and the Theory of the Firm. *J. Law Econ.* 26, 375–390. https://doi.org/10.1086/467041.

Demsetz, H., 1988. The Theory of the Firm Revisited. *J. Law Econ. Organ.* 4, 141–161.
Demsetz, H., 1974. *Toward a Theory of Property Rights.* SpringerLink 163–177.
Desai, M. A., 2009. The Decentering of the Global Firm. *World Econ.* 32, 1271–1290.
Desai, M. A., Dharmapala, D., 2009. Corporate Tax Avoidance and Firm Value. *Rev. Econ. Stat.* 91, 537–546.
Desai, M. A., Foley, C. F., Hines, J. R., 2006. The Demand for Tax Haven Operations. *Journal of Public Economics*, 90(3), 513–531. https://doi.org/10.1016/j.jpubeco.2005.04.004.
Dewey, J., 1926. The Historic Background of Corpoate Legal Personality. *Yale Law J.* xxxv, 20.
Dicken, P., 2007. *Global Shift: Mapping the Changing Contours of the World Economy.* SAGE Publications.
Dine, J., 2012. Jurisdictional Arbitrage by Multinational Companies: A National Law Solution? *J. Hum. Rights Environ.* 3, 44–69.
Dine, J., 2014. Stopping Jurisdictional Arbitrage by Multinational Companies: A National Solution? *European Company Law* 11(2). https://kluwerlawonline.com/journalarticle/European+Company+Law/11.2/EUCL2014014 (Accessed 20 September 2021).
Dizkırıcı, A. S., 2012. Comparison of Istanbul with Hong Kong and Singapore for Regional Treasury Centers. *İşletme Araştırmaları Derg.* 4, 31–44.
Dodge, W. S., 2011. Corporate Liability under Customary International Law Remarks. *Georget. J. Int. Law* 43, 1045–1052.
Donnan, H., Wilson, T. M., 2021. *Borders: Frontiers of Identity, Nation and State.* Routledge.
Donohoe, M. P., 2015. The Economic Effects of Financial Derivatives on Corporate Tax Avoidance. *J. Account. Econ.* 59, 1–24.
Dörrenbächer, C., Geppert, M., 2011. *Politics and Power in the Multinational Corporation: The Role of Institutions, Interests and Identities.* Cambridge University Press.
Dourado, A. P., 2016. The EU Anti Tax Avoidance Package: Moving Ahead of BEPS? *Intertax* 44, 440–446.
Dowd, T., Landefeld, P., Moore, A., 2017. Profit Shifting of U.S. Multinationals. *J. Public Econ.* 148, 1–13.
Duhoon, A., Singh, M., 2023. Corporate Tax Avoidance: A Systematic Literature Review and Future Research Directions. *LBS J. Manag. Res.* 21, 197–217.
Dunning, J. H., 1988. The Eclectic Paradigm of International Production: A Restatement and Some Possible Extensions. *J. Int. Bus. Stud.* 19, 1–31.

Dunning, J. H., Lundan, S. M., 2008. *Multinational Enterprises and the Global Economy*. Edward Elgar Publishing.

Dyreng, S. D., Hanlon, M., Maydew, E. L., 2010. The Effects of Executives on Corporate Tax Avoidance. *Account. Rev.* 85, 1163–1189.

Dyreng, S. D., Hoopes, J. L., Wilde, J. H., 2016. Public Pressure and Corporate Tax Behavior. *J. Account. Res.* 54, 147–186.

Dyreng, S. D., Lindsey, B. P., Thornock, J. R., 2013. Exploring the Role Delaware Plays as a Domestic Tax Haven. *J. Financ. Econ.* 108, 751–772.

Dyreng, S. D., Mayew, W. J., Williams, C. D., 2012. Religious Social Norms and Corporate Financial Reporting. *J. Bus. Finance Account.* 39, 845–875.

Eden, L., 2009. Taxes, Transfer Pricing, and the Multinational Enterprise, in: Rugman, A.M. (Ed.), *The Oxford Handbook of International Business*. Oxford University Press, pp. 591–619.

Eden, L., 1998. *Taxing Multinationals: Transfer Pricing and Corporate Income Taxation in North America*. University of Toronto Press.

Eden, L., Byrnes, W., 2018. Transfer Pricing and State Aid: The Unintended Consequences of Advance Pricing Agreements. Rochester, NY. https://papers.ssrn.com/abstract=3244058 (Accessed 14 November 2023).

Eden, L., Dacin, M. T., Wan, W. P., 2001. Standards across Borders: Crossborder Diffusion of the Arm's Length Standard in North America. *Account. Organ. Soc.* 26, 1–23.

Eden, L., Lenway, S., Schuler, D. A., 2005. From the Obsolescing Bargain to the Political Bargaining Model, in: *International Business and Government Relations in the 21st Century*. Cambridge University Press, pp. 251–272.

Eicke, R., 2009. *Tax Planning with Holding Companies – Repatriation of US Profits from Europe: Concepts, Strategies, Structures*. Kluwer Law International B.V.

Einfeld, C., Blomkamp, E., 2022. Nudge and Co-Design: Complementary or Contradictory Approaches to Policy Innovation? *Policy Stud.* 43, 901–919.

Ellicott, J., 1969. United States Controls on Foreign Direct Investment: The 1969 Program. *Law Contemp. Probl.* 34, 47.

Engel, K., 2000. Tax Neutrality to the Left, International Competitiveness to the Right, Stuck in the Middle with Subpart F. *Tex. Law Rev.* 79, 1525.

Epstein, G. A., 2005. *Financialization and the World Economy*. Edward Elgar Publishing.

EU Commission, 2019. Antitrust: EC opens formal investigation against Amazon [WWW Document]. *European Commission*. https://ec.europa.eu/commission/presscorner/detail/en/ip_19_4291 (Accessed 14 August 2025).

European Commission, 2016. COMMISSION DECISION of 30.8.2016 ON STATE AID SA.38373 (2014/C) (ex 2014/NN) (ex 2014/CP) implemented by Ireland to Apple (Decision No. C(2016) 5605 final).

European Commission, 2015a. Action Plan on Corporate Taxation – Taxation and Customs Union – European Commission.

European Commission, 2015b. Commission decides selective tax advantages for Fiat in Luxembourg and Starbucks in the Netherlands are illegal under EU state aid rules [WWW Document] *European Union*. https://europa.eu/rapid/press-release_IP-15-5880_en.htm (Accessed 14 August 2025).

European Parliament, 2019. REPORT on financial crimes, tax evasion and tax avoidance [WWW Document]. *European Parliament*. www.europarl.europa.eu/cmsdata/162244/P8_TA-PROV(2019)0240.pdf (Accessed 14 August 2025).

Fagre, N., Wells, Louis T., 1982. Bargaining Power of Multinationals and Host Governments. *J. Int. Bus. Stud.* 13, 9–23.

Fama, E. F., 1980. Agency Problems and the Theory of the Firm. *J. Polit. Econ.* 88, 288–307.

Fayerweather, J., 1972. The Internationalization of Business. *Ann. Am. Acad. Pol. Soc. Sci.* 403, 1–11.

Ferran, E., 1999. *Company Law and Corporate Finance*. Oxford University Press.

Fichtner, J., 2016. The Anatomy of the Cayman Islands Offshore Financial Center: Anglo-America, Japan, and the Role of Hedge Funds. *Rev. Int. Polit. Econ.* 23, 1034–1063.

Fiechter, P., 2011. Reclassification of Financial Assets under IAS 39: Impact on European Banks' Financial Statements. *Account. Eur.* 8, 49–67.

Findley, M. G., Nielson, D. L., Sharman, J. C., 2014. *Global Shell Games: Experiments in Transnational Relations, Crime, and Terrorism*. Cambridge University Press.

Fischel, D. R., 1981. Race to the Bottom Revisited: Reflections on Recent Developments in Delaware's Corporation Law. *Northwest. Univ. Law Rev.* 76, 913.

Fleischer, V., 2010. Regulatory Arbitrage. *Tex. Law Rev.* 89, 227–239.

Fleming, J. C. J., Peroni, R. J., Shay, S. E., 2014. Getting Serious about Cross-Border Earnings Stripping: Establishing an Analytical Framework. *North Carolina Law Rev.* 93, 673.

Fligstein, N., 1993. *The Transformation of Corporate Control*. Harvard University Press.

Foroudi, P., Melewar, T. C., Gupta, S., 2017. Corporate Logo: History, Definition, and Components. *Int. Stud. Manag. Organ.* 47, 176–196.

Forstater, M., 2018. Reading the Missing Profits of Nations. *Taxnotes* 160, 1259–1268.

Forte, R. P., 2016. Multinational Firms and Host Country Market Structure: A Review of Empirical literature. *J. Int. Trade Econ. Dev.* 25, 240–265.

Freedland, F., 1955. History of Holding Company Legislation in New York State: Some Doubts as to the New Jersey First Tradition. *Fordham Law Rev.* 24, 369.

Freedman, J., 2008. Financial and Tax Accounting: Transparency and 'Truth', in: Schön, W. (Ed.), *Tax and Corporate Governance, MPI Studies on Intellectual Property, Competition and Tax Law*. Springer Berlin Heidelberg, Berlin, Heidelberg, pp. 71–92.

Freyer, T., Morriss, A. P., 2013. Creating Cayman as an Offshore Financial Center: Structure & Strategy since 1960. *Ariz. State Law J.* 45, 1297.

Friedrich, J., 2021. Regulatory Arbitrage in the Intersection of Accounting Standards and Tax Laws: The Case of Synthetic Leases. *Account. Econ. Law Conviv.* 11, 201–232.

Friedrich, J., Thiemann, M., 2021. The Economic, Legal and Social Dimension of Regulatory Arbitrage. *Account. Econ. Law Conviv.* 11, 81–90.

Froud, J., Johal, S., Leaver, A., Williams, K., 2006. *Financialization and Strategy: Narrative and Numbers*. Routledge.

Galbraith, J. K., 2007. *The New Industrial State*. Princeton University Press.

Galilei, G., Finocchiaro, M. A., 1997. *Galileo on the World Systems: A New Abridged Translation and Guide*. University of California Press.

Garcia-Bernardo, J., 2021. *Offshore Finance and Corporate Tax Avoidance*. Ipskamp, Amsterdam.

Garcia-Bernardo, J., Fichtner, J., Takes, F. W., Heemskerk, E. M., 2017. Uncovering Offshore Financial Centers: Conduits and Sinks in the Global Corporate Ownership Network. *Sci. Rep.* 7, 6246.

Garcia-Bernardo, J., Janský, P., 2021. *Profit Shifting of Multinational Corporations Worldwide*. ICTD Work. Pap., Institute of Development Studies, Brighton, pp. 1–72.

Garcia-Bernardo, J., Jansky, P., Torslov, T., 2019. Decomposing Multinational Corporations' Declining Effective Tax Rates (No. 2019/39), Working Papers IES. Charles University Prague, Faculty of Social Sciences, Institute of Economic Studies.

Gelter, M., 2019. Centros and Defensive Regulatory Competition: Some Thoughts and a Glimpse at the Data. *Eur. Bus. Organ. Law Rev.* 20, 467–492.

Gelter, M., 2009. Tilting the Balance between Capital and Labor – the Effects of Regulatory Arbitrage in European Corporate Law on Employees. *Fordham Int. Law J.* 33, 792.

Gemmell, N., Kneller, R., Sanz, I., 2011. The Timing and Persistence of Fiscal Policy Impacts on Growth: Evidence from OECD Countries. *Econ. J.* 121, F33–F58.

Gerber, D., 2010. *Global Competition: Law, Markets, and Globalization*. Oxford University Press, Oxford.

Gereffi, G., Humphrey, J., Sturgeon, T., 2005. The Governance of Global Value Chains. *Rev. Int. Polit. Econ.* 12, 78–104.

Gereffi, G., Korzeniewicz, M., 1994. *Commodity Chains and Global Capitalism*. ABC-CLIO.

Gerner-Beuerle, C., Mucciarelli, F. M., Schuster, E.-P., Siems, M. M., 2017. The Law Applicable to Companies in Europe: Study and Possible Reform. *Eur. Co. Law* 14, 148–149.

Gerring, J., Oncel, E., Morrison, K., Pemstein, D., 2019. Who Rules the World? A Portrait of the Global Leadership Class. *Perspect. Polit.* 17, 1079–1097.

Gilpin, R., 2011. *Global Political Economy: Understanding the International Economic Order*. Princeton University Press.

Gindis, D., 2009. From Fictions and Aggregates to Real Entities in the Theory of the Firm. *J. Institutional Econ.* 5, 25–46.

Giraud, A., Petit, S., 2017. Tax Rulings and State Aid Qualification: Should Reality Matter. *Eur. State Aid Law Q. ESTAL* 2017, 233.

Glaeser, E. L., Shleifer, A., 2003. The Rise of the Regulatory State. *J. Econ. Lit.* 41, 401–425.

Gloukhovtsev, A., Schouten, J. W., Mattila, P., 2018. Toward a General Theory of Regulatory Arbitrage: A Marketing Systems Perspective. *J. Public Policy Mark.* 37, 142–151.

Golden, J. M., 2006. Patent Trolls and Patent Remedies. *Tex. Law Rev.* 85, 2111.

Gole, W. J., Hilger, P. J., 2009. *Due Diligence: An M&A Value Creation Approach*. John Wiley & Sons.

Graetz, M. J., 2016. *Follow the Money: Essays on International Taxation – Introduction* (SSRN Scholarly Paper No. ID 2784804). Social Science Research Network, Rochester, NY.

Gramlich, J., Whiteaker-Poe, J., 2013. Disappearing Subsidiaries: The Cases of Google and Oracle. *Account. Rev.* 97(1), 201–232.

Grandy, C., 1989. New Jersey Corporate Chartermongering, 1875–1929. *J. Econ. Hist.* 49, 677–692.

Graz, J.-C., 2019. *The Power of Standards*. Cambridge University Press.

Greenfield, K., 2008. *The Failure of Corporate Law: Fundamental Flaws and Progressive Possibilities*. University of Chicago Press.

Greggi, M., 2019. Transfer Pricing and Tax Law – BEPS Actions 8, 9, 10 and the Italian System: An Assessment, in: Kraft, W.W., Striegel, A. (Eds.), *WCLF Tax und IP Gesprächsband 2017: Immaterielle Werte als zentrale Komponente internationaler Steuerstrategien*. Springer Fachmedien Wiesbaden, Wiesbaden, pp. 205–220.

Greguras, F., Bassett, B., Zhang, J., 2008. *2008 Update to Doing Business in China via the Cayman Islands*. Fenwick & West LLP.

Gross, P. S., 2004. Tax Planning for Offshore Hedge Funds – the Potential Benefits of Investing in a Pfic (SSRN Scholarly Paper No. ID 559645). Social Science Research Network, Rochester, NY.

Grosse, R., 1996. The Bargaining Relationship between Foreign MNES and Host Governments in Latin America. *Int. Trade J.* 10(4), 467–499.

Grubert, H., Mutti, J., 1991. Taxes, Tariffs and Transfer Pricing in Multinational Corporate Decision Making. *Rev. Econ. Stat.* 73, 285–293.

Gumpert, A., Hines, J. R., Schnitzer, M., 2016. Multinational Firms and Tax Havens. *Rev. Econ. Stat.* 98, 713–727.

Guvenen, F., Mataloni, Jr., Raymond J., Rassier, D. G., Ruhl, K. J., 2021. Offshore Profit Shifting and Aggregate Measurement: Balance of Payments, Foreign Investment, Productivity, and the Labor Share (Working Paper No. 23324), Working Paper Series. National Bureau of Economic Research.

Haberly, D., Wójcik, D., 2017. Earth Incorporated: Centralization and Variegation in the Global Company Network. *Econ. Geogr.* 93, 241–266.

Haberly, D., Wójcik, D., 2015a. Tax Havens and the Production of Offshore FDI: An Empirical Analysis. *J. Econ. Geogr.* 15, 75–101.

Haberly, D., Wójcik, D., 2015b. Regional Blocks and Imperial Legacies: Mapping the Global Offshore FDI Network. *Econ. Geogr.* 91, 251–280.

Hadari, Y., 1973. The Structure of the Private Multinational Enterprise. *Mich. Law Rev.* 71, 729–806.

Hall, S., 2017. Rethinking International Financial Centres through the Politics of Territory: Renminbi Internationalisation in London's Financial District. *Trans. Inst. Br. Geogr.* 42, 489–502.

Hannah, L., 2013. *The Rise of the Corporate Economy*. Routledge.

Hardman, J., 2021. Reconceptualising Scottish Limited Partnership Law. *J. Corp. Law Stud.* 21, 179–217.

Harrigan, K. R., 1986. *Managing for Joint Venture Success*. Simon and Schuster.

Harrington, B., 2016. *Capital without Borders*. Harvard University Press.

Hathaway, T., 2020. Neoliberalism as Corporate Power. *Compet. Change* 24, 315–337.

Hayes, T. M., 1997. Checkmate, the Treasury Finally Surrenders: The Check-the-Box Treasury Regulations and Their Effect on Entity Classification. *Wash. Lee Law Rev.* 54, 1147.

Heath, C. J., 2024. Taxing 'Borrow' in 'Buy/ Borrow/Die'. *N. Y. Univ. Law Rev.* 99, 717–781.

Helliar, C., Dunne, T., 2004. Control of the Treasury Function. *Corp. Gov. Int. J. Bus. Soc.* 4, 34–43.

Hespe, K., 2013. Preserving Entity Shielding: How Corporations Should Respond to Reverse Piercing of the Corporate Veil. *J. Bus. Secur. Law* 14, 69.

Hill, F. G., 1967. Veblen, Berle and the Modern Corporation. *Am. J. Econ. Sociol.* 26, 279–295.

Hill, M. D., Kelly, G. W., Lockhart, G. B., Ness, R. A. V., 2013. Determinants and Effects of Corporate Lobbying. *Financ. Manag.* 42, 931–957.

Hines, J. R., 1988. Taxation and U.S. Multinational Investment. *Tax Policy Econ.* 2, 33–61.

Hines, J. R., Rice, E. M., 1994. Fiscal Paradise: Foreign Tax Havens and American Business. *Q. J. Econ.* 109, 149–182.

Hirschman, A. O., 1978. Exit, Voice, and the State. *World Pol.* 31(1), 90–107.

Hirschman, 1990. *Exit, Voice and Loyalty: Responses to Decline in Firms, Organizations and States*, New ed. Harvard University Press, Cambridge, MA.

Holland, J., 2005. A Grounded Theory of Corporate Disclosure. *Account. Bus. Res.* 35, 249–267.

Hong, Q., Smart, M., 2010. In Praise of Tax Havens: International Tax Planning and Foreign Direct Investment. *Eur. Econ. Rev.* 54, 82–95.

Hoopes, J. L., Robinson, L., Slemrod, J., 2018. Public Tax-Return Disclosure. *J. Account. Econ.* 66, 142–162.

Hope, O.-K., Ma, M. (Shuai), Thomas, W. B., 2013. Tax Avoidance and Geographic Earnings Disclosure. *J. Account. Econ.* 56, 170–189.

House of Commons, Committee of Public Accounts, 2013. *Tax Avoidance–Google: Ninth Report of Session 2013–14*. HC 112. The Stationery Office, London.

Howson, P., 2017. *Due Diligence: The Critical Stage in Mergers and Acquisitions*. Routledge, London.

Hussinki, H., King, T., Dumay, J., Steinhöfel, E., 2024. Accounting for Intangibles: A Critical Review. *J. Account. Lit.*, 53(1), 1–28.

Hymer, S., 1982. The Multinational Corporation and the Law of Uneven Development, in: Letiche, J.M. (Ed.), *International Economics Policies and their Theoretical Foundations*. Academic Press, pp. 325–352.

Indap, S., 2024. J&J's Latest Texas Two-Step Strategy on Brink of Victory. *Financial Times*, 15 July.

Irogbe, K., 2013. Global Political Economy and the Power of Multinational Corporations. *J. Third World Stud.* 30, 223–247.

Jaffé, W., 1924. Review of The Capitalization of Goodwill. *Rev. Déconomie Polit.* 38, 107–109.

Jensen, M. C., Meckling, W. H., 1976. Theory of the Firm: Managerial Behavior, Agency Costs and Ownership Structure. *J. Financ. Econ.* 3, 305–360.

Jogarajan, S., 2018. *Double Taxation and the League of Nations, Cambridge Tax Law Series*. Cambridge University Press, Cambridge.

Johannesen, N., 2022. The Global Minimum Tax. *J. Public Econ.* 212, 104709.

Johannesen, N., 2014. Tax Avoidance with Cross-Border Hybrid Instruments. *J. Public Econ.* 112, 40–52.

Jones, G., 2002. *Merchants to Multinationals: British Trading Companies in the Nineteenth and Twentieth Centuries*. Oxford University Press, Oxford.

Jones, G., 1981. *State and the Emergence of the British Oil Industry*. Springer.

Josephson, M., 1962. *The Robber Barons: The Great American Capitalists, 1861–1901*. Harcourt, Brace & World, New York.

Juenger, F. K., 1988. Forum Shopping, Domestic and International. *Tulane Law Rev.* 63, 553.

Kahan, M., Kamar, E., 2003. *The Myth of State Competition in Corporate Law* (SSRN Scholarly Paper No. ID 334120). Social Science Research Network, Rochester, NY.

Karayan, J. E., Swenson, C. W., Neff, J. W., 2002. *Strategic Corporate Tax Planning*. John Wiley & Sons.

Kay, N. M., 2000. *Pattern in Corporate Evolution*. Oxford University Press.

Kaye, T. A., 2014. The Offshore Shell Game: U.S. Corporate Tax Avoidance Through Profit Shifting. Chapman *Law Rev.* 18, 185.

Keightley, M., 2013. *An Analysis of Where American Companies Report Profits: Indications of Profit Shifting*. Fed. Publ.

Kellard, N. M., Kontonikas, A., Lamla, M. J., Maiani, S., Wood, G., 2022. Risk, Financial Stability and FDI. *J. Int. Money Finance* 120, 102232.

Kelleher, R. B., Krislert, S., Timmons, J. F., 2009. Lobbying and Taxes. *Am. J. Pol. Sci.*, 53(4), 893–909.

Kelly, L., 2015. Looking to the Future: Life after the Double Irish. *Int. Tax Rev.* 26, 56.

Kerber, W., 1999. Interjurisdictional Competition within the European Union. *Fordham Int. Law J.* 23, S217.

Kim, I. S., Milner, H. V., 2019. Multinational Corporations and their Influence Through Lobbying on Foreign Policy. *Multinatl. Corp. Chang. Glob. Econ.* 9, 497–536.

King, T. A., 2006. *More than a Numbers Game: A Brief History of Accounting*, 1st ed. Wiley, Hoboken, NJ.

Kogut, B., Kulatilaka, N., 1994. Operating Flexibility, Global Manufacturing, and the Option Value of a Multinational Network. *Manage Sci.* 40(1), 123–139.

Krcmaric, D., Nelson, S. C., Roberts, A., 2024. Billionaire Politicians: A Global Perspective. *Perspect. Polit.* 22, 357–371.

Kreider, J. S., 1933. A Brief History of the Growth of Anti-trust Legislation in the United States. *South. Calif. Law Rev.* 7, 144.

Kudrle, R., 2019. *The Continuing Turmoil in International Business Taxation. Presented at the International Studies Association Annual Conference*, Toronto.

Kurki, V. A., 2019. *A Theory of Legal Personhood*. Oxford University Press.

Lambooy, T. E., Diepeveen, R. A., Nguyen, K., 2013. The Opacity of a Multinational Company's Organization, Legal Structure and Power, in: P. G. M. de Rijk, M. E. van der Vlugt, B. P. A. van de Walle (Eds.), *Corporations and Corporate Governance: A Dutch Perspective*. Boom Juridische Uitgevers, The Hague, pp. 13–28.

Lamoreaux, N. R., 2004. Partnerships, Corporations, and the Limits on Contractual Freedom in U.S. History: An Essay in Economics, Law, and Culture, in: K. Lipartito, D. B. Sicilia (Eds.), *Constructing Corporate America: History, Politics, and Culture*. Oxford University Press, New York, pp. 29–65.

Landwehrmann, F., 1974. Legislative Development of International Corporate Taxation in Germany: Lessons for and from the United States. *Harv. Int. Law J.* 15, 238.

Langenbucher, K., 2021. Regulatory Arbitrage: What's Law Got to Do with It? *Account. Econ. Law Conviv.* 11, 91–117.

Lanz, R., Miroudot, S., 2011. Intra-firm Trade: Patterns, Determinants and Policy Implications. *OECD Trade Policy Papers*, No. 114. OECD Publishing, Paris.

Laundry, M. E., 1967. The GmbH &(and) Co. Kommanditgesellschaft: German Partnership Vehicle for Joint Ventures. *Bus. Lawyer ABA* 23, 213.

Leamer, E. E., 1995. *The Heckscher-Ohlin Model in Theory and Practice, Princeton Studies in International Finance. Internat. Finance Section, Department of Economic*, Princeton University Press, Princeton, NJ.

Lee, J., 2024. Foreign Lobbying through Domestic Subsidiaries. *Economics & Pol.* 36(1), 80–103.

Lee, Y., Gordon, R. H., 2005. Tax Structure and Economic Growth. *J. Public Econ.* 89, 1027–1043.

Lenaerts, K., 2003. The Principle of Subsidiarity and the Environment in the European Union: Keeping the Balance of Federalism, in: Krämer, L. (Ed.), *European Environmental Law*. Routledge. pp. 117–166.

Levin, C., Pryor, M. L., Landrieu, M. L., Mccaskill, C., Tester, J., Baldwin, T., Heitkamp, H., Mccain, J., Johnson, R., Portman, R., Paul, R., Ayotte, K., Bean, E. J., Roach, R. L., Katz, D. H., Goshorn, D. J., Kerner, H. J., Hall, S., Patout, B. M., Wittman, S. D., Robertson, M. D., U.S. Senate, Permanent Subcommittee on Investigations, 2013. *Permanent Subcommittee on Investigations 304*. U.S. Government Publishing Office.

Lewellen, K., Robinson, L. A., 2013. *Internal Ownership Structures of U.S. Multinational Firms.*

Loar, W. N. I., 1982. Use Tax Collection Jurisdiction: Why Not a Unified Nexus Standard. *Am. J. Tax Policy* 1, 119.

Lokken, L., 2005. Whatever Happened to Subpart F – U.S. CFC Legislation after the Check-the-Box Regulations. *Fla. Tax Rev.* 7, 185.

Loomis, S. C., 2012. The Double Irish Sandwich: Reforming Overseas Tax Havens St. *Mary's L. J.* 43(4), 825–858.

Loretz, S., Sellner, R., Brandl, M.-B., Arachi, G., Bucci, V., van't Riet, M., Aouragh, A., 2017a. Aggressive tax planning indicators; Final Report [WWW Document]. Taxation Papers - Working Paper. https://taxation-customs.ec.europa.eu/system/files/2018-03/taxation_papers_71_atp_.pdf (Accessed 14 August 2025).

Loretz, S., Sellner, R., Brandl, M.-B., Arachi, G., Bucci, V., van't Riet, M., Aouragh, A., 2017b. Aggressive tax planning indicators: Final Report. Tax. Pap.-Work. Pap. 2017.

Lovdahl Gormsen, L., 2016. EU State Aid Law and Transfer Pricing: A Critical Introduction to a New Saga. *J. Eur. Compet. Law Pract.* 7, 369–382.

Lukes, S., 2021. *Power: A Radical View.* Bloomsbury Publishing.

Majone, G., 1997. From the Positive to the Regulatory State: Causes and Consequences of Changes in the Mode of Governance. *J. Public Policy* 17, 139–167.

Majone, G., 1994. The Rise of the Regulatory State in Europe. *West Eur. Polit.* 17, 77–101.

Manesh, M., 2011. Contractual Freedom under Delaware Alternative Entity Law: Evidence from Publicity Traded LPs and LLCs. *J. Corp. Law* 37, 555.

Mann, M., 2008. Infrastructural Power Revisited. *Stud. Comp. Int. Dev.* 43, 355.

Marian, O., 2013. Jurisdiction to Tax Corporations. *Boston Coll. Law Rev.* 54, 1613.

Marian, O., 2017. The State Administration of International Tax Avoidance. *Harv. Bus. Law Rev.* 7, 1.

Marjosola, H., 2021. The Problem of Regulatory Arbitrage: A Transaction Cost Economics Perspective. *Regul. Gov.* 15, 388–407.

Marshall, A., 2009. *Principles of Economics: Unabridged Eighth Edition.* Cosimo, Inc.

Martin, J. W., 2018. *Banana Cowboys: The United Fruit Company and the Culture of Corporate Colonialism.* University of New Mexico Press.

Matheson, T., Perry, V., & Veung, C., 2013. Territorial vs. Worldwide Corporate Taxation: Implications for Developing Countries. *IMF Work. Pap.* 13(205), i.

Mathis, K., Tor, A., 2021. *Law and Economics of Regulation*. Springer Nature.
Mattei, U., 1997. *Comparative Law and Economics*. University of Michigan Press.
Mattingly, D., 2020. Blocker Alchemy. *Tax Notes Fed.* 169(5), 757–764.
Maurer, B., 2000. *Recharting the Caribbean: Land, Law, and Citizenship in the British Virgin Islands*. University of Michigan Press.
Maurer, B., 1995. Writing Law, Making a 'Nation': History, Modernity, and Paradoxes of Self-Rule in the British Virgin Islands. *Law Soc. Rev.* 29, 255–286.
Mayo, J., 1979. Before the Nitrate Era: British Commission Houses and the Chilean Economy, 1851–80. *J. Lat. Am. Stud.* 11, 283–302.
Mazzi, B., 2013. *Treasury Finance and Development Banking: A Guide to Credit, Debt, and Risk*. John Wiley & Sons.
McLean, B., Elkind, P., 2013. *The Smartest Guys in the Room: The Amazing Rise and Scandalous Fall of Enron*. Penguin.
Mendoza, E. G., Tesar, L. L., 2005. Why Hasn't Tax Competition Triggered a Race to the Bottom? Some Quantitative Lessons from the EU. *J. Monet. Econ.* 52, 163–204.
Mercuro, N., Medema, S. G., 2020. *Economics and the Law: From Posner to Postmodernism and Beyond*. Princeton University Press.
Meussen, G., 2007. Cadbury Schweppes: The ECJ Significantly Limits the Application of CFC Rules in the Member States. *Eur. Tax.* 47, 13–18.
Meyer, J. A., 2010. Dual Illegality and Geoambiguous Law: A New Rule for Extraterritorial Application of U.S. Law. SSRN Electron. J.
Micheler, E., 2021. *A Real Entity Theory of Company Law*. Oxford University Press, Oxford.
Miljkovic, D., 1999. The Law of One Price in International Trade: A Critical Review. *Appl. Econ. Perspect. Policy* 21, 126–139.
Millo, Y., Spence, C., Valentine, J. J., 2025. *Inertia: Sticky Relationships and Ossified Ideas in Financial Markets*. Columbia University Press, New York.
Mintz, J., 2004. Conduit Entities: Implications of Indirect Tax-Efficient Financing Structures for Real Investment. *Int. Tax Pub. Fin.* 11, 419–434.
Mitchell, L. E., 2008. *Corporate Irresponsibility: America's Newest Export*. Yale University Press.
Modigliani, F., Miller, M. H., 1958. The Cost of Capital, Corporation Finance and the Theory of Investment. *Am. Econ. Rev.* 48, 261–297.
Monès, S. de, Prat, B., Mueller, H., Pappalardo, B. E., Menéndez, U., Durand, P.-H., Mandelbaum, J.-F., Klein, M., Niemann, A., Manzitti, A., Lasarte, G. C., Benítez, G. M., Airs, G. J., 2010. Abuse of Tax Law across Europe (Part Two). *EC Tax Rev.* 19(3), 123–137.

Moon, W. J., 2021. Delaware's Global Competitiveness. *IOWA LAW Rev.* 106.

Morgan, J., 2016. Corporation Tax as a Problem of MNC Organisational Circuits: The Case for Unitary Taxation. *Br. J. Polit. Int. Relat.* 18, 463–481.

Mourant, 2021. A quick guide to directors' duties - Cayman Islands exempted companies. Retrieved from www.mourant.com/file-library/media---2021/a-quick-guide-to-directors--duties-in-the-cayman-islands---april-2021.pdf

Muchlinski, P., 2001. Corporations in International Litigation: Problems of Jurisdiction and the United Kingdom Asbestos Cases. *Int. Comp. Law Q.* 50, 1–25.

Nakamoto, T., Chakraborty, A., Ikeda, Y., 2019. Identification of Key Companies for International Profit Shifting in the Global Ownership Network. *Appl. Netw. Sci.* 4, 58.

Nessy, E., Rahayu, N., 2019. Avoiding Tax using Hybrid Mismatch Arrangement Schemes in Indonesia. In *1st Asia Pacific Business and Economics Conference (APBEC 2018)*, Atlantis Press.

Nesvetailova, A., 2017. *Shadow Banking: Scope, Origins and Theories*. Routledge.

Nesvetailova, A., Palan, R., 2014. Elsewhere, Ideally Nowhere: Shadow Banking and Offshore Finance. Politik.

Nesvetailova, A., Palan, R., Petersen, H., Phillips, R., 2020. Iffs and Commodity Trading: Opportunities for Identifying Risks in Energy Traders' Financial Conduct Using Groups' Corporate Filings.(CITYPERC Working Paper, No. 2021-03). City, University of London, City Political Economy Research Centre (CITYPERC).

North, D. C., 1990. *Institutions, Institutional Change and Economic Performance*. Cambridge University Press.

North, D. C., 1982. *Structure and Change in Economic History*, Unknown ed. W. W. Norton & Company, New York; London.

Nougayrede, D., 2016. The Use of Offshore Companies in Emerging Market Economies: A Case Study. *Columbia J. Eur. Law* 23, 401.

Nye, J. S., 1974. Multinational Corporations in World Politics. *Foreign Affairs* 53(1), 153–175.

Ocean Tomo, 2021. Intangible Asset Market Value Study.

OECD, 2021. 130 countries and jurisdictions join bold new framework for international tax reform – OECD [WWW Document]. www.oecd.org/tax/beps/statement-on-a-two-pillar-solution-to-address-the-tax-challenges-arising-from-the-digitalisation-of-the-economy-july-2021.htm (Accessed 14 August 2025).

OECD, 2025. *OECD Benchmark Definition of Foreign Direct Investment*, 5th ed. OECD Publishing. https://doi.org/10.1787/7f05c0a3-en

OECD, 2013. *Addressing Base Erosion and Profit Shifting*. OECD Publishing, Paris. https://doi.org/10.1787/9789264192744-en.

OECD, 2012. *Hybrid Mismatch Arrangements: Tax Policy and Compliance Issues*. OECD Publishing, Paris. https://doi.org/10.1787/dcb1b67a-en.

OECD, 1998. *Harmful Tax Competition: An Emerging Global Issue*. OECD Publishing.

O'Hara, E. A., Ribstein, L. E., 2009. *The Law Market*. Oxford University Press.

Olson, M., 2009. *The Logic of Collective Action*. Harvard University Press.

OpenOil, 2018. OpenOil [WWW Document]. OpenOil. http://openoil.net/

Orts, E. W., 2013. *Business Persons: A Legal Theory of the Firm*. Oxford University Press, Oxford.

Palan, R., 2015. Futurity, Pro-cyclicality and Financial Crises. *New Polit. Econ.* 20, 367–385.

Palan, R., 2010. International Financial Centers: The British-Empire, City-States and Commercially Oriented Politics. *Theor. Inq. Law* 11, 149–176.

Palan, R., 2006. *The Offshore World: Sovereign Markets, Virtual Places, and Nomad Millionaires*. Cornell University Press.

Palan, R., 1999. Susan Strange 1923–1998: A Great International Relations Theorist. *Rev. Int. Polit. Econ.* 6, 121–132.

Palan, R., Murphy, R., Chavagneux, C., 2013. *Tax Havens: How Globalization Really Works*. Cornell University Press.

Palan, R., Petersen, H., Phillips, R., 2021. Arbitrage spaces in the offshore world: Layering, 'fuses' and partitioning of the legal structure of modern firms. Environ. Plan. Econ. Space 0308518X211053645.

Palan, R., Phillips, R., 2022. Arbitrage Power and the Disappearing Financialized Firm. *Finance Soc.* 8, 22–41.

Panayi, C. H., 2015. *Advanced Issues in International and European Tax Law*. Bloomsbury Publishing.

Panayi, C. H., 2013. *European Union Corporate Tax Law*. Cambridge University Press.

Panayi, C. H., 2009. Corporate Mobility in Private International Law and European Community Law: Debunking Some Myths. *Yearb. Eur. Law* 28, 123–176.

Panayi, C. H., 2006a. Treaty Shopping and Other Tax Arbitrage Opportunities in the European Union: A Reassessment – Part 1. *Eur. Tax.* 46, 104–111.

Panayi, C. H., 2006b. Treaty Shopping and Other Tax Arbitrage Opportunities in the European Union: A Reassessment – Part 2. *Eur. Tax.* 46, 139–155.

Papke, L. E., 2000. One-Way Treaty with the World: The U.S. Withholding Tax and the Netherlands Antilles. *Int. Tax Pub. Fin.* 7, 295–313.

Paquier, S., 2001. Swiss Holding Companies from the Mid-nineteenth Century to the Early 1930s: The Forerunners and Subsequent Waves of Creations. *Financ. Hist. Rev.* 8, 163–182.

Park, S., 2018. Related Party Transactions and Tax Avoidance of Business Groups. *Sustainability* 10, 3571.

Partnoy, F., 2018. The Law of Two Prices: Regulatory Arbitrage, Revisited. *Georgetown Law J.* 107, 1017.

Partnoy, F., 2009. *FIASCO: Blood in the Water on Wall Street*, Main-reissue ed. Profile Books, London.

Penrose, E. T., 2009. *The Theory of the Growth of the Firm*. Oxford University Press.

Peppitt, M., 2008. *Tax Due Diligence*. Spiramus Press Ltd.

Peters, J., 2004. Conduit Entity Rules Are Key to IP Planning. *Int. Tax Rev.* 16, 25.

Petrin, M., Choudhury, B., 2018. Group Company Liability. *Eur. Bus. Organ. Law Rev.* 19, 771–796.

Phillips, R., Gardner, M., Robins, A., Education, U. S. P., Surka, M., Education, U. S. P., 2017. The Use of Offshore Tax Havens by Fortune 500 Companies 60.

Phillips, R., Petersen, H., Palan, R., 2021. Arbitrage Spaces in the Offshore World: Layering, 'Fuses' and Partitioning of the Legal Structure of Modern Firms. *Environ. Plan. A* 55(4), 1041–1061.

Phillips, R., Pyle, J., Palan, R. P., 2021. The Amazon Method: How to take advantage of the international system to avoid paying tax (Policy Report). CITYPERC, London.

Picciotto, S., 1992. *International Business Taxation: A Study in the Internationalization of Business Regulation*. Weidenfeld and Nicolson, London.

Pistor, K., 2019. *The Code of Capital: How the Law Creates Wealth and Inequality*. Princeton University Press.

Pitcher, A., Soares de Oliveira, R., 2022. Authoritarian Power in the Global Economy. *Democr. Autocracy* 20.

Poitras, G., 2021. Origins of Arbitrage. *Financ. Hist. Rev.* 28, 96–123.

Polak, P., 2010. *Centralization of Treasury Management in a Globalized World* (SSRN Scholarly Paper No. ID 1702687). Social Science Research Network, Rochester, NY.

Polak, P., Robertson, D. C., Lind, M., 2011. *The New Role of the Corporate Treasurer: Emerging Trends in Response to the Financial Crisis* (SSRN Scholarly Paper No. ID 1971158). Social Science Research Network, Rochester, NY.

Polak, P., Roslan, R. R., 2009. Regional Treasury Centres in South East Asia – The Case of Brunei Darussalam. *Manag. J. Contemp. Manag. Issues* 14, 77–101.

Posner, R. A., 1974. Theories of Economic Regulation. Working Paper Series.
Post, J. E., Preston, L. E., Sauter-Sachs, S., 2002. *Redefining the Corporation: Stakeholder Management and Organizational Wealth*. Stanford University Press.
Poulantzas, N., 1978. *Political Power and Social Classes*. Verso Books, London.
Pressey, A. D., Mathews, B. P., 2003. Jumped, Pushed or Forgotten? Approaches to Dissolution. *J. Mark. Manag.* 19, 131–155.
Publications Office of the European Union, 2021. Annual Report on Taxation 2021: review of taxation policies in the EU Member States. Brussels: Publications Office of the European Union. http://op.europa.eu/en/publication-detail/-/publication/db46de2a-b785-11eb-8aca-01aa75ed71a1/language-en (Accessed 24 May 2021).
Quentin, C., 2020. Corporations, Comity and the 'Revenue Rule': A Jurisprudence of Offshore. *Lond. Rev. Int. Law* 8, 399–424.
Raustiala, K., 2011. *Does the Constitution Follow the Flag?: The Evolution of Territoriality in American Law*. Oxford University Press.
Reurink, A., Garcia-Bernardo, J., 2021. Competing for Capitals: The Great Fragmentation of the Firm and Varieties of FDI Attraction Profiles in the European Union. *Rev. Int. Polit. Econ.* 28, 1274–1307.
Ribeiro, S. P., Menghinello, S., De Backer, K., 2010. The OECD ORBIS Database: Responding to the Need for Firm-Level Micro-Data in the OECD (OECD Statistics Working Papers No. 2010/01).
Ribstein, L. E., 2000. The Evolving Partnership. *J. Corp. Law* 26, 819.
Ribstein, L. E., 1991. Limited Liability and Theories of the Corporation. *Md. Law Rev.* 50, 80.
Richard, K., 2018. Are All Tax Rulings State Aid: Examining the European Commission's Recent State Aid Decisions. *Houst. Bus. Tax Law J.* 18, 1.
Richberg, D. R., 1927. Value. By Judicial Fiat. *Harv. Law Rev.* 40, 567–582.
Riles, A., 2013. Managing Regulatory Arbitrage: A Conflict of Laws Approach. *Electron. J*. https://doi.org/10.2139/ssrn.2335338
Rindfleisch, A., 2020. Transaction Cost Theory: Past, Present and Future. *AMS Rev.* 10, 85–97.
Robé, J.-P., 2020. *Property, Power and Politics – Why We Need to Rethink the World Power System*. Bristol University Press, Bristol.
Robé, J.-P., 2016. Globalization and Constitutionalization of the World Power System, in: J.-P. Robé, A. Lyon-Caen, S. Vernac (Eds.), *Multinationals and the Constitutionalization of the World Power System*. Routledge, pp. 14–52.
Robé, J.-P., 2011. The Legal Structure of the Firm. *Account. Econ. Law* 1.
Robertson, C., 2010. *The Passport in America: The History of a Document*. Oxford University Press.

Robertson, R., 1995. Glocalization-Time-Space and Homogeneity-Heterogeneity, in: Featherstone, M., Lash, S., Robertson, R. (Eds.), *Global Modernities*. SAGE, pp. 25–44.

Rock, E., Wachter, M., 2001. Dangerous Liaisons: Corporate Law, Trust Law, and Interdoctrinal Legal Transplants. *Northwest. Univ. Law Rev.* 96, 651.

Rodriguez, A. F., 2008. Most-Favored-Nation Clause in International Investment Agreements – A Tool for Treaty Shopping, *J. Int. Arbitr.* 25, 89.

Rose, A. K., Spiegel, M. M., 2007. Offshore Financial Centres: Parasites or Symbionts?*. *Econ. J.* 117, 1310–1335.

Rosenbloom, A.H. (Ed.), 2002. *Due Diligence for Global Deal Making: The Definitive Guide to Cross-Border Mergers and Acquisitions, Joint Ventures, Financings, and Strategic Alliances*, 1st ed. Bloomberg Press, Princeton, NJ.

Rosenzweig, A. H., 2012. Thinking Outside the (Tax) Treaty. *Wis. Law Rev.* 2012, 717.

Ross, S. A., 1976. The Arbitrage Theory of Capital Asset Pricing. *J. Econ. Theory* 13, 341–360.

Rowlingson, K., McKay, S., 2011. *Wealth and the Wealthy: Exploring and Tackling Inequalities Between Rich and Poor*, 1st ed. Bristol University Press.

Russell, J. A., 1873. *A Treatise on Mercantile Agency*, 2nd ed. H. Sweet, London.

Saittakari, I., Ritvala, T., Piekkari, R., Kähäri, P., Moisio, S., Hanell, T., Beugelsdijk, S., 2023. A Review of Location, Politics, and the Multinational Corporation: Bringing Political Geography Into International Business. *J. Int. Bus. Stud.* 54, 969–995.

Samuels, W. J., 1972. Ecosystem Policy and the Problem of Power. *Environ. Aff.* 2, 580.

Samuelson, P. A., 1948. International Trade and the Equalisation of Factor Prices. *Econ. J.* 58, 163–184.

Sandler, D., 1998. *Tax Treaties and Controlled Foreign Company Legislation: Pushing the Boundaries*. Kluwer Law International B.V.

Schizer, D. M., 1999. Sticks and Snakes: Derivatives and Curtailing Aggressive Tax Planning. *South. Calif. Law Rev.* 73, 1339.

Schjelderup, G., Stähler, F., 2024. The Economics of the Global Minimum Tax. *Int. Tax Pub. Fin.* 31, 935–952.

Scott, J., 2014. Check the Box for Tax Avoidance, *Forbes*. www.forbes.com/sites/taxanalysts/2014/02/19/check-the-box-for-tax-avoidance/ (Accessed 10 June 2019).

Seabrooke, L., Wigan, D., 2017. The Governance of Global Wealth Chains. *Rev. Int. Polit. Econ.* 24, 1–29.

Seabrooke, L., Wigan, D., 2016. Powering Ideas through Expertise: Professionals in Global Tax Battles. *J. Eur. Pub. Pol.* 23, 357–374.

Sec U.S. Securities and Exchange Commission. n.d. Search Filings. EDGAR. Retrieved from www.sec.gov/edgar/searchedgar/companysearch.html (Accessed 30 July 2025).

Seligman, J., 1976. A Brief History of Deleware's General Corporation Law of 1899. *Del. J. Corp. Law* 1, 249.

Sikka, P., 2003. *The Role of Offshore Financial Centres in Globalization* (SSRN Scholarly Paper No. ID 467682). Social Science Research Network, Rochester, NY.

Sikka, P., Hampton, M. P., 2005. The Role of Accountancy Firms in Tax Avoidance: Some Evidence and Issues. *Account. Forum, Tax Avoid. Glob. Dev.* 29, 325–343.

Silber, N. I., Wei, J., 2015. *The Use of Foreign Blocker Corporations by U.S. Nonprofits: Should Blockers Be Blocked?* (SSRN Scholarly Paper No. ID 2860107). Social Science Research Network, Rochester, NY.

Singer, P., 2011. *The Expanding Circle: Ethics, Evolution, and Moral Progress.* Princeton University Press.

Skinner, G., 2015. Rethinking Limited Liability of Parent Corporations for Foreign Subsidiaries' Violations of International Human Rights Law. *Wash. Lee Law Rev.* 72, 1769.

Slemrod, J., Yitzhaki, S., 2002. Tax Avoidance, Evasion, and Administration*, in: Auerbach, A.J., Feldstein, M. (Eds.), *Handbook of Public Economics.* Elsevier, pp. 1423–1470.

Soares, R., 2021. Researching Africa and the Offshore World (Working Paper). The Oxford Martin Programme on African Governance, Oxford, p. 29.

Song, S., 2014. Subsidiary Divestment: The Role of Multinational Flexibility. *Manag. Int. Rev.* 54(1), 47–70

Speck, S. G., 2015. The Social Boundaries of Corporate Taxation. *Fordham Law Rev.* 84, 2583.

Spengel, C., Heckemeyer, J. H., Nicolay, K., Bräutigam, R., Stutzenberger, K., 2018. Addressing the Debt-Equity Bias within a Common Consolidated Corporate Tax Base (CCCTB): Possibilities, Impact on Effective Tax Rates and Revenue Neutrality. *World Tax J. WTJ* 10, 165–191.

Sterling, R. R., 1968. The Going Concern: An Examination. *Account. Rev.* 43, 481–502.

Stern, P. J., 2017. The Corporation in History, in: *The Corporation: A Critical, Multi-disciplinary Handbook.* Oxford University Press, pp. 21–46.

Stewart, J., 2008. Financial Flows and Treasury Management Firms in Ireland. *Account. Forum* 32, 199–212.

Stewart, J., 2005. Fiscal Incentives, Corporate Structure and Financial Aspects of Treasury Management Operations. *Account. Forum, Tax Avoid Glob. Develop.* 29, 271–288.

Stigler, G. J., 1971. The Theory of Economic Regulation. *Bell J. Econ. Manag. Sci.* 2, 3–21.

Stiglitz, J. E., 1985. The General Theory of Tax Avoidance. *Natl. Tax J.* 38, 325–337.

Stopford, J. M., Strange, S., Henley, J. S., 1991. *Rival States, Rival Firms: Competition for World Market Shares.* Cambridge University Press.

Strasser, K. A., 2004. Piercing the Veil in Corporate Groups. *Conn. Law Rev.* 37, 637.

Surak, K., 2023. *The Golden Passport: Global Mobility for Millionaires.* Harvard University Press.

Tang, R. Y. W., Schultz, T. D., 2017. Country-by-Country Reporting: The New OECD Guidelines and IRS Final Regulations. *J. Corp. Account. Finance* 28, 38–47.

Tax Justice Network, 2020. Financial Secrecy Index 2020: FSI results. Retrieved from https://fsi.taxjustice.net/en/introduction/fsi-2020-results

Tax Justice Network, 2019. Corporate Tax Haven Index 2019: CTHI results. Retrieved from https://cthi.taxjustice.net/en/introduction/cthi-2019-results

Tax Justice Network, 2015. *How the U.S.A. Became a Secrecy Jurisdiction.* Tax Justice Network.

TAXUD, European Commission's Publications Office, 2018. Aggressive tax planning indicators: final report. https://taxation-customs.ec.europa.eu/system/files/2018-03/taxation_papers_71_atp_.pdf.

Taylor, G., Richardson, G., Lanis, R., 2015. Multinationality, Tax Havens, Intangible Assets, and Transfer Pricing Aggressiveness: An Empirical Analysis. *J. Int. Account. Res.* 14, 25–57.

Taylor, W. B., 2010. Blockers, Stoppers, and the Entity Classification Rules. *Tax Lawyer* 64, 1.

The Fairtax Mark, 2019. The Silicon Six and Their $100 Billion Global Tax Gap.

Tiebout, C. M., 1956. A Pure Theory of Local Expenditures. *J. Pol. Econ.* 64(5), 416–424.

Tiley, J., Harris, P., Cogan, D. de, 2004. *Studies in the History of Tax Law*, Volume 1. Hart Publishing.

TJN, 2020. FSI [WWW Document]. www.financialsecrecyindex.com/introduction/fsi-2018-results (Accessed 8 May 18).

TJN, 2019. CTHI 2019 Results [WWW Document]. www.corporatetaxhavenindex.org/introduction/cthi-2019-results (Accessed 20 September 19).

Tørsløv, T., Wier, L., Zucman, G., 2020. The Missing Profits of Nations. Natl. Bur. Econ. Res. Work. Pap. 2018, revised April 2020.

Tørsløv, T. R., Wier, L. S., Zucman, G., 2018. The Missing Profits of Nations (Working Paper No. 24701). National Bureau of Economic Research. https://doi.org/10.3386/w24701

Traversa, E., Flamini, A., 2015. Fighting Harmful Tax Competition through EU State Aid Law: Will the Hardening of Soft Law Suffice. *Eur. State Aid Law Q. ESTAL* 2015, 323.

Truman, D. B., 1971. *The Governmental Process: Political Interests and Public Opinion*, 2nd ed. Alfred A. Knopf, New York.

Tsakalis, D., 2021. 2021 Annual Report highlights the contribution of taxation towards a more innovative, business friendly and healthier EU [WWW Document]. Tax. Cust. Union – Eur. Comm. https://taxation-customs.ec.europa.eu/news/2021-annual-report-highlights-contribution-taxation-towards-more-innovative-business-friendly-and-2021-05-18_en (Accessed 14 August 2025)

UBS, 2024. *Global Wealth Report 2023 – in-depth Data on Wealth around the World* | UBS Global.

UNCTAD, 2023. Trade and Development *Report* 2023.

United States. Commerce Department Mandatory Controls on Investment Abroad, 1968. *Int. Leg. Mater* 7, 579–625.

United States. President (1961–1963: Kennedy), 1964. *Public Papers of the Presidents of the United States: John F. Kennedy, Containing the Public Messages, Speeches, and Statements of the President, January 1 to November 22, 1963*. U.S. Government Publishing Office, Washington, DC. http://archive.org/details/publicpapersofpr0000unse_c4u9 (Accessed 23 July 2025).

US Department of the Treasury, 2016. The European Commission's Recent State Aid Investigations of Transfer Pricing Rulings (White Paper). Washington DC.

van Os, R., Knottnerus, R., 2011. *Dutch Bilateral Investment Treaties: A Gateway to 'Treaty Shopping' for Investment Protection by Multinational Companies* (SSRN Scholarly Paper No. ID 1961585). Social Science Research Network, Rochester, NY.

van 't Riet, M., Lejour, A., 2018a. Optimal Tax Routing: Network Analysis of FDI Diversion. *Int. Tax Pub. Fin.* 25, 1321–1371.

Varian, H. R., 1987. The Arbitrage Principle in Financial Economics. *J. Econ. Perspect.* 1, 55–72.

Veblen, T., 1908. On the Nature of Capital. *Q. J. Econ.* 22, 517–542.

Vernon, R., 2013. *Storm over the Multinationals: The Real Issues*. Harvard University Press.

Vernon, R., 1971. *Sovereignty at Bay: The Multinational Spread of U.S. Enterprises*. Longman.

Vernon, R., 1981. Sovereignty at Bay Ten Years after. *Int. Organ.* 35, 517.

Vickery, B., 2023. Getting Your Ducks in a ROE: Understanding and Working with the Register of Overseas Entities. *Leg. Inf. Manag.* 23, 94–98.

Vlcek, W., 2014. From Road Town to Shanghai: Situating the Caribbean in Global Capital Flows to China. *Br. J. Polit. Int. Relat.* 16, 534–553.

Vogel, K., 1988. Worldwide vs. Source Taxation of Income – A Review and Re-Evaluation of Arguments (Part I). *Intertax* 16, 216.

Walker, R. G., 2006. *Consolidated Statements: A History and Analysis.* Sydney University Press.

Warren, A., Eisen, N., 2024. *Did New York Prove Its Civil Fraud Case against Trump? A Comprehensive Analysis.* SSRN Electron. J.

Waterhouse, B. C., 2013. *Lobbying America: The Politics of Business from Nixon to NAFTA.* Princeton University Press.

Weber, M., 2003. *The History of Commercial Partnerships in the Middle Ages.* Rowman & Littlefield.

Wei, X., Palan, R., 2023. Global Corporate Structure of Chinese State-Owned Financial Institutions through Hong Kong. *J. Int. Relat. Dev.* 26, 373–403.

Weissman, A., Newman, D., 2007. Rethinking Criminal Corporate Liability. *Indiana Law J.* 82, 411.

West, A., 2018. Multinational Tax Avoidance: Virtue Ethics and the Role of Accountants. *J. Bus. Ethics* 153, 1143–1156.

Weyzig, F., 2013. Tax Treaty Shopping: Structural Determinants of Foreign Direct Investment Routed through the Netherlands. *Int. Tax Public Finance* 20, 910–937.

Whytock, C. A., 2010. The Evolving Forum Shopping System. *Cornell Law Rev.* 96, 481.

Wilkins, M., 2005. Multinational Enterprise to 1930: Discontinuities and Continuities, in: Chandler, A.D., Mazlish, B. (Eds.), *Leviathans: Multinational Corporations and the New Global History.* Cambridge University Press.

Williamson, J., 1993. Democracy and the 'Washington Consensus'. *World Dev., Special Issue* 21, 1329–1336.

Williamson, O. E., 2010. Transaction Cost Economics: The Natural Progression. *Am. Econ. Rev.* 100, 673–690.

Williamson, O. E., Winter, S. G., 1993. *The Nature of the Firm: Origins, Evolution, and Development.* Oxford University Press.

Williston, S., 1888. History of the Law of Business Corporations before 1800. I. *Harv. Law Rev.* 2, 105–124.

Wirth, G., Arnold, M., Morshäuser, R., Carl, S., Greene, M., 2024. *Corporate Law in Germany.* C. H. Beck.

Wittendorff, J., 2010. Transfer Pricing and the Arm's Length Principle in International Tax Law 1–912.

Wright, R. E., 2013. *Corporation Nation.* University of Pennsylvania Press.

Yablon, C. M., 2006. The Historical Race Competition for Corporate Charters and the Rise and Decline of New Jersey: 1880–1910. *J. Corp. Law* 32, 323.

Ylönen, M., Teivainen, T., 2018. Politics of Intra-firm Trade: Corporate Price Planning and the Double Role of the Arm's Length Principle. New Polit. *Econ.* 23, 441–457.

Zey, M., 1999. The Subsidiarization of the Securities Industry and the Organization of Securities Fraud Networks to Return Profits in the 1980s. *Work Occup.* 26, 50–76.

Zey, M., Camp, B., 1996. The Transformation from Multidivisional form to Corporate Groups of Subsidiaries in the 1980s: *Sociol. Q.* 37, 327–351.

Zey, M., Swenson, T., 1998. Corporate Tax Laws, Corporate Restructuring, and Subsidiarization of Corporate form, 1981–1995. *Sociol. Q.* 39, 555–581.

Zucman, G., 2015. *The Hidden Wealth of Nations: The Scourge of Tax Havens.* University of Chicago Press.

Zucman, G., 2014. Taxing across Borders: Tracking Personal Wealth and Corporate Profits. *J. Econ. Perspect.* 28, 121–148.

Index

accumulation, 22
Amazon, 1, 26, 106, 131, 135, 154, 173
American, xi, xiii, xviii, xix, xx, xxvii, xxxi, 12, 16–18, 22, 24, 26, 69–72, 77, 79, 82, 84, 88, 99, 104–105, 107, 140, 159, 161, 172–175, 180
American Tobacco Company, 19, 22
anti-abuse, 120, 122, 171
Apple, 1, 16, 129–131, 135, 154, 161
arbitrage, xi, xiii, xvii, xxvii, xxviii, xxix, xxx, xxxi, xxxvi, 1–8, 12, 16–17, 20–22, 26–27, 29–31, 33–39, 42, 44–49, 51–61, 63, 74–76, 81, 87–89, 91, 95–96, 99–104, 108–113, 116, 118–119, 122, 124–125, 127, 129, 131, 133–135, 138, 143–144, 153, 156–158, 160–162, 165, 168–171, 174–177, 182–197

Bank of China, 162
Berle and Means, 25
BOC, 162
BP, 41, 165
Britain, 5
British Virgin Islands, 102, 119, 150, 163
British-American Tobacco company, 18, 88
Buffett, Warren, 187

capital export neutrality, 106
Cayman, 88, 97, 102, 108, 119, 136, 149–151, 163
Cayman Islands', 150
CCMCEs, xxxvi, 10, 12–13, 26, 29, 39, 62–63, 77, 82, 84–91, 93–96, 98–101, 107, 109, 111–114, 116–117, 120–122, 124–126, 128–129, 134, 137, 141, 144–145, 147–149, 151, 153, 156, 160, 170, 174, 182–183, 192, 195, 197
CFC, 98–99, 101, 103, 106, 121, 125, 131–132, 172
China, xi, 4, 12, 68, 131, 162, 179
Civil War, 17, 22, 71
Coase, Ronald, 82
Coca-Cola, 25, 127
Commons, John R., xviii, xix, xx, xxiii, xxiv, xxv, xxvi, xxvii, xxix, 24, 38, 47, 68–69, 74, 77, 79, 120, 158
conduit, 93–94, 102, 106, 137, 140, 148, 173
CORPLINK, xiv, 13–16, 37–38, 41–43, 92, 114, 132–133, 140, 154, 161, 164–166, 169, 173–175
corporate groups, xx, xxii, xxvii, xxx, xxxvi, 1, 8, 13, 23–26, 35, 36, 40, 43, 71–72, 78–80, 86, 89, 104, 107, 116–117, 134, 158, 184–187, 189–190, 194–197
corporate power, xiv, xxxvi, 8, 190, 192, 195
corporate treasuries, 107–109, 137
Cyprus, 87, 137

Delaware, 70–73, 76, 79, 88, 139, 146, 149–150, 155, 174
dormant companies, 165–166
Double Irish, Dutch Sandwich, 1, 161
Double Irish and Single Malt, 1
due diligence, 39–41, 143

end-of-chain, 94, 96, 102–103
equity, xiv, xxiii, xxv, 24, 39, 41–42, 92, 110, 125–126, 129–130, 132, 141, 147–148, 155, 159–162, 187, 192, 196

Index 227

equity mapping, 12, 39
European conduit, 135, 138
European Union, 2, 132, 135–140, 173

FDI, 12, 34, 85, 94, 97, 102, 136–137, 140–141, 143
Fleischer, V., 16, 44–49, 90
France, 5, 17, 23, 62–63, 65, 67, 69, 86, 113, 131, 139–140, 151
fuse, 151, 153
fuse corporate structure, 151

Gates, Bill, 187
GDP, xi, 3, 137
general partner, 151
geoeconomic misalignments, 6
Germany, 5, 17, 23, 64, 68, 86, 95, 113, 139–140, 154
global environment, 21
global markets, 19, 194
global value chain, 127
going concern, xxii, xxiv, xxxvi, 9, 23, 79–80, 84, 88
goodwill, xix, xx, xxii, xxiii, xxviii, xxix, 24–27, 74, 78, 80, 117, 144, 185, 195
Google, 1, 161

Heinz, xx, 17
holding company, xv, xix, xxv, 14, 24, 71–72, 74–76, 80, 86, 109, 111, 133
Hong Kong, 102, 109, 119, 162
House of Commons, 1
Hybrid Mismatch Entities, 126

institutional environment, xxvii, 18
intangible property, xx, 17, 24–26, 77–78, 85, 120, 129, 197
internationalization, 17–18, 88
Ireland, 1, 88, 102, 105, 119, 129–131, 136–137, 161
Italy, 5, 17, 151

Jersey, xix, 23–24, 26, 70–74, 76, 78–79, 84, 86–88, 103, 163
jurisdictional arbitrage, xxx, 1–2, 47, 57, 60, 90, 122, 186, 190, 194–195
jurisdictions, xi, xxviii, 5, 8–9, 13, 17, 19–21, 27–28, 31, 33, 45–46, 51, 53, 56–61, 75, 86–88, 90–91, 93–94, 98, 101–103, 105, 108, 111–112, 118, 120–123, 125, 128–129, 131, 133–142, 145–148, 151, 153, 154, 156, 158–159, 161–164, 168–171, 173–174, 177, 186–188, 192

K-10, 161
Kennedy, John F., 1, 16, 98

law of two prices, 54–56, 61
League of Nations, 114, 116, 119
leveraged, 76, 89, 126
leverages, xxii, 25, 27, 29, 31, 39, 47, 50, 55, 75, 98–99, 107, 127, 132, 140, 174, 177–180, 183, 195
limited partnerships, 151, 154
LLC, 152, 155
Luxembourg, 41, 102, 106, 108, 126, 132, 136–137, 148, 154, 173

Malta, 1, 137
Marxism, 22
Marxist, 22, 30
microcosmic event, 8
Microsoft, 187
MNCs, xiii, xiv, xv, xvi, xvii, xx, xxviii, xxix, xxxi, 2–13, 16, 20, 26, 29, 32–35, 39, 41–43, 46, 55–56, 60, 62, 82–91, 93–94, 98–101, 108–110, 112–114, 116, 120–121, 124–125, 129, 139–140, 143–144, 147, 156–157, 160, 164, 173–174, 177–183, 189–195, 197
Morgan, J. P., 76
Musk, Elon, 187

Netherlands, 1, 17, 62, 87–88, 99, 102, 105, 108, 115, 135–138, 154, 172
Netherlands Antilles, 172
New Jersey, 24, 71–72, 74, 76, 84, 86
nexus(es), 11, 26, 32, 35, 128–129
non-financial firms, 132, 134, 170

Obama, Barack, 16–17
OECD, 2, 35, 70, 93, 113, 115–117, 121–122, 126, 131–132, 163, 165, 171–172

OFCs, 2, 4, 54, 88, 102–103, 105–106, 108, 120, 123, 132–134, 136, 140, 150–151, 154, 162–165, 167–168, 172, 174, 193
offshore financial centres, 2, 54, 136, 162
Oracle, 161
Orbis, 13–16, 40, 42–43, 132, 137, 161
ownership pathways, 14

parent company, xxv, 4, 9, 12, 14, 80, 82–85, 93–102, 105–106, 111–112, 115–117, 125, 130, 143, 145–148, 158, 174, 185–186
partnerships, xiv, 10, 36, 84, 90, 95, 100, 106, 144, 151, 154, 160, 162, 173
Partnoy, F., 44, 46, 54–57
Pepsi, 127
Petrochina, 165
Pistor, K., 54–55
political systems, 18, 20, 37, 180

registration, 21, 82
regulatory arbitrage, xxviii, 2, 11, 34–35, 41, 46–50, 54, 57, 60, 75, 88, 103, 111–112, 139, 172, 174, 184, 191
regulatory optimization, 21
regulatory state, 3, 7, 46
residence taxation, 115, 120
Rockefellers, 17, 76
Roosevelt, Theodore, 16–17, 73
rule-based transgressor elite, xxix, xxx, xxxvi, 8, 188–189, 193, 195

Scotland, 62, 154
Second Industrial Revolution, 5
Singapore, 87–88, 102, 108, 136–137, 150, 161
sinks, 102–103
source taxation, 115–117, 125
splitters, 14, 94–95, 99–101, 111–112, 155, 173, 175

stoppers, 104, 106
subsidiaries, xix, xxiv, xxv, xxviii, xxxi, 1, 3–5, 9, 11–14, 16, 20, 23, 25–26, 28, 31, 33–36, 38–40, 42–43, 53, 57–58, 71–72, 75–76, 80, 84–90, 92–107, 109–112, 115–121, 124–135, 139–141, 143–148, 150–154, 157–168, 172–175, 179, 184–186, 190, 192–193
Switzerland, 87, 102, 108, 136–137

tax havens, 46, 59, 102, 105, 117–118, 124, 133, 136–137, 157, 161, 170, 172–173, 188
tax rules, 4, 17, 45, 104, 119, 121, 125, 132, 170
taxation, xi, xvii, xxviii, xxxvi, 3–5, 8, 19–20, 25, 34, 36, 48, 53, 59, 66, 70–72, 87, 91–92, 99, 102–103, 106, 108, 113–119, 122–125, 130–131, 134, 138–139, 143, 148–149, 156, 164, 171, 173, 177, 179, 184–185, 187, 190–191
Tesla, 187, 189
Toyota, 25
treasury, 5, 17, 107–108, 136, 171–173
Trump, Donald, xi, xxx, 155–156, 161

United States, xi, xiii, xviii, xxvi, 1, 3, 5, 17, 22–23, 39, 51, 60, 62, 64, 68, 70–74, 76, 82–83, 86–89, 98, 104–106, 113, 115, 120, 129–130, 132, 151, 158, 164, 170–175, 187, 196
US companies, 85–86, 107, 135, 170, 172–173
US foreign investment, 46
US multinational firms, 136

Wells Fargo, 14–15
William III, King, 44

For EU product safety concerns, contact us at Calle de José Abascal, 56–1°, 28003 Madrid, Spain or eugpsr@cambridge.org.

www.ingramcontent.com/pod-product-compliance
Ingram Content Group UK Ltd.
Pitfield, Milton Keynes, MK11 3LW, UK
UKHW021619130126
466887UK00019B/320